CHRISTIAN HIGH SCHOOL RELIGION SERIES

God's Plan Unfolds

The Church from Nazareth to Nicaea

Student Book

By Andrew Bailey, Ronald Schlegel, and Ronald Stelzer

Editors: Arnold E. Schmidt
Jane Haas

CPH
SAINT LOUIS

Contents

To the Student   4

Unit 1: Great Expectations   5
    1   Wanted: Big Man on Campus   6
    2   "One Nation Under God"   8
    3   Sects and Violence   10
    4   Hear Ye! Hear Ye!   12
    5   That's Incredible!   14
    6   Through the Eyes of Jesus' Stepfather   16
    7   The Synoptic Gospels   18
    8   Trailblazing Fire   21
    9   Review of Unit 1   23

Unit 2: Jesus, the Minister   24
    10   One of the Guys   25
    11   Homecoming, Nazareth High, A. D. 29   27
    12   Hide and Seek   29
    13   The Coach Picks His Team   31
    14   Jesus Breaks the Rules   33
    15   Creatures from Outer Space   35
    16   Building on a Rock   37
    17   You Gotta Have Faith!   39
    18   True Love!   41
    19   Jesus' Secret Code   43
    20   Natural Disasters and Evil Spirits   45
    21   Opportunity Knocks   47
    22   The End of the Beginning and the Beginning of the End   49
    23   Review of Unit 2   51

Unit 3: Jesus, Our Teacher   52
    24   The Fizz in the Soda Pop   53
    25   The Seeds and Deeds of Life   55
    26   How to Be a Super Christian   57
    27   Heart Failure   59
    28   The American Dream   61
    29   Be Prepared!   63
    30   Surprise! Who? Me?   65
    31   God Has Feelings Too   67
    32   Growing Up Childlike   69
    33   Judgment, Heaven, and Hell   71
    34   How's Your Spiritual Health?   73
    35   Review of Unit 3   75

Unit 4: Jesus, Our Hope   76
    36   Big Hit on Broadway!   77

Editorial Secretary: Phoebe Wellman

Write to Library for the Blind, 1333 S. Kirkwood Road, St. Louis, MO 63122-7295, to obtain *God's Plan Unfolds: The Church from Nazareth to Nicaea* (Student Book) in braille or sightsaving print for the visually impaired.

Unless otherwise stated, the Scripture quotations in this publication are from The Holy Bible: NEW INTERNATIONAL VERSION, copyright © 1973, 1978, 1984 by the International Bible Society. Used by permission of Zondervan Bible Publishers.

Scripture quotations marked RSV are from the Revised Standard Version of the Bible, copyrighted 1946, 1952, © 1971, 1973 by the Division of Christian Education of the National Council of the Churches of Christ in the U.S.A., and are used by permission.

Bible quotations marked TEV are from the Good News Bible, the Bible in TODAY'S ENGLISH VERSION. Copyright © American Bible Society 1966, 1971, 1976. Used by permission.

Scripture quotations marked NASB are from the NEW AMERICAN STANDARD BIBLE © The Lockman Foundation 1960, 1962, 1963, 1968, 1971, 1972, 1973, 1975, and are used by permission.

Copyright © 1986 Concordia Publishing House
3558 S. Jefferson Avenue, St. Louis, MO 63118-3968
Manufactured in the United States of America

All rights reserved. No part of this publication may be reproduced, stored in a retrieval system, or transmitted, in any form or by any means, electronic, mechanical, photocopying, recording, or otherwise, without the prior written permission of Concordia Publishing House.

5   6   7   8   9   10   11   12   13   14   06   05   04   03   02   01   00   99   98   97

37 Traps and Ambushes	79
38 What's the World Coming To?	81
39 Last Will and Testament	83
40 When Darkness Reigns	85
41 Winners and Losers	87
42 Who Did It?	89
43 The Last Laugh	91
44 Famous Last Words	93
45 Review of Unit 4	94

Unit 5: The Church Begins 95

46 The Roman World and God's Plan of Salvation	96
47 An Overview of Acts	99
48 The Acts of the Holy Spirit	101
49 Pentecost	103
50 The Church in Jerusalem After Pentecost	105
51 Persecution	107
52 The Church Grows Beyond Jerusalem and Judaism	109
53 Review of Unit 5	111

Unit 6: God's Servant Paul 112

54 Paul's Threefold Background	113
55 Paul's First Missionary Journey	115
56 The Council of Jerusalem	117
57 Paul's Second Missionary Journey: Europe	119
58 Paul's Helpers	121
59 Paul's Third Missionary Journey and Letter Writing	124
60 Paul's Arrest and Imprisonment	126
61 Paul's Fourth Journey: To Rome	128
62 Review of Unit 6	129

Unit 7: The Development of Holy Scripture 131

63 The Old Testament Canon	132
64 The Books of the New Testament Are Written Down and Used	134
65 The New Testament Canon Is Formed	136
66 Scripture in My Language	138
67 Interpreting the Bible	140
68 Review of Unit 7	143

Unit 8: Overview of the Epistles and Revelation 144

69 The Pauline Epistles (Part 1)	145
70 The Pauline Epistles (Part 2)	148
71 Hebrews and James	150
72 The Epistles of Peter and Jude	152
73 The Epistles of John	154
74 Revelation	156
75 Concluding Activities for Unit 8	158

Unit 9: The Church Until About 400 159

76 The Apostolic Fathers	160
77 Worship Life in the Early Church	163
78 Early Church Government	165
79 Roman Religion and Christianity	167
80 Early Church Fathers	169
81 Roman Persecution—Times of Fiery Trial	171
82 In the Days of Constantine	173
83 Review of Unit 9	175

Unit 10: The Church Responds to Heresies 176

84 Early Christian Heresies	177
85 The Apostles' Creed	179
86 Arianism—a Strong Challenge to Orthodoxy	181
87 Athanasius—the Father of Orthodoxy	183
88 Ecumenical Councils—Doctrine by Decree	185
89 The Ecumenical Creeds	187
90 Review of Unit 10	189

To the Student

Have you planned anything lately?

Maybe you've planned a party. You probably went through a "things to do list" that included the following:

When and where will I have the party?

What friends will I invite?

When will I call them to find out who can come?

What food will I get ready? What games will we play? What music will we listen to?

What will I wear?

Plans. We all make some kinds of plans each day. We plan our daily schedules. We plan our homework and our recreation. We plan menus. We plan how to spend our money. We plan for our future. Sometimes our plans work out. Sometimes they fail.

Long, long ago, before the beginning of the world, God made His plan—His perfect plan, His never-failing plan. God's plan of many parts has unfolded for His people since creation.

He tells us through the Old Testament prophets of His plan to send a Savior to save all people from sin.

God reminded His people of His promise of forgiveness as they waited longingly for their Savior through the intertestamental years.

He fulfilled His promise of salvation when He sent His only Son, Jesus, to be the Savior of the world.

Then God revealed His plan to bring the Good News of this Savior to people throughout the world (Acts 1:8).

God's Good News plan unfolds for you too: God loves you so much that He gave His Son, Jesus, to take your sins with Him to His death on the cross. He loves you so much that He promises to take you to heaven to live with our risen Lord. God loves you so much that He includes you in His ever-unfolding plan—a plan that daily includes His gifts of love, forgiveness, patience, care, and opportunities to share Jesus with others.

As you study and discuss the lessons in this course, remember that **"The plans of the Lord stand firm forever, the purpose of His heart through all generations" (Psalm 33:11).**

May the Holy Spirit fill you with knowledge, understanding, and a joyous expression of your Christian faith as you study and discuss God's unfolding plan of salvation for you and all people.

The Editors

Unit 1
Great Expectations

*"Six more days!" Sarah shouted as she made a big **X** on the kitchen calendar. "Robb, aren't you excited?" she asked her brother, who was making a chocolate milkshake.*

"Sure, yeah," answered Robb above the whir of the blender. "But nobody could be as excited as you!"

Sarah had finished packing her luggage two days ago, the same day their Aunt Catherine had phoned to invite both of them to spend a week on her Colorado ranch. She and Robb had accepted immediately, and got their parents' approval that evening after supper.

*The last two days flew by for Sarah. She daydreamed about flying to Colorado and riding horses with her cousins. Neither Sarah nor Robb had ever seen the Rocky Mountains. She hoped they'd have a little snow on their tops. She carefully packed her art tablet and box of pastels, planning to capture the scenery on paper. Sarah made lists and gathered things to take along. Everyday, she made another **X** on the calendar! It was hard for her to wait!*

Think of a time when you waited and waited for a special day to come. How did you wait? What did you do to get ready? How did you feel?

People waited a long time for God to send a Savior. They worked. They traveled. They prayed. They sang. They hoped. They lived. And many even died waiting. They shared their longings with their family members and friends. They looked forward to the Messiah's coming with great expectations. God had made covenants with His Old Testament people, promising them His blessings of love and forgiveness.

The time finally came. God delivered! He kept His promise to send a Savior. Jesus was born and grew to be a man. He fulfilled Isaiah's prophecy that the Servant, God's own Son, would take our punishment upon Himself to the cross **(Isaiah 53:4-5)**.

During this unit, you'll discover more about our heavenly Father's plan for His people and how He kept His promises. Jesus Christ, Savior of us all, fulfilled God's promise of salvation and provided us hope of eternal life. God, through the Holy Spirit, continues to keep us in the faith and provides us with both hope and joy as we get ready for Jesus' second coming, when He will take us to live with Him in heaven.

Session 1
Wanted: Big Man on Campus

He was one in a million. In fact, Lutheran High hasn't been the same since he graduated.

Extremely popular with the entire student body, he was elected student body president by a landslide. (   ) The girls loved him. (   ) A date with him was a girl's dream come true. (   ) You should have seen him draw a crowd with his moves on the dance floor! The cheerleaders even composed and sang songs about him. (   )

He was a tremendous athlete—all-state in three sports. In his first starting assignment, he quarterbacked the team to an upset victory over an arch-rival that was favored by three touchdowns. (   ) He went on to lead the team to an undefeated season and a number one ranking in the state.

He was also undefeated as a wrestler. (   ) But he was best known as a strike-out artist, a pitcher with dazzling velocity and accuracy, as well as a very good hitter. (   )

He was good looking, a fine speaker, and very talented musically, both instrumentally and vocally. (   ) Guitar was his specialty, and he played it so well. (   ) Even the older teachers and administrators liked it. He was often asked to use his talent to lead singing in worship services. The songs he composed were everyone's favorites. (   )

He seemed to be the model young man who could do no wrong. It was quite a shock when he got his girlfriend pregnant. (   ) He accepted the strong disciplinary action of the principal without making excuses. (   ) Even in his humiliating moments, he proved to be a shining example.

Everyone keeps looking back to those glory years for Lutheran High. With each incoming freshman class, there is the hope that there might be another one like him. (   )

Does your school have a folk hero like him?

Does it surprise you that this person is entirely fictional?

Does it surprise you that this person's description compares closely to one outstanding Biblical character?

I think this Bible person is _____

WANTED: THE MESSIAH

Throughout the Old Testament, God promised His people a Messiah—a Savior. The people waited, prayed, and *longed for* their Savior. While they waited, they wondered what the Messiah would be like. In many ways the description of the high school hero is like the ancient Jewish idea of the coming Messiah. The people waited, prayed, and watched for a "hero" to come—someone who was good at everything, someone they would all adore.

What does the Bible tell us about the promised Messiah? Read the following Old Testament prophecies. Then write the Bible reference after each characteristic of the Messiah. You may have more than one reference for each.

**Isaiah 9:6-7   Isaiah 11:1-10   Jeremiah 23:5-6
Daniel 7:13-14   Haggai 2:6-9, 22**

1. Come from God _____

2. Invincible Conqueror _____

3. Peace through strength _____

4. Smart and wise _____

5. Fair, impartial Judge _____

6. Great earthly wealth _____

7. Internationally renowned and revered _____
8. Jerusalem His capital city _____
9. Strong spiritually _____
10. Everlasting reign _____

WANTED: THE KING OF GLORY

The idea of the Messiah and the Messianic kingdom was imbedded deep in the Jews' consciousness. It was not just wishful thinking or a far-out dream. It was a firm expectation rooted in the promises of God to David in **2 Samuel 7:12, 13,** and **16.** In these Bible verses God promised David that his offspring would rule over an everlasting Kingdom established by God.

The Jews then expected the Messiah to be like David, only better. David was their great hero. The high school hero in the introductory part of this lesson is a contemporary version of David. Within the parentheses in the introduction, write the letters of the Bible references that correspond to the descriptive statements about the high school hero. (For example, **1 Samuel 17:34-35** pictures David as an undefeated wrestler. Write *I* after the statement about the high school wrestler.)

(A) 1 Samuel 16:18   (B) 2 Samuel 5:1, 3
(C) Psalms   (D) 1 Samuel 16:23
(E) 2 Samuel 6:14-15   (F) Matthew 21:9
(G) 1 Samuel 17:4   (H) 2 Samuel 6:22
(I) 1 Samuel 17:34-35   (J) 2 Samuel 11
(K) 1 Samuel 17:49   (L) 2 Samuel 12:11-14
(M) 1 Samuel 18:6-7

WANTED: THE SON OF DAVID

David lived about 1,000 years before Christ. Most of the kings who ruled after David led the Jewish people into idolatry and immorality. God sent prophets to warn the Jews of His growing anger with their unfaithfulness. But the people couldn't believe that God would allow anything to happen to the Kingdom that He promised would last forever.

Read **Jeremiah 7:1-11** and **Micah 3:9-12.**

1. On what did the Jews base their confidence?
2. Why was their confidence out of place?

It came as a tremendous shock to the Jewish people when, in 587 B.C., King Nebuchadnezzar of Babylon led his army into Jerusalem, leveled its walls and temple, and burned everything to the ground. For 70 years many Jews were exiled in Babylon. It gave them a lot of time to think things like "Why did God let this happen to us?" They concluded that the prophets' warnings were right. The people had been unfaithful to God and disobedient to His commands. They concluded that they deserved what they got.

When they finally returned to their homeland of Palestine, they had a lot of pieces to pick up. All around them they saw broken cities, a broken temple, and a broken nation. It all reminded them of the prophets' warnings and the broken commandments of God. So, as they began putting the pieces of their nation back together, they committed themselves to remaining faithful to God and His law.

This was the situation when the last Old Testament books were written. The people remembered God's promises to David. These promises provided the hope and determination they needed to go on. At the same time they looked and hoped for the second and greater David to lead them back to glory.

GRANTED: GOD'S PROMISES FOR ME

1. Read **Psalm 145:13** and paraphrase this verse.
2. Describe one important promise God has made and kept for you. Then share it with a friend.

The King of Glory

Willard F. Jabusch — Israeli folksong

Refrain
The King of glory comes, the nation rejoices,
Open the gates before Him, lift up your voices.

Stanzas
1 Who is the King of glory; how shall we call Him?
  He is Emmanuel, the Promised of ages.
2 In all of Galilee in city or village,
  He goes among His people curing their illness.
3 Sing then of David's Son, our Savior and Brother;
  In all of Galilee was never another.
4 He gave His life for us, the Lamb of salvation,
  He took upon Himself the sins of the nation.
5 He conquered sin and death, He truly has risen,
  And He will share with us His heavenly vision.

Copyright © 1966, 1982, Willard F. Jabusch. Administered by OCP Publications, 5536 NE Hassalo, Portland, OR 97213. All rights reserved. Used with permission.

For no matter how many promises God has made, they are "Yes" in Christ.

2 Corinthians 1:20

Session 2

"One Nation Under God"

"We hold these truths to be self-evident: that all men are created equal, that they are endowed by their Creator . . ."

"Congress shall make no law respecting an establishment of religion, or prohibiting the free exercise thereof . . ."

" . . . and to the Republic for which it stands, one nation under God . . ."

Do you recognize these three statements? They are excerpts from very three significant documents in the history of the United States. They tell us a lot about important principles on which this nation was founded.

From the very beginning, most founding fathers of the United States acknowledged God's existence and His will as supreme. However, at the same time, they didn't want to force anyone into religion. People were free to believe or not to believe, to join a religious denomination or not to join. Their religious convictions would not make them any more or less a citizen of the United States. The founding fathers placed a high value on an individual's freedoms.

What are ways the people in the United States demonstrate a commitment to freedom of religion today?

FREEDOM OR CONFORMITY?

Freedom of religion is a relatively new ideal. Throughout history, most nations have been committed to one religion or another. Citizens have been expected to follow the national religion. In the Old Testament times, a nation and its god or gods were closely related. If a nation prospered or was victorious, people concluded that their god was more powerful than the other nation's god. On the other hand, if a nation experienced some natural or man-made catastrophe, people concluded that the nation's god was either weak or angry with its people. The ideal then was not freedom of religion, but conformity and loyalty to the nation's god.

1. Which ideal did the nation of Israel have: freedom of religion or conformity of religion?

When the remnant of Israelites returned to their homeland in Palestine from their exile in Babylon, they had no nation or temple or king. The high priest became the ruling figure. The high priest was the head of both the church and the state. The Israelites had no separation of church and state, nor did they want it. Their church was a national church and their nation was a religious nation. All citizens were expected to be completely loyal to the nation's God. Those who did not believe in their national God or follow His laws were unpatriotic, treacherous, and dangerous to the well-being of the entire nation.

The Israelites were a nation founded by their God. At one time they were just a bunch of slaves in Egypt. But God delivered them with 10 awesome plagues and a miraculous path through the Red Sea. He personally fed and led them through the wilderness. He hand-delivered their law code on Mount Sinai. He brought them to the edge of their new homeland and then He told them what He expected of them. (These expectations are found in Deuteronomy.) It was these expectations that the people subsequently ignored and disobeyed. So their nation of Israel was destroyed and their people were taken into exile.

2. Now the Israelites had returned. It was time to start over. All the people gathered around Ezra, the high priest. Read **Nehemiah 8:1-3, 18.** What happened?

3. Read some of the things Ezra read to the assembly of the Israelite returnees. Then summarize what God's law demands in each of the following Bible passages.

Deuteronomy 7:1-6 _____

_____

_____

Deuteronomy 12:29-32 _____

_____

_____

4. Read **Deuteronomy 28:1-4.** What could the Israelites expect if they did as God commanded?

5. What amazing thing did the Israelites agree to do in response to Ezra **(Ezra 10:1-4)**?

THE INTERTESTAMENTAL PERIOD

Ezra set the tone for the entire 400-year period between the end of the Old Testament and the beginning of the New Testament. The great quest of many Jewish people during the intertestamental period was for purity—racial purity, religious purity, legal purity, and national purity. Never again did they want to incur the wrath of their God. The Israelites struggled to rid themselves of all foreign, contaminating influences that might lead them away from uncompromising devotion to the Lord and the Law.

This was not an easy task in light of the times. From 334 to 323 B.C., Alexander the Great of Macedonia conquered many nations and established a vast empire. As a boy, Alexander had learned in the school of Aristotle, and he had developed a great admiration for Greek culture and religion. Wherever he went, including Palestine, he promoted Greek ideas and civilization by all conceivable means. His promotion included intermarriage. Greek became the universal language, and even the Hebrew Scriptures were translated into the Greek for the sake of Greek-speaking Jews. This famous translation is called the *Septuagint*.

Alexander died a young man in 323 B.C., and his empire was divided among his generals and relatives. The Jews in Palestine were dominated first by the Ptolemies of Egypt and then by the Seleucids of Syria. One of the most tragic periods in Jewish history came at the hands of the Seleucid King Antiochus IV in the mid-second century B.C.

A decree was then issued by Antiochus IV that all Jews were to conform to Syrian laws, customs, and religion. The worship of Greek gods and goddesses was to replace adoration of Jehovah. Distinctively Jewish customs, such as Sabbath observance, the rite of circumcision, and the avoidance of unclean food, were prohibited on penalty of death. Mothers who had their babies circumcised were crucified with their babies hung around their necks. The required daily sacrifices were prohibited. A herd of swine was driven into the temple, and on the altar dedicated to the Olympian Zeus, swine flesh was sacrificed.

(From *Introduction to the Intertestamental Period*, by Raymond F. Surburg [St. Louis: Concordia Publishing House, 1975.] Used by permission.)

Many Jewish people who chose to be faithful to the Lord suffered extremely cruel and inhumane treatment. Finally, the Jews revolted under the leadership of the Maccabean family. The Maccabees and their patriotic followers, experts in guerrilla warfare and terrorism, hid by day and struck by night. In 164 B.C. Jerusalem was recaptured, the temple was cleansed, and pure worship was restored. The Jewish Feast of Hanukkah, which occurs during the season Christians celebrate Christmas, commemorates this purification and rededication.

For the next 100 years, the Jews exercised greater control of their affairs, but their leaders were more concerned about political power than religious purity, and this disillusioned many pious Jewish people.

The Romans came to Palestine in 63 B.C. The Romans were assisted by the family of Herods, who received political power in exchange for their loyalty to Rome. Most famous was Herod the Great, a strong and efficient governor who engaged in a magnificent building program. However, he loved Graeco-Roman culture and his own power more than the Jewish ideals of religious purity and national autonomy. Thus, the Jews hated him. Jesus was born toward the end of this Herod's reign, in the midst of the Jews' continuing struggle to become again "one nation under God."

A PRAYER FOR TODAY

O God, You were with Your people through all the years of the Old Testament. You talked with them. You gave them their daily needs. You showed them where to live, what to eat, and how to love each other. You loved Your people then. And You love us now.

Help me, God, to be Your child. Lead me from temptations to worship anything or anyone before You. Guide me so that I use the freedoms You give me to be a Christian citizen and worker in Your kingdom.

Most of all, God, I thank You for Jesus. Without my Savior, I'd be a hopeless case. Thanks for promising Your Son to Your people. Thanks for keeping Your promise and delivering Him to them—and to me! Thanks for freeing me from the burden of sin and giving me the power to live for You. I'm so glad You make us all one nation—in Christ—under You.
Amen.

Session 3

Sects and Violence

Republicans and Democrats. Conservatives and liberals. Hawks and doves. Right-wingers and left-wingers. The National Association for the Advancement of Colored People. The National Rifle Association. The American Civil Liberties Union. The Moral Majority.

What do these groups of people have in common? Not much, except that they are all categories of people who are more or less organized to promote their shared concerns.

In every country that allows freedom of expression and association, like-minded people will find each other and work together for a common cause. We might expect that the Jews, with their common heritage and Law, would be a unified nation. However, at the time of Christ, the Jews were split into several sects, parties, and groups. The two most often mentioned in the Bible were the Pharisees and the Sadducees.

PHARISEES AND SADDUCEES

What do you know about the Pharisees and the Sadducees? Write **P** or **S** for the following descriptions. You might put both letters on a same blank. Some blanks may be left unmarked.

1. ____ mostly laymen   ____ mostly clergy (priests)
2. ____ unpopular   ____ popular
3. ____ mostly poor   ____ mostly middle class ____ mostly rich
4. ____ religious conservatives ____ religious liberals
5. ____ strong in local synagogues ____ power centered in temple
6. ____ emphasized Law and traditions ____ emphasized festivals and sacrifices
7. ____ preferred status quo ____ eager for new Messianic kingdom
8. ____ small in number   ____ relatively large group
9. ____ hated Rome   ____ appreciated Rome
10. ____ hated Jesus   ____ appreciated Jesus

What I'd like to remember about the Pharisees and Sadducees from our class discussion:

_____

_____

_____

TWO OTHER SECTS

Zealots

The Zealots were another sect among the Jews. As their name implies, this group was very *zealous* for the Jewish cause. In their beliefs, they resembled the Pharisees. In their actions, they resembled the Maccabees. Sometimes Zealots relied on acts of terrorism and guerrilla warfare to make their point against the Roman occupation. They were equally scornful of the Jewish establishment, which collaborated with Rome in order to maintain its positions of privilege and political power. Although the Zealot spirit extends way back into Jewish history, the Zealots, as a distinct sect, were founded in A.D. 6 by Judas of Galilee. One of Jesus'

12 apostles was identified as a Zealot **(Luke 6:15, Acts 1:13).**

Essenes

Another prominent sect, numbering around 4,000, was the Essenes. The Essenes were disillusioned with all other Jewish sects and parties. In their opinion, the Sadducees were too corrupt, the Zealots were too violent, and the Pharisees weren't strict enough. Washing their hands of the entire mess, the Essenes withdrew from society to live in communes in the wilderness area on the western edge of the Dead Sea. Here they renounced worldly possessions and pleasures, practiced celibacy, and emphasized ceremonial purity. Their communes could be compared to the monasteries of the Middle Ages. They expected that their extreme devotion to God would hasten the imminent return of the Messiah. What we know about the Essenes comes entirely from secular historians, as they are not even mentioned in the Bible. Some have speculated that John the Baptizer lived among them for a while.

Each of these four religious sects considered themselves to be patriotic. Each thought they were doing what was best for the Jewish nation. All except the Sadducees believed they were making possible the imminent appearance of the Messiah. All agreed that the Jewish nation was on the verge of a golden age.

REFLECTION QUESTIONS

1. Which sect do you think Jesus would find *most* to His liking? Why?

2. Which sect do you think Jesus would find *least* to His liking? Why?

A PRAYER FOR TODAY

O God, there are so many different kinds of people in this world! Each one is trying to be more powerful, more important, more outstanding than the other. Each group of people seems to have its own goals, its own power, its own sense of direction.

I know You can't agree with them all, God. I know so many don't follow Your Word and Your loving ways. I know they're confused, just like some people were in Old Testament times.

Help me, God, to see more clearly who people are. Help me hear, see, and understand what people believe and what they're working toward. Help me be patient and accept each person as Your child.

Forgive me, God, when I think I'm better than someone else. Forgive me when I shut them out or fail to understand where they're coming from.

Help me live in peace with the people around me, showing them the love You show me through Jesus, my Savior and Lord.

Amen.

Session 4
Hear Ye! Hear Ye!

God had been silent for 400 years. No inspired Word had come through any prophet. The heavens had been strangely silent.

God suddenly broke into history with two astonishing announcements. This exciting breakthrough is recorded for us by the historian Luke.

In the first four verses of his book, Luke tells us that he wrote so we could have the true and complete story of Jesus' life. As you read from the Gospel of Luke for today's session, you will discover a continuing theme of joy, especially in Mary's song and in the angel's messages. Read to find out how Luke tells the Good News of Jesus Christ. Discover how Luke shows that Jesus' coming into the world brings joy, hope, and salvation to each of us sinners.

GOD'S WORD FOR ME

Do you remember the last research paper you wrote? You probably spent a lot of time and energy collecting and organizing your material. Luke wrote his gospel much like you would write an extensive research paper. Through the Holy Spirit, God gave Luke the words he wrote for you.

1. Read **Luke 1:1-4.** The "preface" to Luke's gospel is written in the manner of a Greek historian. With what is this historian-evangelist concerned **(verse 1)**?

2. What reason does Luke give for writing this book?

GOD'S GOSPEL MESSAGE TO ZECHARIAH

1. Read **Luke 1:5-7.** What surprising news do we learn in **verses 6** and **7**?

2. Do you think we can tell how God feels about us by what blessings we do or don't receive? (Talk about this in class.)

3. Read **Luke 1:8-17.** The name *John* means "The Lord, the God of the covenant, has been gracious." Why is the name *John* fitting for him?

4. Read **Numbers 6:1-5** and **Malachi 4:5-6.** Describe how John was to be different and special.

5. What lessons from **Luke 1:18-20** can we learn and apply to our own lives?

GOD'S GOSPEL MESSAGE TO MARY

1. List the similarities you find in **Luke 1:23-38** between God's announcements to Zechariah and to Mary.

2. List the differences.

3. Compare Mary's response **(Luke 1:34)** with Zechariah's **(Luke 1:18)**. Talk about it.

4. The angel told Mary that Jesus would be great and called the Son of the Most High **(verse 32)**. What else was to be special about Jesus **(verse 33)**?

5. The name *Jesus* means "The Lord is salvation." Why do you think Zechariah and Mary were told the names to give their sons, instead of choosing names for their children as parents usually do today?

GOD'S GRACIOUS GIFTS

1. Read **Luke 1:39-45.** After the angel gave Mary the important message, Mary hurried off to tell Elizabeth, who lived about 70 miles away. Elizabeth was one of God's special gifts to Mary. Think of someone special to you. Thank God for him or her.

2. How would you describe Elizabeth after reading **verses 39-56**?

3. What were God's gifts to Mary and Elizabeth?

4. What one important thing does the Bible tell us in this section about unborn babies?

God is good. He gave gifts to His people long ago, and He continues to give us gifts today. Think of three gifts God has given to you. They might be material, physical, or spiritual gifts. Include your thanks to God for His personal gifts to you in today's closing prayer.

MARY'S SONG OF FAITH

1. Read **Luke 1:46-56.** Tell in your own words how Mary felt about God.

2. We often call Mary's song the *Magnificat*. When Mary sang, she "magnified" God. She recognized Him as the holy, mighty, and merciful God who made her an instrument of His redeeming work. Mary saw through His work the fulfillment of all His promises. Find the *Magnificat* in your hymnal and sing or say the words together. Then tell about one time when God showed mercy to you, performed a mighty deed for you, lifted you, or filled you with good things.

THE BIRTH OF JOHN THE BAPTIZER

A baby's birth is a very blessed occasion. Imagine the parents' and relatives' reactions when John was born to Elizabeth and Zechariah.

1. Read **Luke 1:57-66.** God gave Zechariah the gift of the Holy Spirit so he could prophesy. What important words did Zechariah write?

2. In what way did Zechariah change?

ZECHARIAH'S SONG OF CELEBRATION

1. We call Zechariah's song the Benedictus. *Benedictus* means "blessed." Read **Luke 1:67-80.** Zechariah sang about God's love and faithfulness in keeping His promises. He reminds us that God gives forgiveness and salvation for our sins. Find Zechariah's song in your hymnal. Describe how Zechariah felt about God after John was born and named.

2. Read **verses 74** and **75** again. Why does God save us through Jesus Christ?

3. What does *your* name mean? Think of at least one way you can apply the meaning of your name to God's purpose for your life. Tell how you can use your name to celebrate God's gift of salvation to you.

Praise be to the Lord, the God of Israel, because He has come and has redeemed His people.
Luke 1:68

Session 5
That's Incredible!

THE BIRTH

How would you feel if the President of the United States announced that he would speak at your high school graduation ceremony? If the most popular music group in the nation agreed to perform a benefit concert for your school? If the highest paid professional athlete agreed to speak at your athletic awards banquet?

Would you make any special arrangements? Where would these important people stay? Would you provide hotel accommodations? Give up your bedroom? Pitch a tent in your backyard?

Would you activate a publicity committee? Would you announce their coming in the newspapers and on radio and TV? Would there be live news coverage? Would you send specially printed invitations? Whom would you invite? Government leaders? Pastors? Garbage collectors?

What travel arrangements would be made? Would they fly into the nearest airport? Be chauffeured in a limousine? Hitchhike?

*Someone more special than any president or star athlete or popular musical group came to earth many years ago. God Himself arrived in human flesh and blood! The fact that God came at all is amazing enough, but **how** He came is even more incredible.*

1. Read **Luke 2:1-20**. Then list surprising circumstances and incredible aspects of the coming of Baby Jesus.

_____

_____

_____

2. Compare Jesus' birth with your own birth. In what ways was Jesus' more humble? In what ways was it more glorious?

More Humble	More Glorious
_____	_____
_____	_____
_____	_____

3. Compare the angel's appearance to the shepherds (**Luke 2:8-14**) with the angel's appearances to Zechariah (**Luke 1:11-20**) and Mary (**Luke 1:26-38**). In what ways were these angelic appearances similar?

4. What do we learn from the angels about the significance of the Baby born in Bethlehem (**Luke 2:10-11**)?

THE INFANT

1. Read **Luke 2:21-24**. The events recorded in these verses combine to tell us something very significant about Jesus. What is it?

2. **Luke 2:24** and **Leviticus 12:8** tell us something about Joseph and Mary. What is it?

3. Read **Luke 2:25-35**. What additional and surprising insights do we get from Simeon about the significance and destiny of the baby Jesus?

4. What does Simeon see in the future for Mary **(verse 34)**?

5. Read **Luke 2:36-38**. Why do you think it's important that Luke tells us about Anna, the prophetess? Describe how Anna spoke of Jesus and His work.

THE BOY

1. We know very little about Jesus' boyhood. Read **Luke 2:40-52** to find out what Luke tells about the boy Jesus.

2. Suppose you were the same age as Jesus, growing up in the town of Nazareth. Suppose also that He was your best friend and you spent a lot of time together. Use your imagination and what you know about Jesus from **Luke 2:40-52**. Write a letter to your cousin Baruch who lives in Joppa, describing your best friend, Jesus. What does He look like? What are His hobbies? How does He do in synagogue school? How does He get along with His parents and His friends? What do you enjoy doing together? What do you talk about together?

SOMETHING TO THINK ABOUT

Astronaut Jim Irwin, one of America's astronauts who walked on the moon, is a Christian who once gave his personal testimony at a Billy Graham crusade in Milwaukee. He spoke of his experiences in space, but then concluded, "The really amazing thing is not that man set foot on the moon, but that God set foot on the earth."

Considering the fact that God visited this planet and the manner in which He came, what can we conclude about God? Share your thoughts with the class.

_____

The Word became flesh and lived for a while among us. We have seen His glory, the glory of the one and only Son, who came from the Father, full of grace and truth.

John 1:14

Session 6

Through the Eyes of Jesus' Stepfather

An evangelist once told of an experience he had with Jewish believers in Jesus. The evangelist asked, "What was it that brought you to the conviction that Jesus was your Messiah?"

They replied, "That's easy! The genealogies!"

Many people, as they read the Bible, probably skim over the genealogies and wonder what purpose they might serve. Yet the Bible assures us that **"All Scripture is God-breathed and is useful for teaching . . ."** (2 Timothy 3:16). God has used the genealogies to lead people to Christ and to eternal life.

The Holy Spirit knew what He was doing when He inspired Matthew to write his gospel and include what he did. Matthew's gospel contains material that is especially meaningful to the Jewish people. Let's take another look at the birth and boyhood of Jesus, this time through the eyes of the evangelist Matthew.

ROOTS

You will never become the King or Queen of England. Why not? Because you are not tall enough? Smart enough? Beautiful enough? No. You will never sit on the throne of England because you were not born into the English royal family. Matthew establishes right from the beginning that Jesus is the Christ (Jewish Messiah), and that He has the necessary genealogical credentials.

1. **Matthew 1:1** is a very brief summary of Jesus' family tree. Why do you think Matthew singles out the names of Abraham and David?

2. This genealogy doesn't just trace a family tree. In many ways it reminds us about God and His dealings with His people. Skim the names Matthew listed in **verses 2-16**. Write the names that are familiar to you. Then write one thing you learn about God from His dealings with that person.

_____

_____

_____

_____

3. Jewish genealogies did not commonly include women. Which four women are listed by Matthew? Why do you think God wanted Matthew to include these four women in Jesus' genealogy?

The genealogy includes men and women, great and small people, good and bad, Jewish and Gentile people. Jesus is very much a part of the human race He came to save. Throughout this genealogical history we are reminded of God's faithfulness and mercy. Unfailingly, God works out His purpose through all the circumstances of life.

A WEDDING ALMOST RUINED

Matthew now turns his attention to Joseph, Jesus' earthly stepfather, and gives the story of the first Christmas from his perspective.

1. Read **Matthew 1:18**. How do you think Joseph felt when he found out that his bride-to-be was pregnant?

2. What did Joseph decide to do **(1:19)**? Why?

3. Read **Deuteronomy 22:23-24**. How does this part of Scripture help you understand and describe the character of Joseph?

4. According to **Psalm 130:7-8,** who is going to save Israel from all their sins? What does this tell us about Jesus?

5. Read **Matthew 1:21-23**. List four things that these verses tell us about Jesus.

_____

_____

_____

_____

6. Some people believe that Mary was a virgin all her life. Read **verses 24-25**. Write what you believe about Jesus' mother, Mary, and her marriage to Joseph.

_____

_____

_____

7. In one sentence, write the main point Matthew makes in this section **(verses 18-25)**.

WE THREE KINGS?

"We three kings of Orient are . . . "

So begins a familiar Christmas carol. The three kings probably were not kings from the Orient. Matthew doesn't tell us they were kings. (That assumption comes from the prophecy in **Isaiah 60:3**.) Nor does he say how many there were. (The idea that there were three comes from the number of gifts they brought **[Matt 2:11]**). And contrary to many artists' depictions, the Magi did not worship the newborn king at the manger. (They arrived much later at the house where Jesus' family was staying **[2:11]**).

Read **Matthew 2:1-12**. What important contributions to our understanding of Jesus does this section of Scripture make?

ESCAPE AND RETURN

Another part of Jesus' life that is recorded only by Matthew is the escape to Egypt. Read about it in **Matthew 2:13-18**.

1. What kind of a man was Herod? Why did he act the way he did?

2. What do you think God wants us to learn from this narrative?

3. Read **Matthew 2:19-23**. What can you learn from these last few verses?

4. Matthew gives us a wonderful insight into the person of Joseph. Review **Matthew 1:24; 2:13-14; 2:19-21**. What does Joseph demonstrate repeatedly?

Joseph is never quoted directly in the Bible. The important thing is not what he said, but what he *did*. Even more important is the way in which God used Joseph as His instrument. Joseph was completely submissive to God's plans for his life. Joseph does not stand out as a spectacular Bible person, but he was faithful to God.

She will give birth to a son, and you are to give Him the name Jesus, because He will save His people from their sins.
Matthew 1:21

Session 7

The Synoptic Gospels

An old tale from India tells about five blind men who came to an elephant. One felt the elephant's trunk and decided the animal was shaped very much like a large garden hose. The second felt an ear and decided the elephant was similar to a large fan. The third felt the elephant's side and determined that the animal was like a large wall. The fourth wrapped his arms around one leg of the elephant and concluded the elephant was shaped like the trunk of a tree. The fifth blind man grabbed the tail and proclaimed that an elephant was like a rope.

Each of the blind men told the truth from his own perspective. Each had a unique insight into the animal called an elephant, but not one of the blind men had the whole picture.

We are blessed to have four different perspectives from which to view the life of our Lord and Savior, Jesus Christ. Matthew, Mark, Luke, and John each present Christ in a different way in their accounts called "gospels."

The word *Gospel* means "good news." In the Greek language of the New Testament, the word is *euanggelion*, from which we get the English words "evangelism" and "evangelist." *Evangelism* is the important task of telling people the Good News of Jesus Christ. The word *Gospel* is used in both a broad and a narrow sense. Narrowly speaking, the Gospel is the Good News that Jesus died on the cross and rose to life for the sins of the world. In the broader sense, the Gospel is the whole story of Jesus as recorded by Matthew, Mark, Luke, and John.

Each gospel writer, like any historian, is also an editor, deciding what events to tell and what points to emphasize. Sometimes the accounts are very different, as are Matthew's and Luke's accounts of the birth and boyhood of Jesus. In other instances the gospel accounts are very similar. In all cases the gospel accounts are complementary, not contradictory, for each was written by inspiration of the same God. Each is God's true Word, coming to us through the distinctive personalities of Matthew, Mark, Luke, and John.

In this session you will learn more about the distinctive features of each of the first three gospels. Remember that this session contains a lot of generalizations and summaries. We will emphasize the differences, not the similarities. The gospel writers Matthew, Mark, and Luke tell the events in Jesus' life in a similar order and way. Because of this, the first three gospels are called the *synoptic gospels*. Look at the word *synoptic*. Divide the word into two parts and think of other words that use these combinations of letters.

Syn = _____

Optic = _____

What do you think *synoptic* means?

_____

MATTHEW

1. The author:

_____

_____

2. The audience:

_____

_____

3. Who does he say Jesus is?

_____

_____

4. The structure of the book:

_____

_____

5. Themes found in Matthew:

_____

_____

_____

_____

_____

_____

MARK

1. The author:

_____

_____

2. The audience:

_____

_____

3. Who does he say Jesus is?

_____

_____

Distinctive characteristics of Mark:

_____

_____

_____

LUKE

1. The author:

_____

_____

2. The audience:

_____

_____

3. Who does he say Jesus is?

_____

_____

4. Distinctive characteristics of Luke:

_____

_____

_____

STRUCTURE OF THE THREE GOSPELS

Although each synoptic gospel has distinctive features, they all have similar structures. Look at the diagram of the structure of each gospel. Numbers of the chapters have been placed in each section. Skim through the chapters of each gospel. Choose from the list of titles below. Identify each rectangular section of the synoptic gospels. "Ministry in Galilee" and "Travel Account" have been labeled for you. (If a label has a number behind it, it is used in that many gospels.)

The Twelve	*In Jerusalem (3)*	*Passion and Resurrection (3)*
Parables (3)	*Church Discipline*	*Birth—Boyhood Stories (2)*
Last Things	*Up to Jerusalem (3)*	*Sermon on the Mount*

SOMETHING TO THINK ABOUT

Most biographers do a thorough job of describing the entire lives of their subjects. It is evident from the structures of the gospels that Jesus' biographers ignored about 90 percent of His life and described the events of one week (Holy Week) in great detail. Why do you think they did this?

Jesus did many other things as well. If every one of them were written down, I suppose that even the whole world would not have room for the books that would be written.
John 21:25

But these are written that you may believe that Jesus is the Christ, the Son of God, and that by believing you may have life in His name.
John 20:31

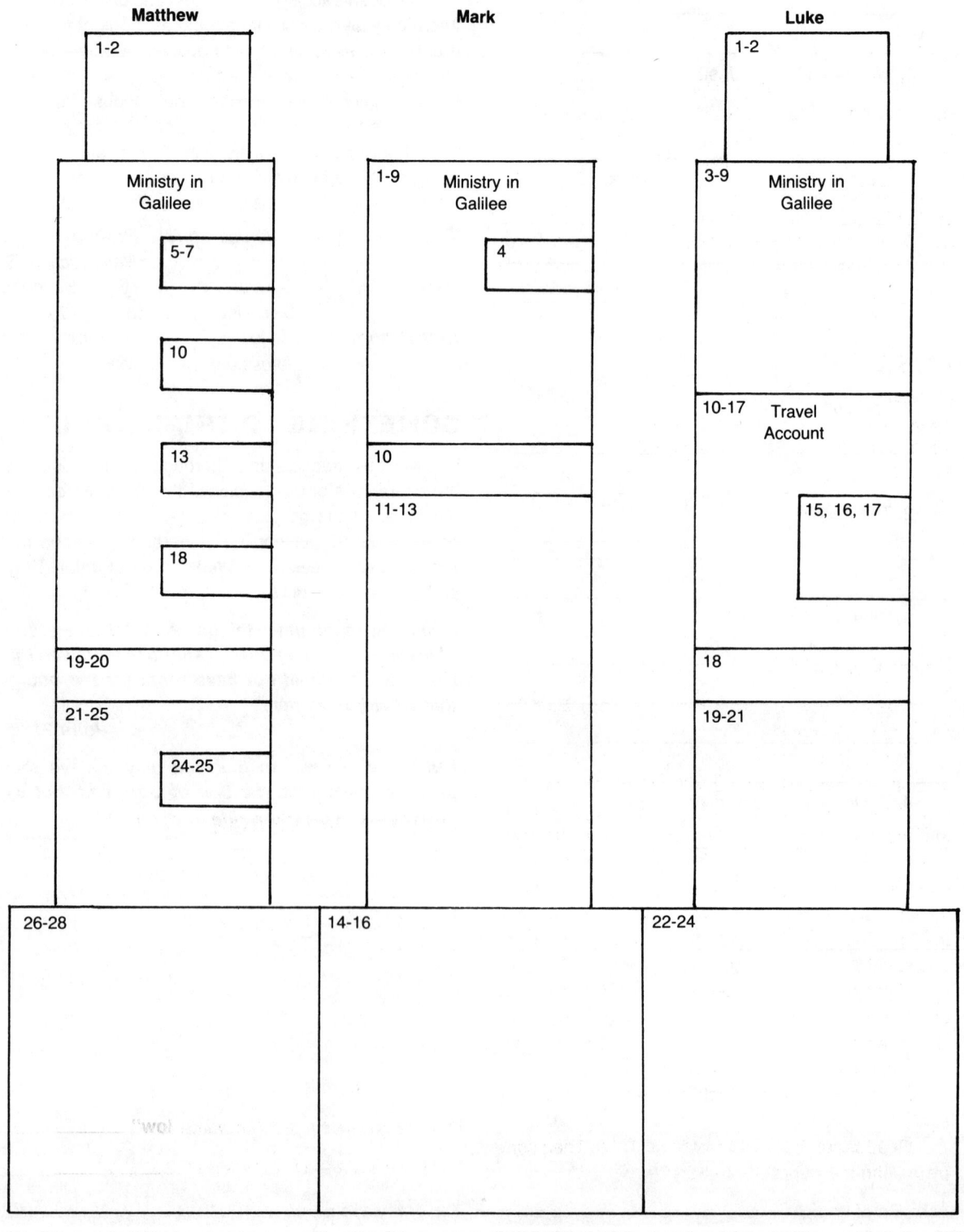

Matthew	Mark	Luke
1-2		1-2
Ministry in Galilee	1-9 Ministry in Galilee	3-9 Ministry in Galilee
5-7	4	
10		
13	10	10-17 Travel Account
18	11-13	15, 16, 17
19-20		18
21-25		19-21
24-25		
26-28	14-16	22-24

Session 8

Trailblazing Fire

About 30 years have passed since the heavens resounded with angelic praises, "Glory to God in the highest, and on earth peace . . . " The Wise Men have long since returned to their home countries. Some of the shepherds who received the angelic birth announcement have probably died by this time. Certainly Zechariah and Elizabeth, Simeon and Anna are dead. Many who heard the witness of the shepherds, the Wise Men, or the others have either died or forgotten all about it. After all, three decades have passed and nothing has happened.

God had to start all over announcing the coming of the Messiah. How would He do it this time? Would He again rely on heavenly angels to proclaim the Messiah's arrival? Would Wise Men arrive from the East? Again God's methods surprise us. He appointed a publicity committee of one—a man with seemingly no knack for public relations—and sent him where nobody lived to proclaim a much different message than the angelic "Fear not." Let's get into God's Word and meet this person.

JOHN'S CALL

1. Read **Luke 3:1-2.** How do these words of God differ from the way a fairy tale usually begins?

2. A seminary is a place where men receive education and training to be pastors. The most exciting day of the year at a seminary is "Call Day," the day that the soon-to-be-graduates receive their first calls. They stand in alphabetical order as their names and their assignments are read aloud in front of an overflow assembly of interested and anxious wives, parents, and friends. Each graduating seminarian receives a call document that explains the details of his call. The document answers such questions as: Where is my church? How many members does it have? What special areas of ministry will I have? What will my salary be? What are the housing arrangements? Do I get a car allowance? How many church workers are on the staff?

Read **Luke 3:3-4** and **Matthew 3:1-4.** Then complete John the Baptizer's call document.

Location of church: _____

Characteristics of his church building: _____

How many members? _____

Means of transportation: _____

Salary: _____

Miscellaneous provisions: _____

JOHN'S MESSAGE

1. John's ministry and message were predicted and summarized by the prophet Isaiah **(Isaiah 40:3-5)** and repeated by Luke **(Luke 3:4-6).** Taken literally, it sounds like John was to head a giant earth moving company! Write what you think the following phrases mean:

"make straight paths" _____

"every valley filled in" _____

"every mountain and hill made low" _____

"crooked roads straightened" _____

"rough ways smoothed" _____

2. Read **Luke 3:7-9.** What did John's audience take great pride in?

3. According to these Bible verses **(3:7-9),** what does John think of their family tree?

4. What does John say is more important than heredity **(3:11-14)?**

5. Write what these figures of speech symbolize **(3:7-17):**

Axe _____

Trees _____

Good fruit _____

Fire _____

JOHN'S EFFECT

1. How did the people respond to John's preaching **(Luke 3:10)?**

2. Review the Ten Commandments in **Exodus 20:1-17** or in Luther's Small Catechism. Now skim **Luke 3:10-14.** Which of the Ten Commandments was John concerned that the people keep?

3. Notice that even some of the unspiritual and unlikely people were deeply moved by John's message **(3:12).** Imagine that you are a first-century Jew, witnessing tax collectors and Roman soldiers ready to change their ways. How would you expect and hope that John would answer these people?

4. If John could preach to people in America today, write what you think he would say to:

An IRS agent _____
_____

A U.S. soldier _____
_____

An employer _____
_____

An employee _____
_____

A church member _____
_____

A high school student _____
_____

JOHN'S IDENTITY

1. Whom did the people think John might be **(Luke 3:15-16)?**

2. What did John think of this **(verse 16)?**

3. Read **verse 17.** A common sight in Jesus' day was a farmer tossing the harvested wheat into the air with a pitchfork. The edible grain would fall back to the threshing floor and the wind would blow away the inedible chaff. What do these figures symbolize?

The winnowing fork _____

The wheat _____

The barn _____

The chaff _____

The fire _____

4. Read **verse 18.** What is so good about John's "good news"?

JOHN'S REWARD

1. What does **verse 19** tell us about the kind of person that John was?

2. What was John's reward **(verse 20)?** Have you ever suffered for doing right? Tell about it.

3. Why do you think God chose someone like John the Baptizer to publicize and prepare for the coming Messiah? Why not angels—or a publicity committee—or at least someone more tactful?

SOMETHING TO THINK ABOUT

God knew that people would not appreciate or receive a Savior unless they were convinced of their lost and sinful condition. The Law prepares us for the Gospel. Do you realize that you, too, are a sinner and need to repent of your sins? We must each continually hear and apply the convicting message of John the Baptizer to ourselves. As Martin Luther said in the first of his famous 95 Theses: "When Our Lord and Master Jesus Christ said, 'Repent' **[Matt. 4:17]**, he willed the entire life of believers to be one of repentance."

Think about these Bible verses. What do they mean for your life? Talk about it with a friend today.

Prepare the way for the Lord.
Luke 3:4

Unless you repent, you too will all perish.
Luke 13:3

Produce fruit in keeping with repentance.
Luke 3:8

[Jesus] will baptize you with the Holy Spirit and with fire.
Luke 3:16

Session 9
Review of Unit 1

Answer the following questions to help you review unit 1.

1. What did the Old Testament people expect as they waited and longed for the Messiah?

2. On what were their expectations based? (List as many of God's promises as you can.)

3. How does the American idea of "one nation under God" differ from the ancient Jewish idea?

4. Describe, from your knowledge of religious sects at the time of Christ, what qualities God appreciates most in a person. Support your statements with specific references to people and events in the first two chapters of Matthew and Luke.

5. "God is full of surprises." Illustrate this statement by referring to what you learned throughout unit 1.

6. Explain why John the Baptizer was an ideal preparer for Jesus.

7. Explain the concept of "righteousness based on mercy" rather than on Law.

8. What are the *synoptic gospels?* Tell briefly about the theme and characteristics of each.

9. Describe what a "call" from God means to you.

10. Write in your own words John the Baptizer's message to the people.

Unit 2
Jesus, the Minister

"Could I see your identification?"

"Take out your driver's license and registration please."

"I'll need to see your passport or your birth certificate."

Identification is important. We need it to get into school functions, to write or cash a check, to drive a car, and to travel in foreign countries. Rights and privileges often hinge on our having proper identification.

Throughout Jesus' ministry, the question people asked most often about Him was "Who is He?" Everything Jesus said and did—and everything that happened to Him—was designed to help people answer this question.

Jesus didn't need to carry identification. His ID was the Word of God. **"Diligently study the Scriptures,"** Jesus said, **"because you think that by them you possess eternal life. These are the Scriptures that testify about Me" (John 5:39).**

As you diligently study the Scriptures during this unit, may the Holy Spirit reveal to you who Jesus is. May He cause you to respond accordingly, and give you joy in God's promise of eternal life!

Session 10

One of the Guys

Who is Jesus?
Some considered Him to be just a carpenter's son. Others were convinced He was demon-possessed. Many viewed Him as a prophet. Actually, Luke clarifies Jesus' identity right from the start of His earthly ministry. Let's discover what Luke tells us.

THE BAPTISM OF JESUS

A pastor's installation at his new congregation, the appearance of a bride at her wedding, the unveiling of a great work of art—all these events are anticipated and greeted with great interest and excitement. What will he be like? What will she look like? Will it look as beautiful as I expect it to?

In this session, we look closely at God's Word as the people eagerly anticipated the unveiling, the first public appearance, the inauguration day of the God-man Messiah for whom the people had been waiting. What kind of beginning will it be? Read **Luke 3:21-22** and **Matthew 3:13-14**.

1. What did John the Baptizer think of the way Jesus began his ministry?

2. Why do you think John felt the way he did?

3. Someone has said, "Go to the Jordan and there find the Trinity." How is the Trinity (three persons in one God) revealed in these verses?

4. How is Jesus identified as the Servant-Son-King-Messiah the Jews have been waiting for? (See **Psalm 2:6-8; Isaiah 42:1** and **6**; and **Isaiah 11:1-2**.)

THE GENEALOGY OF JESUS

Have you ever researched your ancestors' history and made a family tree? How many generations back could you go? Even in our modern day of vast communications and extensive record-keeping, many of us might be able to trace back only a few generations.

Read **Luke 3:21-38**. Isn't it amazing! Jesus could trace his ancestry through David, Abraham, Noah, and back to Adam—the first man God created!

1. How do you think the historian Luke had access to such information?

2. Why do you think he recorded it for us?

THE TEMPTATION OF JESUS

1. A bride and groom's wedding is often followed by a joyous reception and honeymoon. Celebration dances and parties follow the president's inauguration into office. An author and a publisher might schedule a signing party after the publication of a new book. However, Jesus' baptism was followed by a different kind of experience. Read about it in **Luke 4:1-13**. Where did Jesus go? Whose idea was it? What happened there? How long did it last? Why do you suppose this experience was necessary or significant?

2. Compare Jesus' experiences after His baptism with the experiences of the children of Israel. God made way for the Israelites to pass through the Red Sea and led them into the wilderness for 40 years, where He tested their faith and obedience as He continually cared for them. Jesus passed through the waters of His baptism and was led into the wilderness for 40 days, where He was similarly tested and cared for. The children of Israel often failed their tests, but Jesus passed with an A+. What significance might this comparison have?

3. The temptations Jesus faced are similar to temptations humans have always faced.

a. The first is a temptation to pleasure, to fulfill our physical needs and desires the devil's way. It's as old as the Garden of Eden. Think of at least two examples of how Satan might come at us with this kind of temptation today.

b. What kind of temptation is the second one? Give one or two examples of this kind of temptation today.

c. What kind of temptation is the third? Tell how the third temptation demonstrates the devil's cleverness and capacity to deceive.

d. How did Jesus fight these temptations? How does God help you fight temptations in your life?

Jesus overcame temptations through the memorization of, allegiance to, and application of God's Word. We can learn from Jesus' example how important it is to know, understand, and apply God's Word. How about you? Are you able to remember passages from God's Word and use them in everyday situations in your life?

SOMETHING TO THINK ABOUT

We can be grateful that Jesus is not *just* an example for us to follow. If He were only an example, no matter how hard we tried, we could not successfully imitate His perfect life, and we would be condemned for our failure. **The Good News is that Jesus is not merely our example—He is our Substitute.** He, though He was (and is) God, became one *of* us and one *for* us. He lived the perfect life we couldn't live and finally suffered the punishment we deserved. **By His perfect life, innocent death, and glorious resurrection, our sins are forgiven and we have eternal life through faith in Him.**

You became God's special person in the waters of your baptism. God calls you to experience your "40 years" of temptation. God promises that when you die, you will enter your promised land of heaven. **God and His Word are with you always.** That's something to celebrate!

MEMORY WORK
GOD'S WORD IS REAL TO ME

Read the Bible verses at the end of this session. Then ask yourself these questions:
What does God say to me in these words?
What does God mean in these words?
What do these words mean to me today?

If possible, begin today to memorize God's Word. Memorize *exactly* so that you can store God's important messages and information inside your head for your daily life.

Hints on how to memorize:

1. Note the context. How is the verse used?

2. Know the meanings of individual words. Look in a dictionary.

3. Involve many parts of your body. Read the verse aloud several times perfectly. Write the verse several times. Use sign language or your imagination to act out the verse.

4. Visualize the verse. Make it into a picture in your mind or on paper.

5. Break the verse into parts. Memorize one part at a time. Include the reference, too.

6. Review the verse often until it becomes a part of you.

Man does not live on bread alone, but on every word that comes from the mouth of God.
                                Matthew 4:4

For we do not have a high priest who is unable to sympathize with our weaknesses, but we have one who has been tempted in every way, just as we are—yet was without sin. Let us then approach the throne of grace with confidence, so that we may receive mercy and find grace to help us in our time of need.
                                Hebrews 4:15-16

Session 11

Homecoming, Nazareth High, A. D. 29

In July 1969 American astronaut Neil Armstrong became the first human to set foot on the moon. The whole world watched via satellite as he took this "giant step for mankind."

Hometown friends and relatives greeted Armstrong with a great homecoming celebration in Wapakaneta, Ohio. Today, signposts along the highway remind all who pass through Wapakaneta, "This is the hometown of Neil Armstrong." The people also built a space museum and a monument to honor the hometown hero.

Jesus made headline news throughout the region of Galilee 2,000 years ago. We would expect His return to Nazareth, His boyhood home, to be a memorable occasion. It was just that. But no signposts were placed along the highway. No museum or monument was built to proclaim Jesus as the hometown boy who made good. Let's find out what did happen.

EXCEPT IN HIS OWN COUNTRY

Read about Jesus' homecoming in **Luke 4:14-30**.

1. Describe how and why Jesus became well-known and popular. Was it through His miracles? His good looks? His public relations team? What was it?

2. Tell about Jesus' Sabbath Day habit. Did He spend the Sabbath doing His homework? Sleeping in? Worshiping? Catching up on fan mail?

3. If **Luke 4:17-19** is representative of the tone and content of Jesus' teaching and preaching, how would you compare Jesus' methods to those of John the Baptizer?

4. How did Jesus' hometown folks react at first to His words **(verse 22a)**?

5. Explain the people's second thoughts **(verse 22b)**.

6. Why did Jesus' next words **(verses 24-27)** cause so much offense?

7. The homecoming parade "arrives at Nazareth High" **(verse 29)**. How did Jesus manage to excuse Himself from the party **(verse 30)**?

NOT WITHOUT HONOR

Read **Luke 4:31-37**.

1. What was unique about Jesus' teaching?

2. What else amazed people about Jesus **(verse 36)**?

3. What idea is present in both the beginning and the end of this Bible section?

THE REALITY OF JESUS' HOMECOMING

Have you been away from home for a while? What was it like when you came home? How did you feel? Who welcomed you? What kinds of things happened?

Jesus had been alone in the desert for almost a month and a half. We wouldn't call it a vacation for Him. The devil constantly tempted Him. Jesus finally returned to Galilee **"in the power of the Spirit."** How relieved even Jesus must have felt!

Choose one of the following projects. Share your finished product with the class.

1. Imagine you are a reporter covering the story of Jesus' homecoming for *The Nazareth News*. On a separate paper, write a news feature or an editorial for tomorrow's paper.

2. Imagine you are a cartoonist for the same newspaper. Illustrate a cartoon strip about Jesus' homecoming.

3. Write about a time you experienced rejection. Explain how Jesus must have felt when He returned to Nazareth.

4. Imagine you are Jesus writing a letter to your mother, Mary, in Capernaum. Tell about your experiences in Nazareth where you both had lived.

Despite the hostile hometown reception, Jesus' popularity and fame continued to grow. More exciting things are coming. Tune in tomorrow.

He came to that which was His own, but His own did not receive Him. Yet to all who received Him, to those who believed in His name, He gave the right to become children of God.
John 1:11-12

Session 12

Hide and Seek

"Come to the big crusade at the 100,000 seat Metro Coliseum and hear the world-famous evangelist, Razzle Dazzle McFazzle."

Bring your sick! Come, expecting a miracle! Come to our special Friday night service featuring Wheeler Dealer McHealer.

"We've got a great youth group at our church! Last weekend we had over 100 people at the costume dance. Over 50 youth are already signed up to go to next week's Gospel rock concert. Then, on Sunday, we will sponsor the pancake breakfast. That will help raise funds for our new stereo and pool table. We always have big crowds and lots of fun. Won't YOU join us?"

Have you ever attended a big revival? A rally where thousands and thousands of people sang and prayed together? A breakfast or a chili supper that had a tremendous turnout. Would you like to experience this? Do you ever wonder what God thinks about it?

People seem to have a love affair with big numbers. Lots of people! Lots of money! Lots of activity! Lots of excitement! That's where it's all at. The more, the merrier. The bigger, the better! Do you think so?

Jesus had no trouble generating crowds and excitement. He did it without spending money for publicity, coliseums, and TV time. He did it without a large organization or mailing lists and without appealing for funds. In fact, He avoided crowds, forbade publicity, and held many meetings in places too small to accommodate the numbers of people who wanted to hear and see Him.

Let's find out more about how Jesus ministered to the people. Please use notebook paper to answer questions in this session.

AFTER A REST

Read **Luke 4:38-41.**

1. On this same Sabbath Day, a day of rest, how did Jesus spend His morning?
His afternoon?
His evening?

2. The expelled demons knew who Jesus was **(verse 41).** Why do you think Jesus ordered them not to proclaim His identity?

3. What *rest* did Jesus want on this day of rest?

ON THE RUN

Read **Luke 4:42-44.** Then talk about your answers to these questions.

1. Where did Jesus go the next morning?
2. Why did He leave? See also **Mark 1:35.**
3. What did the local people want Jesus to do?
4. Why did Jesus refuse?
5. What did Jesus consider His most important task?
6. What do you think is the most important task of the church today?
7. What would you say the most important task is for you as a Christian?
8. This section is entitled **"On the Run."** What was Jesus running from? What was He running toward?

IN TOUCH

Now read **Luke 5:12-16.**

1. Describe the man's disease and its seriousness.
2. Did this man have faith in Jesus? Explain your answer.
3. Why do you think Jesus touched him?
4. Why do you think Jesus said, "Don't tell anyone"?
5. What happened, and how did Jesus respond **(verses 15-16)**? See also **Mark 1:45.**
6. This section is entitled "In Touch." With whom is Jesus in touch?
7. Is it important for you to make special attempts to spend time alone with God? Why? Why not?

OUT OF SIGHT

Read **Luke 5:17-20.**

1. What was Jesus doing on this day in this house?
2. Describe the paralytic man and his friends.
3. What did Jesus "see" in these people?
4. Look at Jesus' response **(verse 20).** Which statements do you think are true?
   a. Jesus didn't know at first that the man was paralyzed.
   b. The man's spiritual healing was more important than his physical healing.

    c. The man was paralyzed because he was especially sinful.

    d. Jesus and the paralyzed man had been friends for a long time.

    e. Jesus didn't like to be interrupted so rudely.

    5. Now read **Luke 5:21-26.** *Blasphemy* means claiming for oneself what belongs only to God. The power to forgive sins is God's alone. Did Jesus *blaspheme*?

    6. In what three ways did Jesus demonstrate His divine power?

    7. Which is easier to say: "Your sins are forgiven," or "Get up and walk"? Explain your answer.

    8. This section is entitled "Out of Sight." What invisible things did Jesus see? What visible things did the Pharisees *not* see?

SUMMARIZING THIS SESSION

    It was a challenge for Jesus to find time to be alone with His heavenly Father. He stifled those who would publicize His identity or His miracles and thus "crowd out" His devotional life. He took time to be alone with His Father, not to avoid ministering to the people, but to *prepare* Himself for His ministry to people.

    When Jesus returned from His devotional time to His work, His main concern was to preach, not to heal. Healing was an important aspect of His ministry, but its purpose was not to attract attention, crowds, or money. Jesus' mighty acts confirmed that His wonderful words were true. His healing also demonstrated His great compassion, sensitivity, tenderness, humility, and unselfishness.

HOW TO HAVE DAILY QUIET TIME WITH GOD

    1. *Resolve to make a quiet time part of your daily routine* (like brushing your teeth, listening to your stereo, or walking the dog).

    2. *Set aside a quiet time every day,* perhaps in early morning or before you go to bed at night.

    3. *Enjoy quiet time in the same place every day.* Choose a place free from disturbances and distractions.

    4. *Begin quiet time with a prayer.* Ask God to direct your thoughts. Invite Him to speak to you in a personal way through His Word. Use a favorite prayer, or speak to God in conversation.

    5. *Read from the Bible.* Read to enjoy! Use devotional helps, but don't let them become a substitute for God's Word. Read short sections of Scripture at a time. Stop and think about what you're reading. Do you need a place to start? Try Psalms, Proverbs, or one of the New Testament books.

    6. *Close your quiet time with prayer.* Use one of these outlines for a guide:

A—Adoration	P—Praise
C—Confession	R—Repent
T—Thanksgiving	A—Ask
S—Supplication	Y—Yield

    Keep a prayer list (a list of people and things you pray for). Keep a record of God's answers and remember to thank Him. Close with the Lord's Prayer.

    7. *A quiet time might be 10 minutes of the time God gives you. Make time.* It's the most important time in your day. How about beginning your quiet time with God today if you haven't already? God's blessings!

SOMETHING TO THINK ABOUT

Not everyone who says to Me, "Lord, Lord," will enter the kingdom of heaven, but only he who does the will of My Father who is in heaven. Many will say to Me on that day, "Lord, Lord, did we not prophesy in Your name, and in Your name drive out demons and perform many miracles?" Then I will tell them plainly, "I never knew you. Away from Me, you evildoers!"

                                          Matthew 7:21-23

Session 13

The Coach Picks His Team

Who would you choose to help you begin a religious movement that would surpass all world religions and change the course of world history? Politicians? TV stars? Pastors? Business people? Sports heroes?

Jesus began a religious movement. In this session, you'll find out how many and what kinds of people He chose to carry out His great mission.

GONE FISHING

Read **Luke 5:1-11.**

1. What did the people want from Jesus?

Are you as eager as they were to hear God's Word?

Why do you think Jesus wanted to get into a boat?

2. Why would Peter not want to obey Jesus' command to let down the nets?

3. Why did Peter obey Jesus?

Have you ever obeyed Jesus even when it was hard to do? Share your experience with a friend.

4. What was the result of Peter's obedience?

Why did Peter react the way he did **(verse 8)?**

Do you think Peter's response pleased Jesus? Why or why not?

5. How are catching fish and catching men similar? How are they different?

6. What do you think Jesus saw in Peter and his companions that made Him want them on His team?

Would Jesus choose you for His team?

ONE FOR THE MONEY

Read **Luke 5:27-32.**

1. What was Levi's occupation?

Describe Levi's reputation.

Why might Levi be reluctant to obey Jesus' call?

2. Levi held a great banquet to celebrate his call into the ministry. Why do you think he was so happy about it?

Why do you think Levi invited tax collectors and "sinners"?

3. Explain Jesus' response in **verses 31** and **32.**

Is it better to be "righteous" or a "sinner"? Why?

4. In light of this Bible story, do you think you'd "make the cut" for Jesus' team? Explain your answer.

THE FINAL CUT

Now read **Luke 6:12-16.**

1. What does the word *disciple* mean to you?
How many disciples did Jesus have?

2. What did Jesus do before He made His final selection of His team of apostles?

Think of an important decision you have to make. How might praying about your situation help you know what to do?

3. Although Jesus had (and still has) many *disciples,* He chose only a few to be His *apostles.* The word *apostle* means literally to be "sent out." The term *apostle* is used in Scripture to refer only to a select few people: The 12 **(Luke 6)**; Matthias **(Acts 1:21-22)**; Paul (various references), and Jesus **(Hebrews 3:1).**

What are the signs of apostleship according to **2 Corinthians 12:12; Luke 9:1-2; Acts 2:43;** and **5:12?**

4. What was so special about the apostles? See **Luke 11:49; 1 Corinthians 12:28;** and **Ephesians 2:20.**

SOMETHING TO THINK ABOUT

The men Jesus chose weren't rich, famous, or powerful. One had a terrible reputation. Yet Jesus took these men, trained them, and turned the world upside down with them. Jesus demonstrated that He could take ordinary people and do extraordinary things with and through them. Jesus does this today too!

What about you? Have you answered Jesus' call to discipleship? Are you willing to leave everything behind and trust your life to Him?

Jesus might call you to be a pastor, a teacher, or a missionary. Or He might call you to use your skills to serve Him right where you are. Think of a time in the last two days when you had an opportunity to "catch a person" for Jesus. What happened? Tell about it. Then pray that God would help you respond to His call to love Him, share your faith, and serve Him among those around you.

You did not choose Me, but I chose you to go and bear fruit—fruit that will last.
John 15:16

You are a chosen people, a royal priesthood, a holy nation, a people belonging to God, that you may declare the praises of Him who called you out of darkness into His wonderful light.
1 Peter 2:9

Session 14

Jesus Breaks the Rules

Rules. It seems that we love rules. We like to make rules. We aren't comfortable unless we have rules. But it's not always easy to live by the rules.

Many think "religion" is a bunch of rules that need to be kept. Many are fairly comfortable with a religion of rules—dos and don'ts—as long as it's not too difficult to keep them and as long as we don't have to keep them perfectly.

How do you feel about rules?

Many of the "religious" people of Jesus' day weren't comfortable with the Scriptures because they didn't contain enough rules, and the rules that God gave disturbed them. Jesus summarized God's rules, the Ten Commandments, with two brief statements: **"Love the Lord your God with all your heart and with all your soul and with all your strength and with all your mind,"** and **"Love your neighbor as yourself" (Luke 10:27; Deuteronomy 6:5; Leviticus 19:18).** If we would keep these rules, we wouldn't need any others.

Because of sin, we *cannot* and do not keep God's rules. So we manufacture other rules we *can* keep. By keeping these man-made rules, we imagine that we please God, but at times our rules prevent us from doing what God requires.

Jesus experienced a head-on collision with the religion of man-made rules. Many resented Jesus. He was labeled a "rule-breaker." Jesus threatened those who became comfortable with their system of manufactured rules and self-satisfying ways. Let's find out how this happened.

BREAKFAST

Read **Luke 5:33-35.**

1. What rules were Jesus' disciples breaking?

2. Jesus tells His disciples a parable. What do you think the following stand for in the parable?

The guests of the bridegroom _____

The bridegroom _____

The time when the bridegroom is taken away _____

_____

3. Briefly tell Jesus' position on *fasting*.

4. Should a Christian *fast* today? Why or why not?

LEFTOVERS AND HAND-ME-DOWNS

Read **Luke 5:36-39.**

1. Jesus tells two short parables. What do you think the following things stand for?

Patch from a new garment _____

An old garment _____

New wine _____

Old wineskins _____

2. What point does Jesus make?

3. Tell what you think Jesus means in **verse 39.**

WHO'S THE BOSS?

Read **Luke 6:1-5.** To understand better what's happening here, read these Old Testament references and match each with the point it makes.

a. **Exodus 20:8-10**
b. **Leviticus 24:5-9**
c. **Deuteronomy 23:24-25**
d. **1 Samuel 21:1-6**

_____ 1. According to God's ceremonial law, the bread of the Presence was to be eaten only by the priests.

_____ 2. God commanded His people to remember the Sabbath Day by refraining from normal workday activities.

_____ 3. When David and his men were desperately hungry, and the only food available was the bread of the Presence, the priests gave it to them to eat.

_____ 4. God's law permitted hungry people to eat freely the grain from others' fields.

5. According to the Pharisees, what were Jesus' disciples doing wrong?

6. Explain why Jesus felt the disciples were doing right.

7. What do you think Jesus meant when He said, **"The Son of Man is Lord of the Sabbath" (verse 5)?**

GOING TO CHURCH

Read **Luke 6:6-11.**

1. Why did the Pharisees go to church?

2. The Pharisees and Jesus asked different kinds of questions. Place **P** in front of questions that are typical of the Pharisees. Place **J** in front of questions that Jesus is more likely to ask.

_____ a. Is it legal?
_____ b. Is it right?
_____ c. Is it merciful?
_____ d. To do or not to do? That is the question.
_____ e. To do good or to do evil? That is the question.
_____ f. Is it against the rules?
_____ g. Is it honoring to God and helpful to people?

3. How did Jesus spend His Sabbath Day? How did the Pharisees spend theirs **(verses 10-11)?**

4. Who kept the Sabbath Day holy?

5. Briefly tell how you keep the Sabbath Day holy. What do you do? Why?

DEAR ABELARD

Imagine that you write an advice column for your school newspaper. You have received these letters. Write your responses.

Dear Abelard,
Our school has a rule that says we're not to leave the lunch room until we have finished eating. I was sitting close to the cafeteria door when a classmate slipped and fell in the hallway. She was really hurting, choking back the tears, and all her books and papers were scattered all over the floor. But she was outside the lunch room. Should I have helped her?
                                        Very sincerely yours,

Dear Dudley,
_____
_____

Dear Abelard,
    We're supposed to be in our seats when the bell rings for class to begin. But I can't talk to my friends and get from one class to another in such a short time. My friendships are important to me. I don't miss *that much* by coming into class a little late. What do you say?
                                        Rightfully yours,

Dear Marabelle,
_____
_____

Dear Abelard,
    *My boyfriend tells me that if I really loved him, I would go to bed with him. I **do** really love him. What should I do?*
                                        Love and kisses,

Dear Juliet,
_____
_____

SOMETHING TO THINK ABOUT

What does Jesus say to you through these Bible words? What important promise does He give you?

They worship Me in vain; their teachings are but rules taught by men.
                                        Matthew 15:9

If you obey My commands, you will remain in My love.
                                        John 15:10

Session 15

Creatures from Outer Space

Can you recognize a Christian in a crowd? In a small group?

Does being a Christian make a difference in your attitudes, values, and life-style?

Jesus' "Sermon on the Mount" suggests that He would like your answers to these questions to be "Yes!"

In His sermon to the people, Jesus paints a picture of a disciple. Jesus uses the word *disciple* for *Christian*. If we renamed **Matthew 5—7**, we might call it *Jesus' Teaching on Discipleship*.

What makes a disciple? What's a disciple like? How does a disciple think and act?

You'll discover in this session that a disciple is indeed a strange creature. Disciples are so "different"—so unnatural and so supernatural—that we might call them "creatures from outer space."

THE NATURE OF A DISCIPLE

Read **Matthew 5:1-2**.

Who is Jesus teaching through His Sermon on the Mount?

The first part is called the "Beatitudes." We might think of these as "the attitudes we ought to be."

As you consider these Christ-like attitudes, you will probably conclude that these are much different than the attitudes people usually demonstrate. That's because these attitudes come only from a supernatural power at work within us—Christ Himself.

Use separate paper and the following guide to take notes on the "Beatitudes."

QUALITIES OF A DISCIPLE	OPPOSITE QUALITIES
1. Blessed are the poor in spirit, for theirs is the kingdom of heaven.	Cursed are the _____ for theirs is _____
2. Blessed are those who mourn, for they will be comforted.	Cursed are those who _____ for they will _____
3. Blessed are the meek, for they will inherit the earth.	Cursed are the _____ for they will _____
4. Blessed are those who hunger and thirst for righteousness, for they will be filled.	Cursed are those _____ for they will _____
5. Blessed are the merciful, for they will be shown mercy.	Cursed are the _____ for they will _____
6. Blessed are the pure in heart, for they will see God.	Cursed are the _____ for they will _____
7. Blessed are the peacemakers, for they will be called sons of God.	Cursed are the _____ for they will _____
8. Blessed are those who are persecuted because of righteousness, for theirs is the kingdom of heaven.	Cursed are those who _____ for theirs is _____

The first four beatitudes are basically passive. We are the needy receivers. These four can be summarized:

_____
_____

The last four beatitudes are basically active. We actively oppose the temptations and work of the devil. A disciple who has been filled with God's provision wages a battle of personal purity and conducts himself toward others (the needy and the antagonistic) in a way that reflects what God has done for him in Christ. These four can be summarized:

_____
_____

A disciple lives in the light of eternity, while the nondisciple sees only the "here and now." The disciple is so sure of and eager for his or her heavenly reward that he or she rejoices in spite of and even because of earthly difficulties **(verse 12)**. The disciple lives as a citizen of heaven, a "creature from outer space."

35

THE FUNCTION OF A DISCIPLE

Disciples have important earthly missions. Their heavenly-mindedness makes them a blessing to earth. Jesus calls disciples "the earth's salt and light." Read **Matthew 5:13-16**.

1. List beneficial qualities of salt.

2. How was salt used **(Leviticus 2:13; 2 Kings 2:19-22)**?

3. What do you think Jesus meant when He said, **"You are the salt of the earth"**?

4. Now list benefits of light.

5. It's been said that we are each a "light reflector," just as the moon has no light within itself, but reflects the light of the sun. Read **Genesis 1:3; John 1:4-5; John 12:46;** and **1 John 1:5-7**. What is the Source of our light?

6. Our good works are meant to be plainly evident to all, but their purpose is not to bring praise and credit to ourselves. What is the purpose of our life of "discipleship" **(verse 16)**?

THE RIGHTEOUSNESS OF A DISCIPLE

What makes a disciple a disciple? What does it take for us to qualify? Is it a matter of gritting our teeth and trying harder? Maybe we just don't have it in us!

1. In Jesus' day, the Pharisees gritted their teeth and kept trying harder, only to strike out with Jesus. Read **Matthew 5:17-20**. What reward can the Pharisees and all who depend on themselves expect to receive for their self-righteousness?

2. How can anyone be righteous enough to be a disciple? See **Jeremiah 33:15-16**.

3. Jesus explains why the Pharisees' righteousness isn't nearly good enough. (Their righteousness might be good enough to make second string in the Little League, but it's not the big league righteousness that God expects. His standards are high.) Read **Matthew 5:21-26**. What would it take perfectly to fulfill God's commandment, **"Do not murder"**?

4. Read **verses 27-28**. What place do dirty jokes, porno magazines and movies, and other such things have in the life of a disciple?

5. What point does Jesus make in **verses 29-30**?

6. Read **verses 31-32**. What would Jesus say to a married disciple who considers divorce because he or she is no longer in love?

7. How would your language and the language you hear in your school have to change to reflect true discipleship **(verses 33-37)**?

8. When Jesus gives us His righteousness by virtue of His perfect life, death, and resurrection, and when we receive it by faith in Him, then we become disciples—a different sort of people altogether. We become new creations in Christ Jesus. (See **2 Corinthians 5:17**.) To the people of this world, we might act like "creatures from outer space" or from another world. That's because we are! We get our new nature from God Himself. This new nature shows itself in many ways. The remainder of **Matthew 5** gives examples.

Read **verses 38-42**. Jesus' audience was first-century Jewish people living in Palestine. How would Jesus phrase these ideas if He were speaking to you, a late 20th-century high school student in America?

9. Read **verses 43-47**. How does God feel about people who are loving and friendly toward all those who are loving and friendly to them? Think of someone who has treated you unkindly or unfairly. How have you acted toward that person?

10. Those who persecute you provide you with your best opportunity to demonstrate your discipleship—your new nature in Christ. Think of a personal strategy to help you love your enemies. Put your plan in writing and review it often.

11. What is your life goal as a disciple of Jesus?

Let your light shine before men, that they may see your good deeds and praise your Father in heaven.
Matthew 5:16

Be perfect, therefore, as your heavenly Father is perfect.
Matthew 5:48

Session 16

Building on a Rock

Remember the story of *The Three Little Pigs?* The first two little pigs built their houses of straw and sticks, and the big bad wolf blew those houses down. The third little pig, though, built his house sturdily with bricks and mortar and the wolf couldn't blow his house down, no matter how hard he huffed and puffed.

In His Sermon on the Mount, Jesus instructed His disciples how to withstand the huffing and puffing of the big bad devil. Jesus warns that those who don't hear His words and practice them will find their houses built on slipping, sliding sand. But those who live God-centered lives build their houses on a solid rock foundation that even the storms of judgment will not shake.

Discover Jesus' wise counsel concerning discipleship in **Matthew 6** and **7**.

A DISCIPLE'S RELIGIOUS EXERCISES

The Jewish people had three traditional religious practices: almsgiving, praying, and fasting. Jesus teaches that there is a right way and a wrong way of doing religious exercises.

Almsgiving

1. Read **Matthew 6:1-4.** What is the wrong way to give to the needy?
2. What reward does a wrong-way giver receive?
3. About whom is a wrong-way giver most concerned?
4. What is the right way to give according to Jesus?
5. Jesus says people should see our good deeds **(Matthew 5:16),** and He also says we should give secretly **(Matthew 6:3-4).** How would you explain this contradiction?

_____

_____

Praying

6. Read **Matthew 6:5-8.** What are the two wrong ways to pray that Jesus mentions?
7. What prayer is found in **verses 9-15?**
8. Jesus gives extra instruction on the Fifth Petition. What does He say will hinder our prayers from being answered?
9. What is the end result of not having our sins forgiven?
10. Can you afford to live each day holding grudges and trying to get even with someone? What could it cost you?

Fasting

11. Read **verses 16-18.** What is the wrong way to fast?
12. What is the reward for fasting the wrong way?
13. What word does Jesus use to describe the person who gives, prays, or fasts the wrong way?
14. Think about what you have read in **verses 1-18.** Summarize in one sentence what a *hypocrite* is:

_____

_____

A DISCIPLE'S POSSESSIONS

1. Many times, we earthlings set our hearts on the things that money can buy. What's the problem with gathering earthly treasures?
2. What's so great about having heavenly treasures?
3. Your heart is the center of your will, and your will is the center of your being. **Matthew 6:21** tells us that our destiny is tied to the destiny of the things we treasure most. What do *you* treasure most? What will ultimately happen to your treasure?
4. Read **verses 22-23.** What your heart sets its affection on, your eyes focus on, and vice versa. What are three things that appeal to your eyes and capture your attention?

Darkness is a metaphor for evil; *light* pertains to God. Your eyes are the windows to your heart. Are your eyes bringing darkness or light into your life?

5. Some people try to have it both ways. They want to set their hearts on the things of this world *and* on the things in heaven. What does Jesus say about this approach to life **(verse 24)?**
6. Read **verses 25-34.** Some say that Jesus' words are totally unrealistic. We *do* need earthly and

37

material things. Why do you think Jesus reminds us we don't have to worry about such things as food and clothes?

7. What can we do to make sure our material needs are met? A disciple would answer this question by saying:

_____

_____

8. What's the difference between planning for tomorrow and worrying about tomorrow?

9. Summarize in one sentence a disciple's attitude toward material possessions:

_____

_____

A DISCIPLE'S RELATIONSHIPS

The quality of our lives depends more on the *quality* of relationships we have with people than on the *quantity* of our possessions. Jesus guides His disciples in their building relationships through His words in **Matthew 7**. As your teacher leads a discussion of this chapter, use the following as an outline for taking notes.

1. Judge not **(Matthew 7:1-2)**
2. Cricitize not **(7:3-5)**
3. Force not **(7:6)**
4. Depend not **(7:7-12)**
5. Follow not **(7:13-14)**
6. Be not deceived **(7:15-23)**

BE PREPARED

1. According to Jesus, what two things are necessary if we are to be wise **(7:24-27)**?

2. What do you think the storm symbolizes?

RESPONDING IN PRAYER

You've just completed studying Jesus' dissertation on discipleship. Now write a prayer based on Jesus' words and your level of discipleship. You might include elements of praise, thanksgiving, confession of sin, and requests for God's forgiveness and help in specific situations in your life. This is an opportunity for you to tell God your thoughts, confessions, and commitments.

Ask and it will be given to you; seek and you will find; knock and the door will be opened to you. For everyone who asks receives; he who seeks finds; and to him who knocks, the door will be opened.
Matthew 7:7-8

Session 17

You Gotta Have Faith!

Faith in Christ is the most important thing a person can have. Faith opens the door to all of the spiritual blessings only God can give. The word *faith* appears more than 250 times in the New Testament. Jesus looked for faith, tested faith, and encouraged faith when He lived on earth. He became concerned and sad when He didn't find it in people. When He did find faith in a person, He was happy and amazed. The Bible tells us, **"Without faith it is impossible to please God" (Hebrews 11:6).**

What is this thing called faith? Pray that through today's session you might understand faith better and grow in it.

JESUS ESTEEMS FAITH

Read **Luke 7:1-10.**

1. What was the centurion's problem?

2. How did the centurion communicate with Jesus?

3. Why did he never speak directly to Jesus?

4. Look carefully at **verses 4-7.** Compare what the Jewish leaders thought of the centurion with what the centurion thought of himself.

5. Explain what the centurion recognized about Jesus **(verses 7-8).**

6. How did Jesus feel about the centurion?

7. Think about your own life and faith in Jesus. Have you ever amazed anyone with your demonstration of faith?

JESUS ELICITS FAITH

Read **Luke 7:11-17.** Many times Jesus performed His mighty acts in response to a person's faith.

1. What great miracle did Jesus perform outside the town of Nain?

2. What moved Jesus to do what He did?

3. What was the result of Jesus' raising the dead man?

4. Do miracles come from faith? Or does faith come from miracles?

JESUS ENCOURAGES FAITH

Read **Luke 7:18-35.**

1. What is surprising about John the Baptizer's question **(verse 19)**?

2. Why might John ask such a question? (See **Luke 3:20.**)

3. Compare **Isaiah 29:18-19; 35:5-6;** and **Luke 7:21-22.** How does Jesus encourage John's faith?

4. **Isaiah 61:1** prophesies that the Messiah would **"proclaim freedom for the captives and release for the prisoners."** Did Jesus fulfill this promise for John?

5. Read **Luke 7:23.** Why might someone "fall away" (lose faith) "on account of" (because of) Jesus?

6. **Luke 7:24-28** tells us Jesus' evaluation of John. What specifically does Jesus respect about John? How has John been an example of faith throughout his life?

7. What do you think **verse 28** means?

8. What is **"God's way" (verses 29-30)**?

FOR PERSONAL REFLECTION

1. Was there ever a time in your life when God seemed far away and you were tempted to "fall away" or lose faith in Jesus? Can you understand any purpose in God allowing you to go through such an experience?

2. On the basis of what you've learned in this session, read the following statements. Each leaves much to be said about the love and power Jesus has for our lives. Write an improved statement for each. Be ready to share these with the class.

a. Faith is knowing all the answers on a religion exam.

_____

_____

b. Faith is just positive thinking.

_____

_____

c. Faith is how we earn our salvation.

_____

_____

d. Faith is self-confidence.

_____
_____

[Abraham] did not waver through unbelief regarding the promise of God, but was strengthened in his faith and gave glory to God, being fully persuaded that God had power to do what He had promised.

Romans 4:20-21

Session 18

True Love!

Love! Everybody talks about it. Popular vocalists sing about it. But what is it? How do you know when it's real? Is it something you just fall into? Does it have to do with cute looks, nice clothes, a loss of appetite, shiny teeth, or sex? What does Jesus know about love? How could He? He probably never even had a girlfriend.

Have you ever wondered about that? Might Jesus have dated and gotten married if He wanted to? In today's lesson we will see that Jesus received a far more extravagant expression of love from one girl than any guy in your school has ever received.

Why did this one certain girl become so loving toward Jesus? Was it His dashing good looks **(Isaiah 53:2)**? Was it the sports car He drove **(Matthew 21:5)**? Was it all the money He had **(2 Corinthians 8:9)**? Was it His nice house and prestigious neighborhood **(Matthew 8:20; John 1:46)**? Was it the hit tunes His group sang **(Matthew 26:30)**? Let's get to the bottom of this.

JESUS ANOINTED BY A SINFUL WOMAN

Read **Luke 7:36-50.** Then discuss the following questions in small groups. Have one person in each group function as the secretary, recording the consensus of the group on each of the questions. Share your answers and insights with the whole class.

1. Why do you think Simon the Pharisee invited Jesus to his house for dinner? How did Simon feel toward Jesus? (See especially **verses 39, 44-46.** Be able to support your answer.)

2. What feelings did the woman have toward Jesus that were different from Simon's feelings?

3. According to this Bible story, what is the basis of true love? What was the woman's greatest need? Are they the same?

4. Why do you think Jesus never got married?

5. How can a person show how much he or she loves Jesus today? (See **John 14:15; 15:12; 21:15-17.**)

6. How can a person show how much he or she loves others? (See **John 15:13** and **1 Corinthians 13:4-7.**)

FAITH, LOVE, AND FORGIVENESS

In session 17 you talked about the essential role of faith in the Christian's life. One of the great truths of the Reformation is that we are saved through faith alone. But faith is never alone within a Christian's heart. If faith is genuine, it cannot help but express itself in various ways. The most excellent and perfect expression is Christian *agape* love. This is true love—the love Jesus showed for us through His obedient death and resurrection. Christians loving one another becomes possible only through God's grace. He first loved and forgave us. Love comes to us from God Himself through Jesus. Love and forgiveness for God and for others become our responses to God's love and grace.

SHOWING LOVE TO OTHERS

Choose one of the following situations to roleplay with one or two classmates. Or create your own real-life drama. Show how you can demonstrate the love of Jesus to others in various situations. Present your dramatization to the class.

1. You and your mom have had an argument over whom you can date and how late you are allowed to stay out at night. You realize you came down hard on your mom and said some terrible things. You would—

2. You have a friend stay over and you are watching a special video, but your brother keeps interrupting and annoying you. You would—

3. Your dad wakes you up at nine on Saturday morning. He calls it a "reasonable hour" to get up and get going. He wants you to help him cut and stack firewood the whole day. You would—

4. Your grandma lives only a few miles from you, but hasn't seen you for two months. She missed your winter concert and wondered if you'd come by and play your piano pieces for her soon. You would—

5. Your older sister had an exhausting week at her real estate office. She's tired and crabby. You want to show her how much you care about her. You would—

6. Your biology teacher hasn't been himself lately. He is less friendly and more distant than usual. You wonder what's happening in his life. You would—

LOVE DEVOTION

Lord, we thank You for the privilege of calling You our loving Father.
  Thank You, Heavenly Father.
For making each of us a member of Your family:
  Thank You, dear Father.
For giving us Jesus, our Savior, to be our Brother:
  We thank and praise You, Father.
For Your love and forgiveness through our Brother Jesus:
  Thanks, Lord, and keep it coming!
For helping us show to those around us the love and forgiveness You alone can give:
  Thank You, Lord.
All: Thank You for Your gifts to us! All that we are, and all that we have, we give to You, Lord, and to Your service. Amen!

We love because He first loved us.
1 John 5:17

Session 19

Jesus' Secret Code

Can you see the message in the configuration above?

Once you recognize the message, it becomes so obvious that it's hard to imagine not seeing it.

Many people look at life the same way you might have stared at the message—completely confused as to what it's all about. The answer to the puzzle of life and for the puzzle above is the same—JESUS. When we believe in and follow Jesus as our Lord and Savior, the Holy Spirit comes to us and dispels the darkness. A whole new world of meaning is opened to us. Jesus is the Light for our lives.

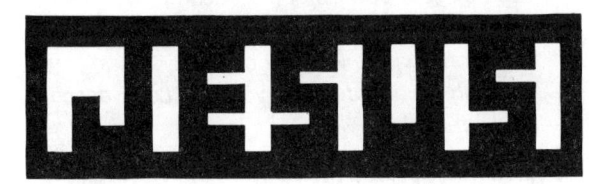

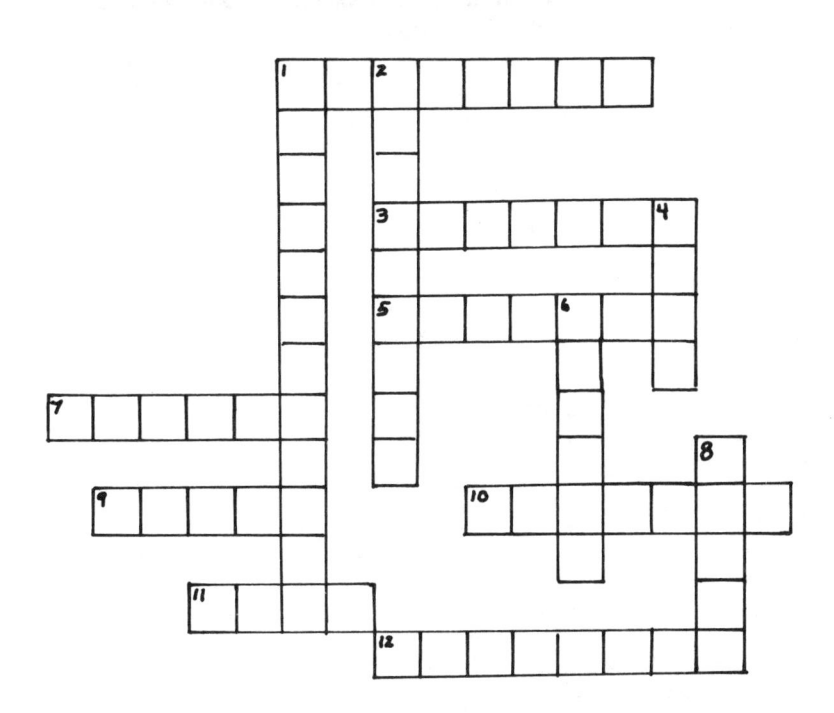

Jesus' parables opened a whole new world of meaning for His disciples, but left others completely in the dark. Jesus preferred to teach about God's kingdom using parables. The purpose of these was both to reveal and conceal. Parables revealed the secrets of the Kingdom to those who believed in Jesus, but parables concealed these same secrets from stubborn unbelievers. To those who saw the light, the light grew brighter. Those who were in the dark continued in their darkness.

THE PARABLE OF THE SOWER

Carefully read **Luke 8:1-15,** then complete the puzzle based on this selection of Scripture. (A correct answer may include two words having no space between.)

Across
1. Jesus' teaching method
3. Jesus' favorite topic
5. Method of planting; to _____
7. Jesus or God
9. Financial supporters
10. Good soil's rate of yield
11. Word of God
12. Those who hear and retain

Down
1. What it takes to be productive
2. Those who fail testings
4. Experienced exorcism
6. Life's worries, riches, pleasures
8. Birds of the air

What sorts of things cause people to fall short of the spiritually productive and eternal life God wants for them?

_____

In one sentence, summarize the lesson of the parable of the sower.

EYES AND EARS

Read **Luke 8:16-18**.

How do **verses 16-18** emphasize the following three concerns of God?

1. Concern for the spread of the Word
2. Concern for how God's Word is received
3. Concern for productive Christian lives

MOTHERS AND BROTHERS

Read **Luke 8:19-21**.

1. Why did Jesus' mother and brothers want to see Jesus **(Mark 3:21)**?

2. To whom does Jesus feel most closely related?

3. Does this section **(verses 19-21)** remind you of any other events or teachings we have studied? What are they?

4. Why do you think some people willingly hear God's Word and put it into practice and others don't **(Philippians 2:13)**?

COME, HOLY GHOST, GOD AND LORD

Use the second and third stanzas from *Lutheran Worship,* 154, as a personal or class prayer.

*Come, holy Light, guide divine,
Now cause the Word of life to shine.
Teach us to know our God aright
And call Him Father with delight.
From ev'ry error keep us free;
Let none but Christ our master be,
That we in living faith abide,
In Him, our Lord, with all our might confide.
Alleluia! Alleluia!*

*Come, holy Fire, comfort true,
Grant us the will Your work to do
And in Your service to abide;
Let trials turn us not aside.
Lord, by your pow'r prepare each heart
And to our weakness strength impart
That bravely here we may contend,
Through life and death to you, our Lord, ascend.
Alleluia! Alleluia!*

We have not received the spirit of the world but the Spirit who is from God, that we may understand what God has freely given us.

1 Corinthians 2:12

Session 20

Natural Disasters and Evil Spirits

What kind of exams did Jesus give His disciples? Did He ask His disciples to sit down every few weeks, sharpen their pencils, and take a test? Do you suppose Jesus graded on a curve?

As far as we know, Jesus didn't give His disciples written examinations. His oral examinations were few and short, consisting of only one or two questions such as, **"Who do you say I am?" (Luke 9:20),** or **"Do you truly love me?" (John 21:16).**

Most of Jesus' exams took place in real life situations. He didn't have to ask His disciples if they had learned their lessons; He just *watched* them. In the Bible basis for this session, Jesus gives His disciples a "living test." As you read and discuss the Bible verses today, ask yourself, **Do Jesus' disciples know yet who Jesus really is? Do they trust in Him? What grade would you give them? Would *you* pass the test Jesus gave to His disciples?**

NATURE RECOGNIZES ITS LORD

1. Read **Luke 8:22-25.** What do you learn about Jesus from this event?

2. What "living tests" have you experienced in your life?

THE SUPERNATURAL RECOGNIZES ITS MASTER

1. Read **Luke 8:26-31.** What are characteristics of demon possession as found in this man?

2. What is *Abyss?* See **Revelation 9:1-2; 11:7; 17:8; 20:1-3;** and **Matthew 25:41.**

3. Read **verses 32-34.** How large was the herd of pigs? See **Mark 5:13** also.

4. How do you think those people tending the pigs felt?

5. If Jesus had been arrested for destroying an-

other's property and you were appointed His defense attorney, how would you argue His case?

_____
_____

6. What do you learn from this incident with the pigs?

_____
_____

7. Explain why the people of this region asked Jesus to leave. How does their request compare to Peter's request in **Luke 5:8?**

_____
_____

8. What evidences of demonic possession or influence are present in our world today?

_____
_____

I RECOGNIZE MY GOD

Both Jesus' majesty and mercy have been depicted in this session. He is revealed as the sovereign Lord, ruling over the fiercest forces of nature and the supernatural, and as the loving Savior, rescuing us from the otherwise overwhelming powers of earth and hell. Jesus is also shown to be in complete control of Himself and His emotions.

What comfort do you receive from this session's reading and discussion? Explain one way this session will change the way you live.

_____
_____
_____
_____

SOMETHING TO THINK ABOUT

For God did not give us a spirit of timidity, but a spirit of power, of love, and of self-discipline.
2 Timothy 1:7

Session 21

Opportunity Knocks

Jesus wanted everyone to have the opportunity to receive the blessings of the Kingdom. So He traveled from place to place, and where He could not go Himself, He sent His disciples to preach and to heal. When people responded to the Good News of the Kingdom, they experienced God's love and power. Indeed, God **"wants all men to be saved and to come to a knowledge of the truth"** (1 Timothy 2:4). However, when people were stubbornly unreceptive to Christ's kingdom message, Jesus offered His gracious invitation to others.

A HEALED MAN SENT

Read **Luke 8:37-39.**

1. The Gerasenes did not want what Jesus had to offer them. How did Jesus respond?

2. What further chance did Jesus provide for the Gerasenes?

3. Do you think it was easy or difficult for the healed demoniac to be Christ's witness? Why?

4. Are you like the Gerasenes or the healed man? Why?

A SICK WOMAN HEALED

Read **Luke 8:40-48.**

1. Jesus returned to the great crowds on the northwest side of the Sea of Galilee. How would you describe the emotional state of the synagogue ruler?

2. How do you suppose this ruler felt as Jesus proceeded to his house?

3. How do you suppose Jairus felt when Jesus stopped to talk with the woman?

4. How did the woman feel? (See **Leviticus 15:25-27.**)

5. What was Jesus' purpose in drawing attention to what the woman had done?

A DEAD GIRL RAISED

Read **Luke 8:49-56.**

1. Jesus said the girl was **"not dead, but asleep."** Was that true?

2. Read **John 11:11-14, 25-26,** and **John 5:24-25.** How does Jesus think of "death"?

3. How did the mourners respond to Jesus **(verse 53)**?

4. How did Jesus respond to them **(verses 51 and 56)**?

5. Why do you think Jesus ordered the parents *not* to do the very thing He ordered the man to do in **Luke 8:39?**

TWELVE DISCIPLES SENT

Read **Luke 9:1-6.**

1. How does Jesus show His concern for the lost in this section?

_____

_____

2. How are the disciples to respond to those who will not accept their ministry? (Compare **Acts 18:6.**)

_____

_____

SOMETHING TO THINK ABOUT

When Jesus comes to us with His saving Word, we must not wait for a more convenient time **(Acts 24:25)**. The apostle Paul urges us to realize that **"now is the time of God's favor, now is the day of salvation" (2 Corinthians 6:2).** Come to Jesus confidently and quickly, knowing that **"whoever comes to Me I will never drive away" (John 6:37).**

We have no guarantee that there will be a tomorrow to respond personally to His message or to share it with our neighbor. In that light, let's hear, read, share, learn, and tell the Good News *today:* **"Jesus loves you! He died to save you from your sins. He will take you to live with Him in heaven when you die. God is love!"**

Today I will tell _____ that Jesus loves him or her. With God's help, this is what I'll say and do:

_____

_____

_____

_____

This salvation, which was first announced by the Lord, was confirmed to us by those who heard Him.
Hebrews 2:3

Session 22

The End of the Beginning and the Beginning of the End

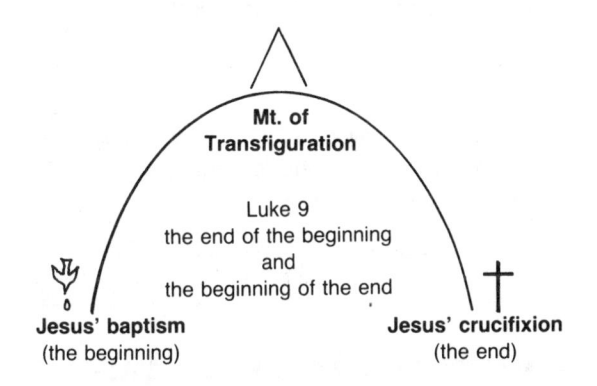

Luke 9 marks a turning point in Jesus' ministry. We can call it "the end of the beginning and the beginning of the end."

In the beginning of Jesus' ministry, the focus was on His growing popularity as He went from victory to victory, demonstrating power over nature, the supernatural, disease, and death. Now the focus shifts to the growing opposition to Jesus, which culminates in His crucifixion. This chapter helps us understand more clearly who Jesus is (clarification of identity) and what His purpose is (clarification of mission). The disciples no longer ask, **"Who is this?" (Luke 8:25)** but confess Him as **"the Christ of God" (Luke 9:20).** Jesus also shifts the focus from leading His disciples to a recognition of Him as Messiah (identity) to instructing them thoroughly concerning the role of the Messiah (mission) and the role of His followers (discipleship).

The following diagram illustrates the centrality of **Luke 9** to the Gospel of Luke and the ministry of Jesus.

Carefully read and study the eight sections in **Luke 9.** Then write how each section demonstrates one or more of the main points of this chapter. The first section has been done for you as an example.

JESUS SENDS OUT THE TWELVE (Luke 9:1-9)

The End of the Beginning and the Beginning of the End:

Jesus begins to prepare the disciples for His departure, when they must carry on His ministry. He gives them more responsibility and intensive training. Jesus begins to draw the attention and concern of the political authorities, who had already executed Jesus' forerunner. This reference to Herod is like a distant thunder that warns of an approaching storm.

JESUS FEEDS THE FIVE THOUSAND (Luke 9:10-17)

Clarification of Jesus' Identity:

Clarification of Discipleship:

PETER'S CONFESSION OF CHRIST (Luke 9:18-27)

Clarification of Jesus' Identity:

Clarification of Jesus' Mission:

Clarification of Discipleship:

THE TRANSFIGURATION (Luke 9:28-36)

Clarification of Jesus' Identity:

The End of the Beginning and the Beginning of the End:

_____

_____

Clarification of Discipleship:

_____

_____

THE HEALING OF A BOY WITH AN EVIL SPIRIT (Luke 9:37-45)

The End of the Beginning and the Beginning of the End:

_____

_____

WHO WILL BE THE GREATEST? (Luke 9:46-50)

Clarification of Discipleship:

_____

_____

SAMARITAN OPPOSITION (Luke 9:51-56)

The Beginning of the End:

_____

_____

Clarification of Jesus' Mission and Discipleship:

_____

_____

THE COST OF FOLLOWING JESUS (Luke 9:57-62)

Clarification of Discipleship:

_____

_____

SUMMING UP AND PERSONALIZING LUKE 9

You have read and studied this complex chapter. Now answer these questions in your own words according to what you believe.

1. What is Jesus' *identity*? Who is Jesus to *you*?

_____

_____

2. What is Jesus' *mission*? What did He do and what does He continue to do for *you*?

_____

_____

3. What is involved in being Jesus' *disciple*? Describe the commitment, the feelings, and the actions you have as Jesus' disciple.

_____

_____

SOMETHING TO THINK ABOUT

Your teacher may choose to give you a test during session 23. Remember the test Jesus gave Peter in **Luke 9:20**? His was a single question. You might have to answer many test questions. However, Jesus asks each of us the same important question that He asked Peter. **"Who do you say I am?"**

A PRAYER FOR TODAY

Dear God, help me, like You helped Your servant Peter, to have the right answers. Help me especially to understand what those answers mean to my life in the body of Christ. Let me be Your instrument. Use me to Your glory. Let Your Holy Spirit move me and work through me that others may see and know Jesus and Your saving grace through Him. I praise and thank You for giving my life challenge, purpose, and meaningful service to You. I trust You for the courage and power I need to say daily, "You are Christ, the Son of God!" In Jesus' name. Amen.

For even the Son of Man did not come to be served, but to serve, and to give His life as a ransom for many.

Mark 10:45

Session 23
Review of Unit 2

Answer these questions to help you review sessions 10—22.

1. Who is Jesus Christ? Was His identity obvious when He lived and taught on earth? Why or why not? What were Jesus' identification papers **(John 5:39)**?

2. Where did Jesus go after His baptism and why?

3. Describe what it was like for Jesus when He returned to His hometown, Nazareth.

4. Why did Jesus need quiet time with God? Why is it also important for you to spend time alone with God?

5. Tell the difference between a *disciple* and an *apostle*. What was so special about apostles?

6. What is a disciple's "righteousness" and where does it come from?

7. What is the kingdom of God and how is "greatness" measured in it?

8. What is *faith*? What are results of faith in Jesus?

9. Define *agape* and *eros* regarding love.

10. What is a parable and why did Jesus teach using parables?

11. Explain the words *life* and *death* as Jesus used them in reference to one's spiritual condition.

12. What is the cost and what are the rewards of following Jesus?

Unit 3
Jesus Our Teacher

"I never knew haiku could be so much fun to write!" exclaimed Jonathan as he told his dad about his creative writing class.

"Sounds like fun, Jon," replied Mr. Stanford. "You must have a good teacher to get you so excited about writing haiku!"

"Yeah! And next week our class is going to start putting together a new school newspaper. I'm going to try out for the sports editor's job. Wow! There's so much to learn! But Mrs. Strock makes it interesting and fun!" Jonathan ran to get ready for basketball practice.

Teachers. They teach, instruct, train, discipline, guide, and educate others. Good teachers impart knowledge, share experiences, guide studies, listen, and bring out the best capabilities in their students.

Think of a teacher who has made learning exciting and fun for you. What did she say? What did he do? Why do you remember that class experience? Why are you thankful for that teacher?

We know Jesus as our Master Teacher. He was the greatest teacher ever!

Imagine having been a student of Jesus when He lived on earth.

Who might have been in your class? Were Jesus' followers male? Female? Old? Young? Rich? Poor? Educated? Uneducated?

Where would you and Jesus' other students have gone to have Jesus teach you? To a school with your own desk? Along a dusty road?

When would you have had class hours with Jesus? Do you think He required His followers to spend six hours per day with Him for 200 school days?

What would you have heard Jesus say, and what would you have seen Jesus do as He taught you and the others? Did He teach one subject or more? Did He have a lesson plan? Cover a book from cover to cover? Lecture? Use visuals? Give assignments? Calculate grades?

Why do you think Jesus would have taught you and His followers? In what ways would Jesus have shown you that He wanted to teach?

Our Teacher Jesus has much instruction to offer us through God's Word and His example. He teaches us about life—that life we live on earth as mortals and that eternal life God gives us when we die through His grace and love for Jesus' sake.

May you grow in love and respect for Jesus and His teaching, and may the Holy Spirit ever strengthen your faith in Him, your Master Teacher, through this unit and forever after.

Session 24

The Fizz in the Soda Pop

Have you ever taken a swig of a soft drink that had lost its fizz? There's not much excitement in the drink without the carbonation.

A Christian's witness to others about Jesus is like the fizz to a soft drink. A Christian who shares Jesus Christ with others bubbles with peace and happiness. Jesus knew the joy and excitement that comes with being a verbal witness for Him. He also knew that most people won't witness unless they get a direct command and a lot of encouragement. So He gathered His followers together and sent them on a witnessing assignment. Sure enough, when they came back, they were bubbling with enthusiasm about their experience.

YOU ARE MY WITNESSES!

Put yourself in this situation:

A group of young people is meeting together next Saturday morning at a local congregation. Their purpose is to survey the neighborhoods surrounding the church. As part of the survey they will give a brief witness of their faith in Jesus Christ and invite unchurched people to come to the worship services of the local congregation. You have been asked to lead them in a Bible study before they go out. The Bible study is **Luke 10:1-24.**

Go through this section verse by verse and note all the insights and applications you might share to motivate, encourage, and instruct them as they go out into the neighborhood as Christ's witnesses. The first verse has been done as an example for you.

Verse 1: Notice the Lord "appointed" people for the task of witnessing. He did not ask for volunteers and He did not make it optional. Jesus also has commanded *us* to be His witnesses. When we share Christ with others, we are merely being obedient and faithful to our Lord. Notice also that Jesus appointed 70 (or 72) to go out in His name. Witnessing is not just a job for full-time church workers (12 apostles), but for lay people as well. (Compare **Acts 8:1** and **Acts 8:4**.) Notice also that Jesus sent them out "two by two." (The apostolic church followed the same practice as the rule of **Deuteronomy 19:15**.) In this way, partners could share the experience together, encourage each other, and let people know that calling people to Christ is calling them into a *community* of faith. The church is the body of Christ, not isolated individuals.

Verses 2-24: On separate paper, write the insights and applications for your Bible study. Be prepared to share them with the class.

GO AND TELL ABOUT JESUS!

We read again and again that Jesus says we must not only *hear* God's Word, but also *put it into practice*. This is especially true about witnessing. It isn't the learning about witnessing but the *doing* of it that puts the fizz into your Christian life and into the lives of others.

Your personal assignment:

Share the Gospel of Jesus Christ with some people who you suspect need to hear it. The Gospel can be said in many ways, but the basic content is summarized in Jesus' words, **"God so loved the world that He gave His one and only Son, that whoever believes in Him shall not perish but have eternal life" (John 3:16).** A more complete summary might be: All people are sinful and deserve to be be condemned to hell (**Romans 3:23** and **Ephesians 2:1-3**). But the God-man

Jesus Christ suffered and died on the cross to take the punishment we deserved upon Himself **(Isaiah 53:5; 1 Corinthians 15:3).** He also rose from the dead and promises eternal life to all who turn from their sins and trust Jesus Christ as their Savior **(Luke 24:46-48; Romans 1:16).**

How might you fulfill this assignment from your Lord and Savior?(*He*, not your teacher, gives this assignment to you!) See **Luke 24:48** and **Acts 1:8.** Here are some suggestions:

1. Pray before you witness. Ask God to bless your time and words with the person. Ask Him to fill you and your friend with His Spirit, that you might be effective and that he or she might be open to hear and receive the Good News.

2. Start by asking important questions of someone you feel comfortable with. That person might be a relative, neighbor, friend outside of school, or a co-worker. You might tell the person that you're taking a survey as part of a school assignment. Ask if he or she would help you by answering a few questions. Then ask key questions (such as those from the Kennedy Evangelism Program):

Are you sure that if you died tonight you would go to heaven?

If you died and God asked you, "Why should I let you into heaven?" what would you say?

After the person responds, you might simply ask, "May I tell you the way I would answer these questions?" Then simply share the Gospel of Christ in your own words. Tell what Jesus has done for you.

3. Go with people from an outreach group in your congregation when they make calls.

4. Help organize and/or participate in a youth evangelism program such as a *Discipleshop* or *Gospel Communication Clinic.*

5. Share the Gospel of Christ with persons having special needs, such as those in nursing homes, homes for people with mental handicaps, hospitals, and shut-ins.

When you have completed your witnessing experience, write a report telling whom you shared Jesus with, their reactions, how each of you felt in this experience, and results, if any.

Remember, too, that when we share the Good News of Jesus, we might share the joy of a person coming to faith in Him or we might never know the results of our witnessing. God gives us His command, empowers us to do His work, and blesses it in His way and time.

You will receive power when the Holy Spirit comes on you; and you will be My witnesses in Jerusalem, and in all Judea and Samaria, and to the ends of the earth.

Acts 1:8

Session 25

The Seeds and Deeds of Life

Television preacher Robert Schuller has often said, "You can count the number of seeds in the apple, but you can't count the number of apples in a seed." The miracle of life and growth is indeed one of the most astonishing and impenetrable mysteries of our world.

Jesus used three short parables to illustrate the growth of God's kingdom. With the help of your teacher and classmates, see if you can understand and apply Jesus' parables to your life.

SEEDS OF LIFE

1. Read **Luke 13:18-21.** What is Jesus telling us about God's kingdom?

_____

_____

2. See also **Mark 4:26-29.** What do we learn here about God's kingdom?

_____

_____

DEEDS OF LIFE

Sammy and Billy overheard their mother saying how much she would like an apple tree in her backyard. Sammy ran to the grocery store and bought a bag of apples. Then he ran home, got the ladder out of the garage, and taped the apples to the limbs of the maple tree in the backyard. Billy had a different idea. He planted an apple seed. Who had the better idea?

Do the apples make the apple tree or does the apple tree make the apples?

Jesus taught that spiritually alive people will do things that demonstrate that they *are* spiritually alive. In other words, you can tell a good person not by how he or she is dressed or decorated, but by the good things that naturally grow out of his or her life. Good deeds don't make a good person, but a good person makes good deeds. One of Jesus' most well-known and well-liked parables illustrates this point. Read the parable of the good Samaritan in **Luke 10:25-37.**

1. How does the legal expert expect to inherit eternal life?

_____

_____

2. Why isn't he satisfied when Jesus said he answered correctly?

_____

_____

3. Carefully compare the legal expert's question in **verse 29** with Jesus' question in **verse 36.** How do they differ?

_____

_____

_____

4. What came first: the good Samaritan or the good deed?

_____

5. In the story of the good Samaritan, determine whom the following statements describe. Place **L** in

55

front of statements that apply to the lawyer, **P** in front of those that apply to the priest or Levite, and **S** in front of those applying to the Samaritan.

_____ Tries to convince himself and others that he's a good person

_____ Ignores others' needs

_____ Tries to figure out what he doesn't have to do

_____ Unself-consciously responds to human need

_____ Doesn't want to get involved if it costs or inconveniences him

_____ Loves his enemies

Now read the list once more and put **M** (for "Me") by those statements which best describe yourself.

Probably the one man in the story that best personifies each of us is the man who was beaten and robbed. We each have been robbed of our life and health by Satan. However, Jesus, our Good Samaritan, has saved our lives and provides continually for our restoration.

Thank and praise Him!

God demonstrates His own love for us in this: While we were still sinners, Christ died for us.
Romans 5:8

Love your enemies and pray for those who persecute you, that you may be sons of your Father in heaven.
Matthew 5:44-45

Session 26

How to Be a Super Christian

What does being a Christian involve? How does a Christian who is really "on the ball" act? How can you tell "a really good Christian"? What kind of a guy or gal is Jesus most pleased with? Is it one who never gets in trouble? Is it one who is president of the youth group at church and never misses any of the meetings? Is it one who is most involved in community projects? Is it one who gets the best grades in religion class? This session will show us the kinds of things about which Jesus is most concerned.

TWO KINDS OF GOOD CHRISTIANS

Two sisters, Mary and Martha, had a very important guest. Jesus had come to stay at their house. Fortunately, Mary and Martha were pretty well off, and they had a nice big home that could accommodate Jesus and His disciples. To prepare a meal for such a large and important group of visitors must have been quite an undertaking. The pressure was on, and it would take everyone's cooperation if everything was going to get done. Read what happened in **Luke 10:38-40**.

1. What was Martha doing?

2. What was Mary doing?

3. Describe how Martha felt about what was happening at their home while Jesus was there.

4. Do you think Jesus' response **(verses 41-42)** surprised Martha? Why or why not?

5. What were Martha's mistakes?

6. What is the "one better thing" that Mary chose?

7. Name good things that tend to crowd out the one better thing in your life.

COMMUNICATION IS A TWO-WAY STREET

Good relationships require communication, and communication involves both listening and speaking. One-way telephone conversations are usually discourteous, boring, and short. Some Christians have a very undeveloped relationship with Christ because they lack one or both of the elements of communication. Some listen but do very little speaking. Others always have something to say but never take time to listen.

Mary demonstrated the importance of listening to God's Word. Now we will learn the importance of communicating with God and the proper way of doing it. We call this communication *prayer*.

1. Read **Luke 11:1-4**. Compare **Matthew 6:9-13**. How do these two passages differ?

2. How do you explain these differences between the Gospels of Matthew and Luke? What is the *real* Lord's Prayer? When did Jesus teach it?

3. When we paraphrase, we say the same thing in different words. Write your paraphrase of the Lord's Prayer.

4. Read **Luke 11:5-8.** What does Jesus teach us about prayer here?

5. Read **Luke 11:9-10.** What does Jesus teach us about prayer in these verses?

6. Read **Luke 11:11-13.** What point does Jesus make?

PRAYER AND FAITH

1. Read Jesus' prayer parable in **Luke 18:1-8.** What does this parable say to you to give you strong encouragement always to pray and not give up?

2. What does Jesus' question in **verse 8** mean to you? How does it relate to the parable?

3. What is the relationship between prayer and faith?

Two Christian behaviors that God values include sitting at Jesus' feet, listening attentively to His Word, and kneeling before God in fervent prayer.

Jesus is primarily concerned about our relationship to Him. The one thing needful is what God gives to us. The work we do for Him is a fruit of that relationship.

How would you evaluate your Christian life by these two criteria—Bible study and prayer?

Pray this prayer or make up one of your own:

Dear Lord, you've caused all of Your Word, our Scripture, to be written so that I can learn from You. Please help me remember to listen to Your Word, read it by myself and with others, mark it, and learn from it, so that it will become an integral part of my life. Give me patience and guide me as I search and struggle through my life. I pray in the name of Jesus, who fills me with the Spirit and keeps me in the faith each day. Amen.

Without faith it is impossible to please God, because anyone who comes to Him must believe that He exists and that He rewards those who earnestly seek Him.
Hebrews 11:6

Session 27

Heart Failure

Each year in the United States nearly 600,000 people die as a result of heart attacks. Approximately 45 million Americans are currently suffering from one or more forms of heart and blood vessel disease. Heart disease is our greatest national health problem.

However, many more people have heart problems that aren't recorded in the statistics furnished by the American Heart Association. These are people who are spiritually sick and dying from hardness of heart. The Bible refers to the "heart" as the seat of the will. Many people in Jesus' day (and today, too) refuse to repent of their sins and believe in Jesus Christ. It was heartbreaking for Jesus to have people whose hearts were dead set against Him. Jesus expressed His heartache with these words: **"O Jerusalem, Jerusalem, you who kill the prophets and stone those sent to you, how often I have longed to gather your children together, as a hen gathers her chicks under her wings, but you were not willing!"** (Luke 13:34).

Jesus' identity as Israel's Messiah could not be denied, except by those who simply refused to believe despite the overwhelming evidence. So it was in Jesus' day, and so it is today. A man convinced against his will is of the same opinion still.

THE BLASPHEMOUS HEART

One deadly heart ailment is *blasphemy*. Read about it in **Luke 11:14-28**.

1. Jesus' enemies could not deny that He had amazing power. But what did they say about Jesus' ability to do miracles?

2. Tell whom the characters represent in **verses 21-22**. "A strong man": _____

"Someone stronger": _____

3. What decision does Jesus call for in **verse 23**?

4. What warning does Jesus give in **verses 24-26**?

5. What similar conversations from earlier chapters in Luke do **verses 27-28** remind you of?

THE SKEPTICAL HEART

Skepticism is the heart ailment that demands proof, but is never satisfied that there is enough evidence to prove something. Read **Luke 11:29-32**.

1. Jesus is to the Jews as Jonah was to the Ninevites. How so?

2. Compare **Matthew 12:40** with the section of Luke's gospel. In what way is Jesus like Jonah?

3. How does the Queen of the South (**1 Kings 10:1-13**) compare with the skeptical Jewish people of Jesus' day?

THE UNFAITHFUL HEART

Read **Luke 11:33-36**.

The "eye" refers to the heart, which, like the lamp, allows us to see. Jesus isn't a lamp under a bushel basket. He is a lamp set on a stand for everyone to see. His Word and His works are clear. But just as a nonfunctioning eye deprives the body of seeing light (even though the light is present), so also the unfunctioning eye of unbelief can deprive a person of the Light that God graciously gave the world—Jesus Christ.

Let's call a person's spiritual "eye" his or her *heart*. A person's heart is either "good" (literally single, simple, without duplicity or ulterior motive) or "bad" (literally evil, wicked, depraved, malignant). The scribes and Pharisees couldn't "see" the obvious (that Jesus was their Messiah) because their organ of sight (the heart) was no good. The bad heart has motives other than to know and to do God's Word; therefore, it cannot recognize Jesus, and it directs the entire body against Him and His kingdom.

Think of a time in your life when your "sight" wasn't so good and you didn't have a clear view of Jesus' love for you. What happened? How did Jesus give you light to see more clearly?

THE HYPOCRITICAL HEART

The hypocritical heart is more concerned with appearance than substance. It pretends to be something that it is not.

Read Jesus' strong words of condemnation directed against symptoms of hypocrisy in **Luke 11:37-54.**

On this occasion Jesus was again invited to dine at a Pharisee's house. The Pharisees were offended that Jesus did not first wash His hands. The legalistic Pharisees were not concerned about germs or hygiene, but with Gentile cooties. Their ritualistic washings were their way of asserting their righteousness and separation from the contemptible riffraff of the world (see **Mark 7:1-4**). However, God judges cleanness and uncleanness on the basis of what is inside a person's heart. Read **verses 37-41.**

1. What does Jesus see on the inside of the Pharisees?

2. What kind of heart is represented by **verse 41**?

3. Another symptom of hypocrisy is a lack of proportion or a mix-up of priorities. Jesus talks about this in **verse 42**. Which are more important, the laws of **Deuteronomy 14:22** or **Micah 6:8**?

4. Still another symptom of hypocrisy is concern for our reputation and popularity with people, as opposed to a concern for doing what pleases God. See **verse 43** and also **Luke 6:26** and **John 5:44**. Why is this behavior so dangerous?

5. In **verse 44** Jesus compares the Pharisees to **"unmarked graves."** What does He mean by that? (See **Numbers 19:16**.)

6. The experts of the Law now protest saying, in effect, "You're hurting our feelings!" Does Jesus apologize for being a rude dinner guest? Tell in your own words what Jesus holds against the experts in the Law.

7. What is **"the key to knowledge" (verse 52)**?

8. What was the result of the pleasant little dinner party the Pharisee had planned **(verses 53-54)**?

HYPOCRISY DIAGNOSED

1. According to **Luke 12:4-5**, what is the cause of hypocrisy?

2. According to **Luke 12:1-3**, what is the end result of hypocrisy?

The American Heart Association wants everyone to recognize the warning signs of a heart attack. These signs include great pain in the center of the chest; pain radiating to the shoulder, arm, neck, or jaw; shortness of breath; and also unusual sweating or nausea.

Jesus has given warning signs of hypocrisy, the heart attack of the soul. Since hypocrisy is one of the leading causes of spiritual death, let's review the warning signals of this potentially fatal disease. Check any that may apply to you:

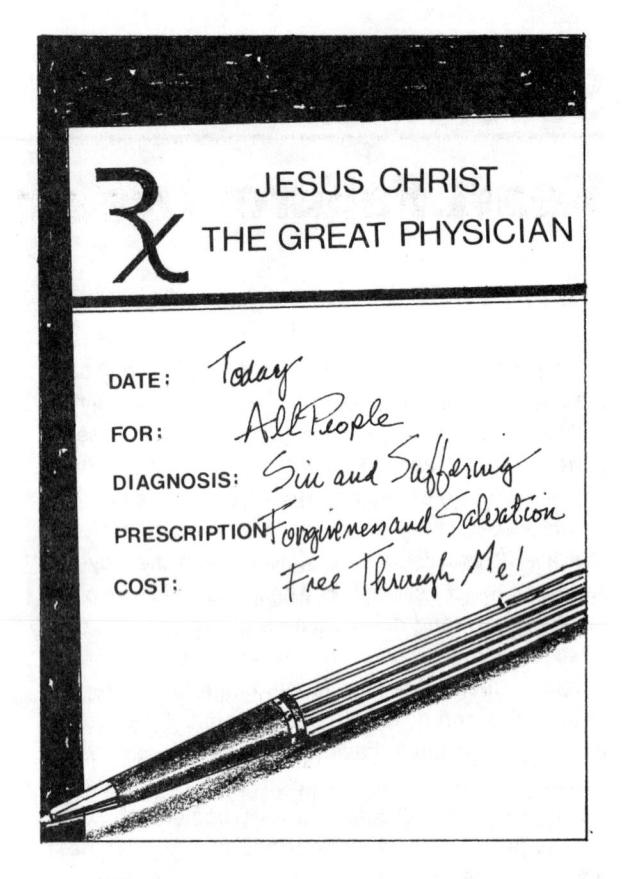

JESUS CHRIST THE GREAT PHYSICIAN

DATE: Today
FOR: All People
DIAGNOSIS: Sin and Suffering
PRESCRIPTION: Forgiveness and Salvation
COST: Free Through Me!

_____ concern with externals (appearance, what's on the outside) over internals (substance, what's on the inside)

_____ lack of proportion; concern for the little things (details, rules) and neglect of the big things (mercy, justice, love)

_____ concern about human approval and popularity, but lack of concern for God's will and approval

_____ concern that others might find out what you are really like

Do any of these warning signs apply to you? If so, here's good news! The disease of hypocrisy need not be fatal. The Great Physician (Jesus) has a 100 percent success rate on all cases that are brought to Him.

Don't ignore your heart problems. Confess them to the Heart Doctor, trust Him to heal you, and then follow His instructions for rehabilitation. Here's more good news: Jesus makes house calls, He's never too busy, and He charges no fee. He's the expert at heart transplants.

It has been said that hypocrisy is the characteristic of the man who attempts to divide his heart between God and self. But God says, **"I will give them an undivided heart and put a new spirit in them; I will remove from them their heart of stone and give them a heart of flesh" (Ezekiel 11:19).**

Session 28

The American Dream

It's not fair!

We're going on strike!

"Nobody else's parents make them come home by 11 o'clock!"

We demand equal rights, equal pay, and no discrimination!

"I'm for tax reform! We carry too much of the burden while others don't do their fair share!"

The corrupt, oppressive regime must be overthrown!

We hear and read statements like these almost every day in the halls of schools, in homes, in newscasts and newspapers, both at home and abroad. People get upset if they think that they're not getting their fair share of the good things of this world. On the other hand, those who have an advantaged position get upset if their possessions or enjoyment of them are challenged or threatened in any way. In this session Jesus deals with people like that—people who are all wrapped up in the world.

HOW TO BE RICH AND FOOLISH

1. Read **Luke 12:13-15.** What was the man who questioned Jesus concerned about?

2. Do you think this man had a right to be upset? Why or why not?

3. Jesus was always helping people. Why didn't He help this man?

4. What was Jesus concerned most about?

5. Read the parable in **Luke 12:16-21.** What reputation do you think the rich man had in his community? Why?

6. Why did God call him a fool?

7. What is God's message for us in this parable?

HOW TO MAKE GOD ANGRY AT YOU

1. We all like to get invitations. It's fun to go out and it's an honor to be invited to a party, a dinner, or to a club. According to **Luke 14:15,** what is the best invitation you could ever receive?

2. Read Jesus' parable in **Luke 14:16-24.** Tell what these people and things represent:

The man preparing a banquet:

_____

The great banquet:

_____

His servant:

_____

Those who got invitations:

_____

The poor, crippled, blind, and lame:

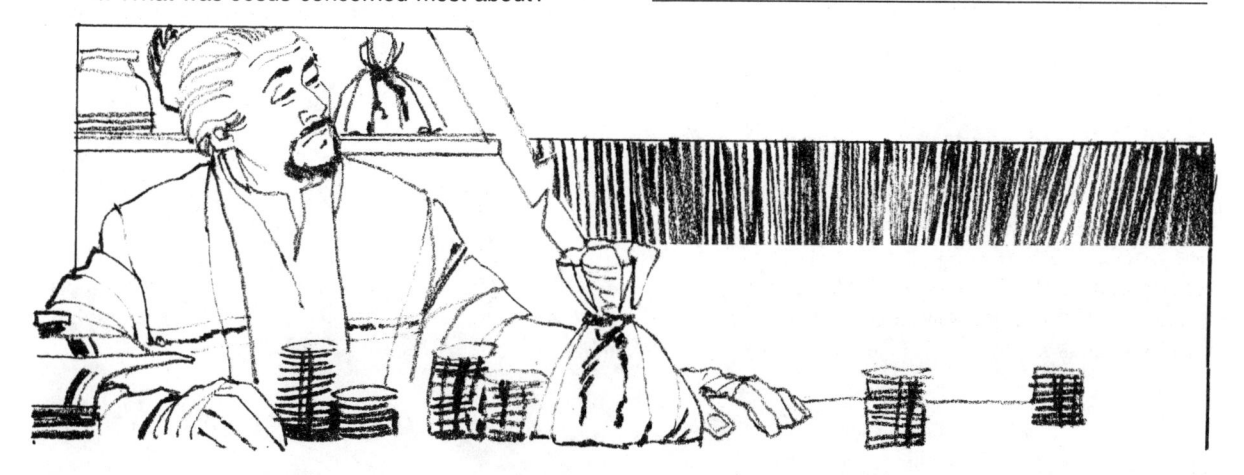

_____

61

Those in the roads and country lanes:
_____

3. What is the lesson in this parable for you?
_____
_____

4. What is the greatest banquet you have ever gone to? Be prepared to share your experience with the class.

5. Look at the following list of excuses for being absent from God's banquet, the feast of forgiveness He offers you through the Lord's Supper. Add others that you can think of. Place **P** by excuses you have used in the past. Place **N** by any you are now using. Place **F** by any you may be tempted to use in the future.

_____ I have a job on Sundays.
_____ Sunday is my only day to relax.
_____ I'm involved in sports and a lot of other activities.
_____ Sunday is my day for staying home with my family.
_____ I'm too tired.
_____ I have no one to go with.
_____ I don't feel like I need to go.
_____ I _____
_____ I _____

6. On the basis of what you've learned in this session, what changes will you make in your life? Whose help will you need to make these changes?
_____
_____
_____
_____

Do not store up for yourselves treasures on earth, where moth and rust destroy, and where thieves break in and steal. But store up for yourselves treasures in heaven, where moth and rust do not destroy, and where thieves do not break in and steal. For where your treasure is, there your heart will be also.
Matthew 6:19-21

How shall we escape if we ignore such a great salvation? This salvation, which was first announced by the Lord, was confirmed to us by those who heard Him. God also testified to it by signs, wonders, and various miracles, and gifts of the Holy Spirit distributed according to His will.
Hebrews 2:3-4

Session 29
Be Prepared!

The motto of the Boy Scouts is "Be prepared." The Boy Scout program is designed to prepare Scouts for survival, for service, for citizenship, and for life. "Be prepared" is a good motto for the Christian as well. This session teaches about the importance of *being* prepared, for *what* we must prepare, and *how* we are to prepare. The importance of preparedness can not be overemphasized. The lack of preparedness will eventually exclude those from eternal life who assume that their own goodness has made their eternity quite secure. Unpreparedness ranks right up there with stubborn unbelief (session 27) and love of money (session 28) as one of the great spiritual killers of humankind.

THE PARABLE OF THE TEN VIRGINS

1. Read the parable in **Matthew 25:1-13**. Then identify what the following represent:

The bridegroom:
_____

The 10 virgins:
_____

The oil:
_____

The wedding banquet:
_____

2. The need to be prepared always relates to some future event. To what future event does this parable point?

3. What do we learn about preparedness from **verses 7-9**?

4. What does this parable tell us about when Christ will return?

5. What will happen to those who are not prepared?

TWO SIMILAR YET DIFFERENT PARABLES

1. Read this parable in **Luke 19:11-27**. What do these represent?

A man of noble birth:
_____

A distant country:
_____

His 10 servants:
_____

10 minas:
_____

His subjects/enemies:
_____

2. Now read the parable of the talents in **Matthew 25:14-30**. This parable is very similar to the parable of the 10 minas, but it does differ in a few significant ways. How does it differ?
_____

3. To what future event do both of these parables point?
_____

4. How can you and how *must* you prepare for this event?
_____

5. What will happen to those who are not prepared?
_____

THE PARABLE OF THE SHREWD MANAGER

Read the parable in **Luke 16:1-13**. Focus on the main point in this parable: the master does not commend the manager for his wastefulness or dishonesty,

63

but only for his shrewdness in making preparations for the future.

1. For what event was the shrewd manager preparing?

2. How did he prepare for this upcoming event?

3. For what event must "the people of the Light" prepare?

4. How are we to prepare for it?

5. This parable teaches us much about our worldly wealth.

   a. Whose wealth is it?

   b. How is it to be used?

   c. What can we gain by it?

MINIPARABLES ON PREPAREDNESS

Read **Luke 12:35-40.**

1. For what event must we prepare?

2. When will this event take place?

3. What surprising reward awaits you and all prepared servants?

4. **Luke 12:41-46** deals with the specific responsibilities of pastors and teachers. What preparations must these people make?

5. **Verses 47-48** indicate there will be differing degrees of punishment in hell. What will determine the severity of punishment?

6. As you review the parables in this session, what indications are given that there will also be varying degrees of rewards and responsibility in God's heavenly kingdom?

SOMETHING TO THINK ABOUT

Being prepared for the return of Jesus Christ involves watching, waiting, and working. It is crucially important that we remember that Christ *is* coming back, that His return will be at an unexpected time, and that, in the meantime, we must be about our Father's business. All of the parables in this section indicate that there will be a significant number of people who appear to be a part of Christ's church who will nevertheless be excluded from the heavenly kingdom because of their unpreparedness.

Are you prepared?

They will see the Son of Man coming on the clouds of the sky, with power and great glory. No one knows about that day or hour, not even the angels in heaven, nor the Son, but only the Father.
Matthew 24:30, 36

We must all appear before the judgment seat of Christ, that each one may receive what is due him for the things done while in the body, whether good or bad.
2 Corinthians 5:10

Session 30

Surprise! Who? Me?

When was the last time you were surprised? Did a friend host a surprise birthday party for you? Were you chosen to be a homecoming attendant? Did you make the soccer team? Were you awarded a computer camp scholarship? Think of a recent surprise in your life.

One of the most wonderful experiences in life is to receive an honor that you never expected. Maybe you thought you'd never make the team or be good enough at computing to get an award. Maybe you thought someone else had the most valuable player award all locked up. Maybe you thought you weren't pretty or popular enough to be voted to the homecoming court.

It feels great to be honored for performance. On the other hand, we can feel totally deflated when we're passed by, especially when we thought we had it coming. When we make plans for the prom and then the person we were counting on turns us down. When we expect to make the team but the coach cuts us. These experiences can be devastating. It's hard to be judged by what we look like, by how well we do something, and by who our friends are. These criteria are "of the world."

Jesus tells us in this session that on Judgment Day there will be a lot of experiences—both wonderful and devastating—for many people. We don't have to expect any bad surprises then if we experience a wonderful surprise now—the surprise of God's love and forgiveness for us in Christ Jesus. Faith in our Lord Jesus Christ, our Savior, is the only criterion by which our heavenly Father will measure us on the Last Day.

THE AVOWED SINNER INSTEAD OF THE SELF-RIGHTEOUS "SAINT"

Read Jesus' parable in **Luke 18:9-14**.
1. Which man was cocksure of his good standing before God?
2. On what was his confidence based?
3. On what did the other man hope?
4. What surprise did God have for them?
5. On what basis do you hope God receives you into eternal life?

THE WALKERS INSTEAD OF THE TALKERS

Read Jesus' parable of the two sons in **Matthew 21:28-32**.
1. Whom does the first son represent?
2. Whom does the second son represent?

Some people talk a good game, but don't produce. They'll promise you one thing and then do quite another. Their walk doesn't match their talk. Their words say one thing but their actions say something entirely different. Are you more likely to talk like the first son or the second son? After which son are you more likely to walk?

3. According to Jesus, who enters the kingdom of heaven, the talkers or the walkers?

THE GENTILES INSTEAD OF THE JEWS

For 2,000 years the Jewish people had longed for, expected, and prayed for the coming of their Messiah-Savior. Yet surprisingly, when the Messiah came He was rejected by the Jewish leaders in the Jewish capital city. In subsequent years the Christian church has been comprised primarily of Gentiles. Read **Luke 13:31-35**.
1. How did Jesus feel about the Jewish people?
2. What was their fatal flaw?
3. How might Jewish people be saved today?
4. What can you do to bring the Gospel to Jewish people you may or may not know?

THE FEW INSTEAD OF THE MANY

Many might have the idea that the majority of people are on their way to everlasting life in heaven. They may think "He was a good man. I'll surely see him in heaven someday." Or "She was such a good church worker. She'll go to heaven now that she has died."

However, the more we listen to Jesus, the more we may begin to wonder.

1. What question did someone ask Jesus in **Luke 13:23**?

2. Read **Luke 13:24-25** and **Matthew 7:13-14**. How does Jesus describe the way to eternal life?

3. How does Jesus describe the way to eternal destruction?

4. Where do the few go? Where do the many go?

THE FAR INSTEAD OF THE NEAR

Some people blindly assume that being a Christian is a matter of what country you live in, what family you belong to, or how much time you spend in or near a church or a Christian school. Read **Luke 13:26-30**.

1. Why were the excluded ones surprised?

2. Who were the included ones?

3. What lesson do you learn from this part of Scripture?

THE DIVIDED INSTEAD OF THE UNITED

1. What did Jesus come to bring according to **Luke 1:79; 2:14;** and **10:5**?

2. Read **Luke 12:49-53**. What does this section of the Bible tell you Jesus came to bring?

3. Explain these two seemingly contradictory passages from questions 1 and 2. (For help, see also **John 14:17** and **Romans 5:1**.)

LUCKY? UNLUCKY? RATHER— BLESSED AND SAVED!

Can you tell how God feels about you by how "lucky" or "unlucky" you are? When things go well, do you say, "Somebody up there likes me"? Do you conclude, as did Maria in *The Sound of Music*, that "Somewhere in my youth or childhood, I must have done something good"? And, if things go badly, do you ask, "Why me?" and try to figure out why God doesn't like you?

1. Read **Luke 13:1-5**. What can we conclude about the Galileans and residents of Jerusalem who were killed?

2. What response does God expect from *all* people?

3. Read the parable in **Luke 13:6-9**. Identify the meanings of these symbols:

The owner of the fig tree:

_____

The fig tree:

_____

The vineyard:

_____

The caretaker of the vineyard:

_____

The one more year:

_____

SOMETHING TO THINK ABOUT

God has a surprise for everyone. Some are surprised now. Others will be surprised later.

The ones surprised now are surprised by God's love and forgiveness. They repent of their sins, trust in Christ, and bear fruits of repentance. They live each day in the Light of Jesus.

Others will be surprised later by the severity of God's judgment and their own exclusion from eternal life.

In which group are you?

If you think you are standing firm, be careful that you don't fall! No temptation has seized you except what is common to man. God is faithful; He will not let you be tempted beyond what you can bear. But when you are tempted, He will also provide a way out so that you can stand up under it.
1 Corinthians 10:12-13

Session 31

God Has Feelings Too

The officers and advisers of the Lutheran Youth Fellowship were having their regular monthly planning meeting. They were discussing a problem they had in Trinity Lutheran Church. A lot of young people were dropping out of the church after their confirmation.

"What can we do to get these people back in church?" asked Anthony. "It really bothers me that these people aren't coming anymore."

"I think we should concentrate on the ones we have," Cherise advised. "You can't win 'em all, you know."

"What a person does after confirmation is his or her own business," suggested Alex. "After all, we're old enough to make our own decisions."

"Frankly, I hope a few of them never do come back," admitted Pat. "If I told you what some of them are into now, you'd be shocked. If they ever did belong here, they sure don't belong now."

"I don't agree!" countered Chris. "Let's plan something special and then make phone calls, write invitations, and even visit them."

"That's a lot of work!" exclaimed Lisa. "And besides, I have too many other things I have to do. I can't be chasing after people who don't want to come anyway."

"Why did I ever agree to be a youth group officer?" thought Peter.

What would you think or say if you were at this meeting?

THE LOST SHEEP AND THE LOST COIN

Read the two parables in **Luke 15:1-10.**
1. Why do you think "sinners" were attracted to Jesus?
2. What do the following elements in Jesus' parables stand for?
The shepherd and the woman:

The 99 sheep and the nine coins:

The one sheep and the one coin:

The friends and neighbors:

3. How did the shepherd feel about his one lost sheep? How did the woman feel about her one lost coin?
4. How did the shepherd feel when he found his lost sheep? How did the woman feel when she found her lost coin?
5. What do we learn about God from these two parables?

THE LOST SON

Read the entire parable in **Luke 15:11-32.**
1. Whom do the three main characters represent?
The younger son:

The father:

The older son:

_____

2. Which of these is the main character in the story? Why?

3. What do we learn about God from the way the father responds to the younger son's request in **verse 12?**

From the way he responds to the younger son's return?

From the way he responds to the older son's reaction?

4. Do you think the older son had a good reason to complain? Why or why not?

5. This parable is Jesus' longest, most well-known, and probably best-loved parable. Why do you suppose people love this parable so much?

SOMETHING TO THINK ABOUT

1. Remembering the message in **Luke 15,** write a brief letter of advice and encouragement to the officers and advisers of the Trinity Lutheran Youth Fellowship. Be prepared to share this with your class.

_____

_____

_____

_____

_____

2. As you take the message of **Luke 15** seriously, what changes will you want to make in your life through your attitudes and actions?

_____

_____

A PARABLE FOR TODAY

I remember a feeling I had when I was about six years old. My mom and dad and sisters and brothers all got in the car and went to the state fair. We'd been to county fairs each year, but this was the first time I'd ever been to a *state* fair.

People were everywhere. We trudged through the crowds on the fairways and in the grandstand. I probably missed seeing things I'd never seen before as I kept my eyes glued on Mom and my hand tightly gripped in hers.

We cheered at the noisy tractor-pulling contest. We sneezed and wheezed through the straw-filled pig and cattle barns. We stood in awe at God's prize-winning pumpkins and flowers in the judging halls. Finally, we found our way to the circus-colored sno-cone stand. I chose last, and I chose cherry. I slurped it slowly, walking far behind the rest of my family, not wanting to let the cold icy treat drip and be wasted. It wasn't long as I walked on the dusty path that I looked up and panicked. I strained my eyes looking for my family. I couldn't see anyone I knew! I stood in the middle of the dirt path, tears ran down my dirt-streaked cheeks, and my sticky sno-cone dripped through its soggy paper cone. Soft plops dropped onto my sneakers and splattered into the dirt. I was lost! I was separated from my family.

It seemed *too* long before Dad found me! But when he came running toward me, weaving in and out of the two-way crowd with his arms outstretched, I felt SO good again! He scooped me up, squished his rough cheek against my wet one, and said, "Thank God! I found you!"

Dad didn't scold me for dawdling along the way. He never implied that I had done anything wrong that day. Instead, he poured out his love and relief in his actions and words. He sang all the way home. I felt so small, so happy, so *found!*

If we feel so wonderful when a loving parent or friend on earth finds us, how exhilarated might we feel when we know that our heavenly Father is rejoicing over finding us as His once lost, separated child!

For the Son of Man came to seek and to save what was lost.

Luke 19:10

Session 32

Growing Up Childlike

It's not easy to be an adolescent. It can be the hardest time in your whole life. You aren't a child. Yet you aren't an adult. There are so many changes in your life. You're adjusting to physical, emotional, and spiritual growth all at once. You constantly change in the ways you relate to your parents, other adults, your school friends, and persons of the opposite sex. Experiencing changes in yourself is sometimes exciting. Often it's scary. Many times it's embarrassing.

Perhaps you'd just like to hold onto the security of family and home, play by the rules, and let the future and all its independence gradually draw you out. Or maybe you'd like to get this "transition time" over with as fast as you can.

Maturing in a God-pleasing way into adulthood takes time and effort. We need to retain elements of our childhood as well as grow in various ways. The trick is for us to distinguish between what is childlike and what is childish—to keep the one and outgrow the other. This session helps us understand typical characteristics of childhood that are important for us to have and keep forever.

SETTING THINGS STRAIGHT

Read Luke **18:15-17**.

1. Whom did the people bring to Jesus?
2. Why do you think the disciples rebuked them?
3. What do you think Jesus meant by what He said in **verse 17**?

CASE STUDY 1: THE POOR YUPPIE—A FLUNKIE IN CHILDLIKENESS

1. Look at **Luke 18:18, 21** and **Mark 10:17**. What good things could you say about this fellow?
2. What did Jesus get at by His responses in **Luke 18:19, 20,** and **22**? What did Jesus try to get the man to realize?
3. What do we learn about the attempt to earn peace with God through keeping the Commandments by the man's questions in **Luke 18:18** and **Matthew 19:20?**
4. How did Jesus feel toward this young man according to **Mark 10:21** and **Luke 18:22?**
5. What unchildlike characteristic did this man show?
6. Read **Matthew 19:23-25** and **Luke 18:23-26**. How did the disciples react to what Jesus had to say? Why do you think they reacted that way?
7. What does it take for a rich person to be saved **(Luke 18:27)?**

CASE STUDY 2: THE PERPLEXED DISCIPLES— STRUGGLES IN CHILDLIKENESS

1. What unspoken question lurks behind Peter's statement in **Luke 18:28?**
2. What rate of interest does Christ promise on investments made in His kingdom **(Matthew 19:29; Luke 18:29-30)?**
3. Read **Luke 18:31-34**. Why do you think the disciples had such difficulty understanding Jesus' very plain and simple words?
4. Explain how the disciples demonstrated both childlikeness and childishness. (Most modern day disciples have this same mixture in their lives. Do you?)

CASE STUDY 3: THE SEEING BLIND BEGGAR—HONOR STUDENT IN CHILDLIKENESS

1. Read **Luke 18:35-43**. Why do you suppose the leaders of the parade wanted the blind beggar to be quiet?
2. How did the blind beggar demonstrate childlikeness?
3. In **Isaiah 11:6** it was prophesied that in the messianic kingdom **"a little child will lead them."** How did the blind beggar contribute to the fulfillment of the prophecy?

CASE STUDY 4: THE GENEROUS CHEATER—HONOR STUDENT IN CHILDLIKENESS

1. Read **Luke 19:1-10.** How did Zacchaeus demonstrate his childlikeness?

2. Compare **Luke 19:8** with **Numbers 5:5-7.** How do you know Zacchaeus was not like the rich young ruler, trying to earn his way to heaven?

3. Jesus called Zacchaeus a **"son of Abraham,"** the father of the faithful. According to **John 8:39,** how are we to recognize a true child of Abraham?

4. Which incident from the life of Abraham compares to the response of Zacchaeus?

KEEPING THINGS STRAIGHT

The rich young ruler, Zacchaeus the tax collector, and the patriarch Abraham were all very rich. Wealth does not in itself damn a person any more than poverty saves a person. One's attachment to material possessions is a good indicator of childlikeness, or lack of it. The rich young ruler's heart was attached to his possessions, not to Christ, therefore Christ demanded he give it all away. Jesus made no such demand upon Zacchaeus or Abraham. He didn't have to. Their childlikeness was evident.

What characteristics of childhood *are* important for us to keep?

_____

_____

Think of ways that you demonstrate godly childlikeness in your life. Personally reflect on these things. You might want to write things down as you reflect for your own benefit. Begin a personal journal. Write about yourself—your attributes and attitudes—for a few minutes each day. Be honest. Read what you've written. Discover your growth. Ask God to help you grow to be childlike in your Christian faith and relationships with Him and others.

I tell you the truth, anyone who will not receive the kingdom of God like a little child will never enter it.
Luke 18:17

When I was a child, I talked like a child. I thought like a child, I reasoned like a child. When I became a man, I put childish ways behind me.
1 Corinthians 13:11

Session 33

Judgment, Heaven, and Hell

The people who lived during the Middle Ages thought a lot about Judgment Day, heaven, and hell. The awesomeness of judgment, the bliss of heaven, and the agony of hell were graphically illustrated in medieval art and architecture. Some of the greatest works of literature (for example, Dante's *Divine Comedy*) focused almost entirely on these themes. Everywhere people turned they were reminded that the goal of this life was to attain life everlasting.

Today we live in a very different world. Modern men and women could conceivably live an entire lifetime doing all the things most people do—going to school, watching television and movies, reading books and magazines, making a living, raising a family, getting involved in the community, retiring, and finally dying, without ever learning anything about what awaits us after this life. What many think they know about life after death comes from studies that totally ignore the testimony of God's Word.

However, Judgment Day, heaven, and hell do not go away just because we choose to ignore them. The Bible tells us that we must all appear before the judgment seat of Christ, and this same Christ has told us a lot about that day and what lies beyond it. God does not intend for us to live in constant anxiety about what lies beyond, like so many did in the Middle Ages. Neither does He want us to be ignoring it or ignorant of it, like so many are today. What you learn in this session is what your loving Savior wants you to know and remember. May it be both an encouragement and a warning to you, and may it influence how you live every day for the rest of your life.

GOD TELLS US ABOUT JUDGMENT DAY, HEAVEN, AND HELL

Fill in the chart on the next page to find out what these Bible stories teach us about judgment, heaven, and hell.

LIVING PREPARED

Jesus will come to earth again. That last day will mark the final separation of those who are saved from those who are lost. Not one will be forgotten. Not one will be overlooked. God will raise to life each dead person to face eternal judgment with those who are still alive.

Only God can save you and me. He has already done this through Jesus' suffering, death, and resurrection. Jesus, by taking our sins with Him to the cross, has made us "right" with God, our Judge. He has granted us a free and total pardon from our sins. He has given us the hope of living forever with Him through Jesus Christ, our Savior. We need only to believe.

How would you feel if Judgment Day would come at this moment? Would you be ready for Jesus? Would you go to heaven? Why or why not?

SOMETHING TO THINK AND PRAY ABOUT

God's kingdom on earth is *here* and *now.* We don't know exactly when He will move us from His earthly kingdom to His heavenly one. Think of how exciting it would be to leave home and enjoy a long, luxurious vacation on a beautiful tropical island or somewhere else you've always dreamed of. For Christians, going home to our Father in heaven is *the most exciting* segment of life!

If you could know in some magical way that tomorrow would be your last day before Judgment Day, how would you spend it?

Since you don't know when Judgment Day will come, how might you best live each new day of your earthly life?

Jesus lived, died, and rose again "that each of us might be His own and live under Him in His kingdom, and *serve Him* in everlasting righteousness, innocence, and blessedness." Read **Matthew 25:35-40** again. How could you serve Jesus through a friend, a family member, or a neighbor this week?

I have fought the good fight, I have finished the race, I have kept the faith. Now there is in store for me the crown of righteousness, which the Lord, the righteous Judge, will award to me on that day—and not only to me, but also to all who have longed for His appearing.

2 Timothy 4:7-8

	The Wheat and Weeds (Matthew 13:24-30, 36-43)	**The Net of Fish** (Matthew 13: 47-50)	**The Sheep and Goats** (Matthew 25: 31-46)	**The Rich Man and Lazarus** (Luke 16:19-31)
What will happen on Judgment Day?				
How are the people of God different from the people belonging to Satan (on earth)?				
How is hell described?				
How is heaven described?				

Session 34

How's Your Spiritual Health?

Periodically we go to a doctor for a checkup. Usually by checking a few basics, this medical professional can determine the state of our health. We might have to stick out our tongue or step on the scale. The doctor listens to our heartbeat and checks our blood pressure, reflexes, and posture. In just a few minutes, the doctor can tell us how healthy we are.

You've learned a lot during this unit about what it means for Jesus to be the Messiah and what it means for someone to be one of His disciples. Remember that the state of our spiritual health is determined not so much by what we *know*, but by what we are putting into *practice*. (What we do gives evidence of what we believe.) In this session, Doctor Jesus (the Great Physician) gives us a spiritual checkup. Perhaps the results of this exam will tell you more about your spiritual health than any unit test or review ever could.

JESUS' FIVE-POINT SPIRITUAL CHECKUP

I. Considerate, Self-denying Love

Read **Luke 17:1-2**. The world is full of temptations and sin, but Jesus doesn't want us to make it any worse than it already is. Our words and deeds either make it easier for others to follow Christ or to fall into sin. We are to be careful what kind of influence we have on others, especially younger people who tend to look up to us and imitate our behavior. From your own experience, list three ways that people in your school influence others to do wrong:

1. _____
2. _____
3. _____

Now list three ways in which you are already or can be an influence for good:

1. _____
2. _____
3. _____

II. Concern for Holiness and Mercy

Read **Luke 17:3-4**. According to Jesus, we should care enough about our fellow Christians ("brothers") to confront them when they are compromising their Christian testimony. We are our brother's keeper. List three times when you cared enough about God's will and your brother's welfare to rebuke (reprimand or criticize) a sin:

1. _____
2. _____
3. _____

List three ways Christians in your school could be more concerned and courageous in rebuking sin:

1. _____
2. _____
3. _____

Jesus is also concerned that we be forgiving toward those who do wrong to us. When people are sorry for their wrongdoings, we are not to hold anything against them, even in the case of repeated offenses. After all, we constantly receive forgiveness for our repeated offenses against God. List three ways in which you have demonstrated or could demonstrate the spirit of forgiveness:

1. _____
2. _____
3. _____

III. Little Faith in a Great God

Corrie ten Boom is one of the most inspirational Christians of the 20th century. Her bold Christian witness in the midst of the horrors of Nazi concentration camps and in subsequent years caused one person to exclaim in admiration, "Corrie, you must have great faith!"

"No," Corrie replied, "I just have faith in a great God."

In **Luke 17:5-6,** Jesus urged His disciples not to focus on the size of their faith, straining as it were to make it grow, but rather to focus on the size of their God, resting their faith in Him. List three "oak trees"(big problems) which you have that you need to *faith-fully* entrust to your great God:

1. _____

2. _____

3. _____

List three ways you have recently demonstrated faith in a great God:

1. _____

2. _____

3. _____

IV. Selfless Service to God

In **Luke 17:7-10** Jesus tells us that we should not expect pats on the back or recognition for merely doing what we are supposed to do, namely, serve God and other people. A true servant of Christ is much more conscious of his or her unworthiness and indebtedness, and does not consider it any great thing to have merely done a duty. List three servantlike duties you could perform without expecting applause, pay, recognition, or thanks:

1. _____

2. _____

3. _____

V. Thankfulness and Praise

Read **Luke 17:11-19.** Many people take God's blessings for granted, and even forget to thank Him for direct answers to prayer. List three ways you have demonstrated thankfulness and have given praise to God:

1. _____

2. _____

3. _____

DISCOVERY TIME

What did you discover about your spiritual health? Did this checkup reveal any areas of concern? Since the beginning of this course, have you become more spiritually fit?

What's the diagnosis? Do you have any need for the medicine of God's forgiveness in Christ? Any indication of a need for dietary supplements of the spiritual food of God's Word? Any need for more spiritual exercise?

Take heart! All your spiritual illnesses can be healed. All your needs are met in Jesus Christ, your Savior!

[Jesus] said to him, "Rise and go; your faith has made you well."

Luke 17:19

For the grace of God that brings salvation has appeared to all men. It teaches us to say "No" to ungodliness and worldly passions, and to live self-controlled, upright and godly lives ... while we wait for the blessed hope—the glorious appearing of our great God and Savior, Jesus Christ.

Titus 2:11-13

Session 35
Review of Unit 3

Answer these questions to help you review sessions 24—34.

1. What is the *apostolic church?* What do those who belong to the apostolic church do?

2. Describe the kingdom of God as completely as you can.

3. Who is your "neighbor"?

4. What is the "one better thing" in your life that sometimes is crowded out by good worldly things?

5. What part does communication have in your relationship with Jesus?

6. What is the relationship between prayer and faith?

7. Describe three spiritual "heart problems" and tell Jesus' diagnosis, prescription, and rehabilitation program for these.

8. God invites us to share His heavenly banquet. What is that banquet on earth, and what does our response to God's invitation indicate?

9. Why is it important that we be prepared for Jesus' second coming? How can we be truly prepared?

10. What warning and what promise does God make to us in **1 Corinthians 10:12-13?**

11. In 25 words or less, personalize **Luke 19:10.**

12. What will happen on Judgment Day?

13. How are the people of God different from those belonging to the devil here on earth?

14. How do Matthew and Luke describe hell?

15. How do Matthew and Luke describe heaven?

Unit 4
Jesus, Our Hope

"Whew!" sighed Christa. *"I finished all the experiments and I learned all the elements and their properties. I'm sure I've got between an A and a B in Chemistry. I **hope** it's an A!"*

Hope. Christa has a sure grade. She hopes, though, for the best.

"Guess what!" Ryan told David excitedly. *"Remember when I told you my dad promised me a car when I turn 16? Well, my birthday's next month, and Dad said we could start looking for my car this Saturday. I **hope** we find the one for me!"*

Hope. Ryan's dad has made a promise. He's sure to keep it. Ryan hopes for *the* car—clean, sporty, fairly new, the one he's been dreaming of for a long time.

We often say "I hope," don't we? "I hope the game doesn't get rained out." "I hope the guy I like asks me to the dance. I hope he likes me as much as I like him." "I hope Mom doesn't hear me come in past the magic hour." "I hope I don't run out of gas." "I hope my girl asks me to her family's cottage at the lake on Saturday." "I hope I can find a summer job." "I hope."

Sometimes the things we hope for are fairly sure things. Maybe a reward someone has already promised us. But we hope it's the color or style or size we like.

Other things we hope for might be long shots. Like when we hope for a date with someone who doesn't even know our name. Or when we hope for a career as a singer when we can't sing in tune.

Hope. We have *one* sure hope. We have one hope we can know and trust will never change. We have one hope we can look forward to no matter what else happens to all our other worldly hopes. **That hope is the hope Jesus gives us for our lives.**

Jesus, our Hope. He is like an anchor for our lives. Because He took away all our sins forever, we can feel firm and secure that, through faith in Him and through the forgiveness our heavenly Father graciously offers us, Jesus will always be our Friend. He will listen when we talk to Him. He will strengthen us when we feel weak. He will show us His way and guide us in making decisions. He will surround us with His unchanging love. And He will take us to live with Him in heaven when we die. Jesus is our *only* Hope for the life that matters—our life with Him, here and in eternity.

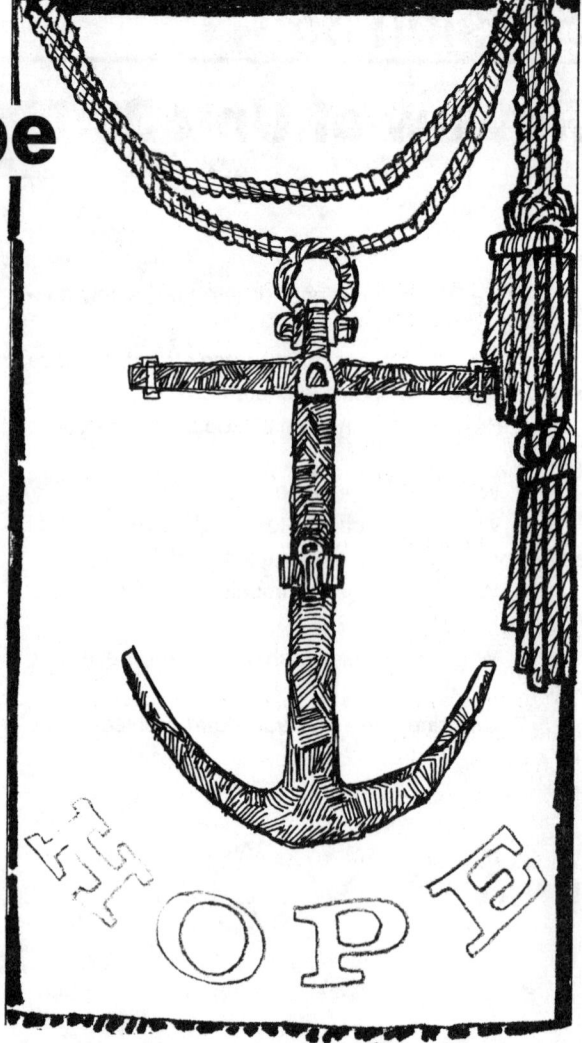

As you read and discuss Jesus' fulfillment of the Old Testament prophecies through His suffering, death, and resurrection, think of Him as God's instrument in His plan to provide you and all people with hope for your life. Thank and praise Him for the hope He gives to you and to everyone who believes in Him.

Put your hope in God.
Psalm 42:5

We wait for the blessed hope—the glorious appearing of our great God and Savior, Jesus Christ, who gave Himself for us to redeem us.
Titus 2:13-14

Session 36

Big Hit on Broadway!

Today we honor our heroes with ticker tape parades. In Jesus' day, when a king was crowned or when a general returned from a successful campaign, the people honored them in much the same way. The fans crowded the streets, waved their victory palms, and shouted words of praise and allegiance.

Palm Sunday was Jesus' one and only "ticker tape parade." The city of Jerusalem bulged to three times its normal population due to all the pilgrim Jews who came to the temple city to celebrate the Passover, the great holiday season commemorating the day when God made the Egyptian pharaoh set the Israelites free. The hotels and motels all had "no vacancy" signs out. Those pilgrims who arrived early were accommodated by residents who had a spare bed or floor space. Others found camping space on the slopes around the city. Jerusalem buzzed because Jesus, the great prophet from Nazareth, was expected to come too. His mighty words and deeds were the hottest topic of conversation. Many speculated about who He was and what great things He might do. Let's go to Jerusalem and get in on the excitement!

JESUS, THE KING

1. Read **Luke 19:28-38.** In what ways did Jesus demonstrate that He is a king?

2. In what ways did the people show that they recognized Him to be a king?

3. In what ways did Jesus show Himself as an unusual sort of king?

JESUS, THE MESSIAH

The Old Testament is filled with many prophecies pertaining to the Messiah. You have already discovered that Jesus fulfilled many of these prophecies. On the first Palm Sunday, Jesus fulfilled more key prophecies concerning the Messiah.

1. Read **Zechariah 9:9-10.** What words of this prophecy were fulfilled by Jesus?

2. Read **Psalm 118:22-27.** What words of this prophetic psalm did Jesus fulfill?

JESUS, THE PROPHET

1. Read **Luke 19:39-44.** How did the Pharisees react to Jesus' Palm Sunday parade?

2. Why do you think they reacted that way?

3. Read **verses 41-42.** Why did Jesus weep during His parade?

4. What did Jesus predict?

5. Has Jesus' prediction come true? If so, how?

6. Have you ever wept over someone's stubborn refusal to accept Jesus? Share your experience with the class.

JESUS, THE PROTESTER-ACTIVIST

Jesus was not a violent man, and it was rare indeed for Him to resort to physical force to make a point. Read **Luke 19:45-46.**

1. What did Jesus do?

2. Why was Jesus so angry?

3. If Jesus had been arrested for vandalism, destruction of others' property, and disturbing the peace, and you were appointed His defense attorney, upon what would you base His defense?

4. Do you ever get angry about anything that happens in church or school chapel? What makes you angry? Why?

JESUS, THE LAMB OF GOD

Palm Sunday is also known as Passion Sunday. It's the beginning of Holy Week, the week of Jesus' suffering and death for the sins of the whole world. Read **Luke 19:47-48.** Then sing or read together the following hymn. Notice the blend of palm and passion, power and pain, majesty and meekness. Jesus is the Victorious Victim.

Ride On, Ride On in Majesty

1. Ride on, ride on in majesty!
   Hear all the tribes hosanna cry;
   O Savior meek, pursue Your road
   With palms and scattered garments strowed.

2. Ride on, ride on in majesty!
   In lowly pomp ride on to die.
   O Christ, Your triumphs now begin
   O'er captive death and conquered sin.

3. Ride on, ride on in majesty!
   The winged squadrons of the sky
   Look down with sad and wond'ring eyes
   To see the approaching sacrifice.

4. Ride on, ride on in majesty!
   Your last and fiercest strife is nigh.
   The Father on His sapphire throne
   Awaits His own anointed Son.

5. Ride on, ride on in majesty!
   In lowly pomp ride on to die.
   Bow your meek head to mortal pain,
   Then take, O Christ, Your power and reign!

Lutheran Worship, 105

We praise Jesus when we sing the Sanctus and we ask for His mercy in the words of the Agnus Dei. Read or sing these words from the hymnal (*Lutheran Worship,* pp. 189-91).

Blessed is the King who comes in the name of the Lord!

Luke 19:38

Session 37

Traps and Ambushes

Jesus' Palm Sunday ride through the streets and His tear through the temple caused His enemies to intensify their efforts to discredit and destroy Him. They devised what they thought to be incriminating questions, knotty problems, and impossible dilemmas for Jesus. They hoped to make Jesus say something that would get Him into trouble with either the Jewish people or the Roman government. This session focuses on the unanswerable questions that Jesus was asked, and the unanswerable questions Jesus asked in return.

WHO GAVE YOU THE RIGHT?

The royal welcome Jesus received on Palm Sunday and the way He responded to it, as well as the way He took charge of what went on in the temple, seemed to imply that He considered Himself acting on the authority of God Himself. It was considered blasphemy—a crime punishable by death—for any man to claim for himself the prerogatives that belonged to God alone or His Messiah-elect. The Jewish leaders hoped to get Jesus specifically to claim the title of Messiah so they might have a pretext to arrest and condemn Him. Apparently the thought that He might very well be the Messiah never occurred to them. They hated Him too much seriously to entertain such a possibility.

1. Read **Luke 20:1-2.** Why do you think Jesus' enemies came out in such a large group to ask Jesus their question?

2. Read **verses 20:3-6.** In your own words, why is Jesus' question so difficult for them?

3. What was John's message that these Jewish leaders refused to heed?

4. Read **verses 7-8.** The Jewish leaders told Jesus they couldn't answer, claiming ignorance. What was Jesus' reply?

SHOULD WE PAY TAXES TO CAESAR?

1. Read **Luke 20:20.** How do Jesus' enemies approach Him this time?

2. Read **verses 21-22.** How do the spies' words compare with the attitude of their hearts?

3. The question Jesus' enemies had devised in **verse 22** was meant to trap Jesus. Either a yes or a no would get Him into trouble. What would happen if Jesus said yes?

4. What would happen if Jesus answered no?

5. Read Jesus' answer in **verses 23-25.** According to Jesus, what do you think belongs to Caesar and what belongs to God?

WHOSE WIFE WILL SHE BE IN THE RESURRECTION?

1. The Sadducees now take a turn at trying to stump Jesus. What do you remember about the Sadducees from session 3?

2. The Sadducees thought their question would make Jesus' teaching about life after death appear ridiculous. (See **Luke 20:27-33.**) They assumed that Jesus' conception of the afterlife was the same as the Pharisees', namely, more of the same, only bigger and better. According to Jesus **(verses 34-36),** how does the next life differ from this one?

3. According to **verses 37-40** and **Matthew 22:29,** what was the Sadducees' problem?

WHOSE SON IS THE CHRIST?

1. It is now Jesus' turn to ask a question. Read what Jesus says in **Luke 20:41-44.** In **verse 42** and in **Psalm 110:1,** who is meant by "The Lord" and "my Lord"?

2. With what point is Jesus trying to confront the Sadducees?

FINAL WARNING

1. Read **verses 45-47.** Tell in your own words what Jesus doesn't like about the teachers of the Law.

2. What end awaits them?

CELEBRATE BEING PART OF CHRIST'S BODY

I See The Lord
I see, Lord, in my tightly clenched fists

79

The representation of myself.
I hold only myself, my cares, my possessions,
    my pride, and my hurts.
[*Tightly clench fists and hold them out in front of you.*]
I shut You out lest You change me.
I shut other people out lest they would know me,
    lest they would hurt me.
In fact, I could strike out with these fists against those
    who would threaten me.
[*Bow head and cover with open hands.*]
But I see in the tight knuckles and tense forearms
    what this is doing to me.
I'm uptight, enslaved, imprisoned with myself.
I'm tired, tense, lonely, and in despair.
I'm only destroying myself.
[*Bring arms up above head; clench fists and look upward.*]
And now, in slowly opening my hands,
I release myself to You, Lord.
Take my guilt, burdens, cares,
    emptiness, and loneliness.
[*Share hugs, handshakes, words of care and forgiveness. Say, for example, "You are important to me." "God's peace be yours." "God loves you and so do I."*]
My arms no longer hurt! My knuckles are no longer tight!
Thank You for release, for freedom, for peace!
With open hands I can no longer shut You out,
    shut out people, strike out against those who threaten me.

[*Slowly raise arms with hands open.*]
Open hands are for helping!
Jesus, fill them with Your love.
Show them what to do, how to witness,
    how to serve.
[*Bring arms down and keep them outstretched as if holding something.*]
Suddenly I am aware of the hurts and needs of other
    persons, of other situations.
In my mind's eye I place them in these hands
    and lift them to You for Your sustaining grace
    and healing touch.
[*Bring hands together and lift them to eye level.*]
No longer alone, I reach out to clasp
    the hand of brother and sister.
I thank You for him and for her.
I pray for her and for him.
Shape us together into the Body of Christ.
Amen.
[*Reach out and clasp the hand of the person on either side of you, keeping hands raised.*]

(From *Resources for Youth Ministry*, 82:2. Copyright 1982 Board for Youth Services, The Lutheran Church—Missouri Synod. Used by permission.)

For the foolishness of God is wiser than man's wisdom, and the weakness of God is stronger than man's strength. It is because of Him that you are in Christ Jesus, who has become for us wisdom from God—that is, our righteousness, holiness, and redemption. Let him who boasts boast in the Lord.
1 Cor. 1:25, 30-31

Session 38

What's the World Coming To?

What's the world coming to?

How will all our international problems turn out?

Some worry that the world is headed for a nuclear holocaust. They hope that scientists and technologists will come up with new defense systems that will protect us from such frightful, annihilating weapons.

Others fear a Communist takeover, resulting in our loss of all freedoms and existence in a state of perpetual slavery.

Still others believe that no matter what people do, the universe will eventually run down, the sun will cease to give its heat, and the earth will be a cold, dark, lifeless planet.

The Jews of Jesus' day were generally much more optimistic about the future than people today tend to be. As we learned in the first few sessions in this course, the Jews' optimism was based on their expectations of the coming Messiah. They looked forward to a future of unending peace and unlimited prosperity. They expected the Son of Man to make Jerusalem His capital and to reign over the entire earth. The things Jesus told His disciples about the coming kingdom of God under the Son of Man sounded very strange to their ears. We examine Jesus' insights into the future in this session.

WHEN THE KINGDOM COMES

Read what Jesus says about the coming of the kingdom of God in **Luke 17:20-37**. The key to understanding Jesus' remarks is to realize that the Son of Man and God's kingdom come at two different times in two different ways.

1. In the left column below you'll find descriptions of the King's and His kingdom's coming. In the middle column, write the number of the verse(s) from **Luke 17** that support the description. In the right column, write **1** if it describes the first coming and **2** if it describes the second.

Description	Reference	Coming
Comes as a sacrificial victim	_____	_____
Establishes itself in men's hearts	_____	_____
Sudden and spectacular	_____	_____
A day of wrath and destruction	_____	_____
Not so obviously recognizable	_____	_____
Complete separation of good and evil	_____	_____

2. Put **X** in front of any choices below that would correctly finish this sentence: **The world will end, and the kingdom of God will come**

_____ in a great nuclear war.
_____ at a time when people are occupied with normal activities.
_____ through the discoveries of modern science.
_____ when all people work together in peace and unity.
_____ by action of the worldwide Communist movement.
_____ without people even realizing it.
_____ after there is no more life on earth.

3. What lesson do we learn from the story of Lot's wife **(Genesis 19:26)**?

SIGNS OF THE END

In **Luke 21:5** we discover the disciples sightseeing in the magnificent city of Jerusalem, much of it recently constructed and renovated by Herod the Great. Jesus, however, looked a few years into the future when the beautiful city of Jerusalem, the pride and joy of Jewish people the world over, would lie in ruins and the Jewish people would cease to exist as a nation in their own land.

The disciples were alarmed at Jesus' dire prediction, and were curious as to when this catastrophe would take place. Jesus used their question as an occasion for not only explaining the events leading up to the fall of Jerusalem, but also for explaining the terrible events that will someday lead up to the destruction of the whole earth. Indeed, the destruction of Jerusalem was a small-scaled preview of the far greater destruction of our universe which will take place when Jesus Christ returns.

Read **Luke 21:8-38** to complete the crossword puzzle.

Across
2. intoxication
3. weighs your heart down
4. troubled by fears
8. when Jesus' words pass away
10. epidemics
13. man-made calamities
14. heavenly body
15. heavenly body
16. survival technique; to _____
18. world hunger
19. heavenly bodies
20. overthrowing governments

Down
1. look out! (two words)
5. bewilderment
6. natural disasters
7. do this to be saved (two words)
9. suffering for Christ
11. ancient symbol of chaos
12. wastefulness
17. vehicle for Christ

LOOK TO THE FUTURE

1. Can and should Christians look to the future with optimism? With pessimism? Why?

2. Think of a frightening or stress-filled situation you have experienced. How did you handle it? Did you rely on God to help you through? How might you face the next tough situation that comes your way?

We live in hope and trust for our future. We can do this only because God kept His promise and sent His Son, Jesus, to save us from sin and eternal death. Jesus gives us the forgiveness of our sins and the hope we need to live with our eyes focused on heaven. When we die, Jesus will give all believers the crown of life eternal. God is trustworthy. He is in control. He loves you and me and shares His kingdom with all who believe in Him. Thank and praise Him!

At that time they will see the Son of Man coming in a cloud with power and great glory. Heaven and earth will pass away, but My words will never pass away.
Luke 21:27, 33

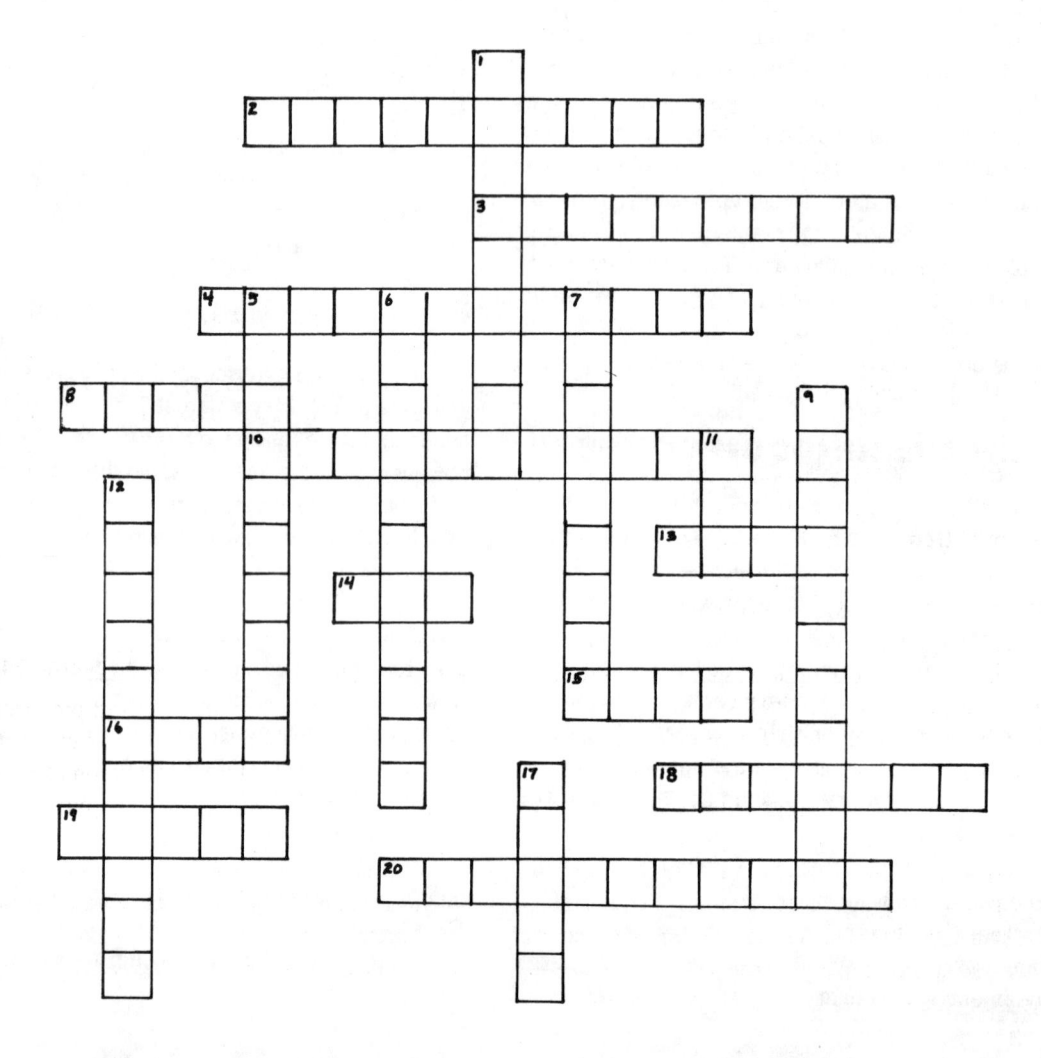

Session 39

Last Will and Testament

A last will and testament is a legal document in which a person declares how his or her possessions should be distributed at the time of death. It doesn't go into effect until the death of the individual, nor can it be altered in any way after the death of the individual.

On the eve of His death, Jesus drew up His last will and testament. He didn't have any money or property to leave His friends. The clothes off His back were already spoken for. The Scriptures had prophesied that these would go to the soldiers through the casting of lots. But Jesus had something much more precious to leave us. In fact, what He left has enriched and sustained millions of Christians the world over through 20 centuries. This inheritance is Jesus' own body and blood, given and shed for us for the forgiveness of sins. This is the New Testament (covenant, agreement) according to which God deals with us. During the Old Testament years, God's people were obligated to observe all the Jewish regulations and sacrifices. In the new agreement, Jesus fulfilled the sacrificial system by making the ultimate final sacrifice of Himself, by which we are made heirs of salvation through faith in Him.

JESUS MADE HIS WILL

1. The Jewish leaders were intent on eliminating Jesus, but they had a problem. What was their problem? What was their solution?

2. God's new covenant with people was instituted on the night of the anniversary celebration of the greatest and most significant event in the history of the Jewish people—the night when God delivered them out of their Egyptian bondage. This event, more than any other, established in the minds of God's people the special relationship they had with the true God. Read about the first Passover in **Exodus 12:1-14.**

On the eve of God's deliverance of all people from their bondage to sin, death, and the devil, Jesus instituted a new memorial celebration that would make the old obsolete. The New Testament now fulfills and replaces the Old. Below are listed elements of the old memorial. Explain how each prefigures and is fulfilled in the New Testament.

a. a lamb **(Exodus 12:3)**
b. year-old males **(verse 5)**
c. without defect **(verse 5)**
d. all the people of the community of Israel **(verse 6)**
e. slaughter **(verse 6)**
f. blood **(verse 6)**
g. eat the lambs **(verse 7)**
h. roasted over the fire **(verse 9)**
i. strike down every firstborn **(verse 12)**
j. bring judgment **(verse 12)**
k. a day you are to commemorate **(verse 14)**

3. Many years before, God had promised to establish a new covenant to take the place of the old. Compare **Luke 22:19-20** with **Jeremiah 31:31-34.** What does God give and promise man in the new covenant?

4. Some unbelievers have considered Jesus' death as evidence that Jesus was a tragic failure, foiled in His attempts to carry out His intentions. Read carefully **Luke 22:7-23** and list evidence that Jesus is really in control of His destiny.

JESUS EXPLAINED HIS WILL

1. How do you think Jesus felt about the disciples' dispute **(Luke 22:24)**?

2. How does Jesus measure greatness?

3. How did Jesus illustrate His will for His disciples **(John 13:3-5, 12-17)**?

4. Some people refuse the role of servant because they want to prove to themselves and to others how important they are. According to **John 13:3-5**, Jesus' sense of self-importance enabled Him to be a servant. Why is it easier to be a servant once your own importance and worth have been established by God?

5. List ways that you could better fulfill Jesus' will for you to be a servant at home, at school, or wherever you are.

6. People not only try to avoid the role of a servant, but also make the mistake of thinking that the key to greatness is in abundant self-confidence. What did Jesus try to teach Peter in **Luke 22:31-34**?

7. What do you think Jesus meant by what He said in **verses 35-38**?

JESUS SUBMITTED HIS WILL

Read **Luke 22:39-46**. In this section, we go with Jesus to the Garden of Gethsemane on the slope of the Mount of Olives. It was at this time Jesus faced His greatest trial and temptation.

1. What indications do you find that this was no small trial for Jesus?

2. According to **Luke 22:32, 40, 41, 44, and 46**, what is the key to overcoming temptation successfully?

3. What was the great temptation Jesus faced?

4. What great temptations do you need to resist in your life? Add these to your prayer list and ask God to help you.

5. About what things in your life do you need to pray the words Jesus prayed, **"Not my will, but Yours be done"**?

SOMETHING TO THINK ABOUT

Of all the great things Jesus did, He wants to be remembered most in that He gave His body and blood as an offering for all sin. For this, we truly thank and praise Him!

If you were to die today, for what would you *be* remembered? If God gives you many more years to live, for what would you *like to be* most remembered?

This is My body given for you; do this in remembrance of Me. This cup is the new covenant in My blood, which is poured out for you.
Luke 22:19-20

Session 40

When Darkness Reigns

In his first epistle, John wrote, **"God is light; in Him there is no darkness at all" (1 John 1:5).**

Jesus said, **"I am the light of the world. Whoever follows me will never walk in darkness, but will have the light of life" (John 8:12).**

And Jesus said of those who followed Him, **"You are the light of the world. . . . Let your light shine before men, that they may see your good deeds and praise your Father in heaven" (Matthew 5:14, 16).**

Wherever God strongly influences people's affairs and the business of nations, God's praises and good deeds abound. People are good, kind, and considerate. You can take them at their word. Those in authority show strength and nobility of character. You can expect to be treated with justice and impartiality in courts of law. You can live in peace, knowing that evil will be punished and goodness will be supported. Religion and morality will prosper.

However, when people live without God's light, beauty, and harmony, the devil and his forces quickly create hell on earth. Results of sin—hatred and cruelty to others—reach frightful dimensions. People unashamedly lie, deceive, gossip, and falsely accuse others. You find corruption and oppression everywhere. Lawlessness abounds, even among leaders of the church and state.

The things you'll study and discuss in this session are the results of times "when darkness reigns." Although we all experience dark, gloomy, depressing times, we can be happy and sure of God's love and forgiveness of all our sins through Jesus Christ. God provided light for our darkness. That light is His Son, Jesus Christ. Pray that He will be the light that dispels the darkness in your life.

DARK DAY—DARK DEEDS

List the dark deeds that show darkness reigned in each of the following:

1. Dark deeds in the garden **(Luke 22:47-53)**

_____

_____

2. Dark deeds in the courtyard of the house of the high priest **(Luke 22:54-62; Matthew 26:74)**

_____

_____

3. Dark deeds in the house of the high priest **(Mark 14:55-65; Luke 22:63-65)**

_____

_____

4. Dark deeds in the Jewish Supreme Court **(Luke 22:66-71)**

_____

_____

5. Dark deeds in the Roman court **(Luke 23:1-7)**

_____

_____

6. Dark deeds in Herod's palace **(Luke 23:8-12)**

_____

_____

7. Dark deeds by Pilate and the people **(Luke 23:13-25; Matthew 27:15-26; John 19:1-16)**

_____

_____

DARK FRIDAY—GOOD FRIDAY

Good Friday. The darkest day in the history of the world. Never has anything so evil been done to anyone so good. Darkness reigned. Death came. Yet, we remember this day as "Good Friday."

Does "Good Friday" seem like an appropriate name for the day Jesus died with our sins on the cross? Why or why not? What name would you choose for that dark day?

A LIGHT DEVOTION

1. Meditate on these questions:
Who is light?

Who is direction?
Who guards and defends?
Who leads and teaches?
Who is truth?
Where is justice?
Where is honesty?
Where is mercy and forgiveness?
Where is life?
Where is hope?
Where is relief from futility?
Where is warmth and comfort?
Where is assurance and confidence?
Where is love?

2. Reflect on God's Word:

Jesus says, "I am the light of the world; he who follows Me will never walk in darkness, but will have the light of life." John 8:12

In Him was life, and that life was the light of men. The light shines in the darkness, but the darkness has not understood it. . . . The Word became flesh and lived for a while among us. We have seen His glory, the glory of the one and only Son, who came from the Father, full of grace and truth. John 1:4-5, 14

For we do not preach ourselves, but Jesus Christ as Lord, and ourselves as your servants for Jesus' sake. For God, who said, "Let light shine out of darkness," made His light shine in our hearts to give us the light of the knowledge of the glory of God in the face of Christ. 2 Corinthians 4:5, 6

3. Respond to God's Light:

(Pray or sing these words to the melody of "Praise God, from Whom All Blessings Flow," *Lutheran Worship,* 461.)

Lord Jesus Christ, the Light of life,
Light up my life and make it right.
Accept my praise; I lift my voice
To shout my thanks in joyful noise.

The world is oft times dark and sad,
But I know things need not be bad
With You as my companion true.
I'll make it Lord. You'll see me through!

Praise Father, Son, and Holy Ghost!
Sing anthems loud with heavenly hosts.
Our lives need not be dark as night.
God sent His Son; the Son is Light!

Christ Jesus is the Light of life.
Christ Jesus makes the darkness bright.
Christ Jesus gives us hope and love.
Thanks be to God, our Father above!

(Adapted from *Resources for Youth Ministry,* 79:3. Copyright 1979 Board for Youth Services, The Lutheran Church—Missouri Synod. Used by permission.)

May Jesus Christ, the Light of the world, light up the dark crevices of your life. May He make all your dark days good days. May you be warmed and blessed in the rays of God's Son! Amen.

Session 41

Winners and Losers

There are winners. There are losers.
What does "winner" mean to you?
Does a winner have the most points on the scoreboard at the end of the game? Does the winner pass the final exam? Get a car? Have a private telephone line?
Who's a "loser" in your eyes?
Does a loser ask three girls to the prom and get turned down every time? Ask three guys to a party and get "no" for an answer each time? Try out for the team and get the job of handing out water bottles?

I think a winner is: _____
_____

I think a loser is: _____
_____

In today's session, you'll consider the account of Jesus' crucifixion and determine who are the winners and losers.

SIMON FROM CYRENE

It was customary for the person sentenced to die by crucifixion to carry his own cross. Jesus did this **(John 19:17)**. However, He needed help along the way. The Roman soldiers forced a passerby to carry Jesus' cross.

1. What do we know about this person? Read **Mark 15:21** and **Romans 16:13**.
2. Tradition tells us that Simon's "misfortune" led to his conversion, and his two sons came to hold prominent positions in the new Christian church. Do you think Simon was a winner or a loser? Why?

DAUGHTERS OF JERUSALEM

On the way to Golgotha, the crucifixion site, the procession passed a group of women who expressed their sorrow by wailing.

1. How did Jesus react toward these women **(Luke 23:27-31)**?
2. Were these daughters of Jerusalem winners or losers? Why?

JESUS CRUCIFIED

Read **Luke 23:32-34**.
Jesus was placed in the company of two criminals. They shared the same sentence. Soldiers drove spikes through Jesus' hands and feet, fastened Him to the wooden cross, then dropped the cross upright into place. While Jesus hung suspended, in agony, the Roman soldiers gambled for His only earthly possession—His clothing.

1. How did Jesus react to those who treated Him this way?
2. Do you think Jesus was a winner or a loser at this point? Why?

THE JEWISH LEADERS

Read **Matthew 27:37-44**.
The Jewish leaders, through much ingenuity and persistence, successfully accomplished what they had set out to do. They had captured, convicted, and crucified their enemy.

1. What does this part of Scripture say that they did?
2. Do you think these Jewish leaders were winners or losers? Why?

ONE DYING CRIMINAL

Both criminals who were crucified with Jesus joined with the spectators in heaping insults on Jesus **(Matthew 27:44)**. However, one dying criminal experienced a change of heart.
Read **Luke 23:39-43**.

1. What observation did this criminal make?
2. What did he request?
3. What promise did he receive?
4. Was this dying criminal a winner or a loser? Why?

JESUS DIED

Read **Luke 23:44-45**.
1. What happened when Jesus died?

2. What is the significance of those events? (See **Amos 8:9** and **Hebrews 9:3-15** and **6:19-20**.)

3. Read Jesus' last words in **John 19:30** and **Luke 23:46**. Did Jesus die a winner or a loser? Why?

THE EXECUTIONERS

Read **Matthew 27:51-53**.

1. What happened when Jesus died?

2. What effect did the manner of Jesus' death and the events surrounding it have on the Roman executioners **(verse 54)**?

3. Do you think the centurion and his coexecutioners were winners or losers? Why?

TWO MEN WHO BURIED JESUS

If Jesus was to be buried, it had to be done before sundown when the Jewish Sabbath began.

Read **Luke 23:50-54** and **John 19:38-42**.

1. Who were the two men who buried Jesus?

2. What does the Bible tell about these men?

3. Why were they afraid openly to identify with Jesus **(John 9:22)**?

4. Were these men winners or losers? Why?

SOMETHING TO THINK ABOUT

At the beginning of this session, you described a winner and a loser.

Having studied and discussed this session, now describe God's idea of a winner: _____

_____

Describe God's idea of a loser: _____

_____

In all these things we are more than conquerors through Him who loved us.

Romans 8:37

Session 42
Who Did It?

WHO? HOW? WHY?

Maybe you've played the popular board game, "Clue." The object of the game is to determine who committed the murder, where it happened, and how it was done.

Let's play a clue game regarding the "murder" of Jesus.

First, read **Luke 23:1-49; Mark 15:21-41;** and **Matthew 27:32-56.** Then prepare a separate paper with these three headings:

Who did it?
How did they do it?
Why did they do it?

Determine *who* was responsible for Jesus' death, *how* they caused His death, and *why* they did it (their motive). The object is to answer the three questions in as many different ways as you can. Get on the case, Sherlock! Be prepared to share your discoveries in class.

STAR WITNESS

Isaiah 53 and **Psalm 22** were written about 700 and 1,000 years before the time of Jesus Christ. Yet, they read like a newspaper account and an editorial about Jesus' crucifixion. Read these two Old Testament passages.

Write in the left column anything from these passages that reminds you of the Good Friday events.

Write in the right column the New Testament book, chapter, and verse(s) that relate to each Old Testament reference.

Old Testament Prophecy	New Testament Fulfillment
_____	_____
_____	_____
_____	_____
_____	_____
_____	_____
_____	_____
_____	_____
_____	_____

VERDICT

Who is the "star witness" in the case of the "murder" of Jesus Christ?
Who is ultimately responsible?
How do you feel when you hear this verdict?

SOMETHING TO THINK ABOUT

LIVING OR DYING?
Many of God's creatures don't know what life is all about.
They laugh and dance, indulge and spend,
and find some satisfaction in pursuing thrill,
excitement, danger, popular acclaim, and
material security.
They follow their selfish instincts
or yield to their craven desires.
They convince themselves that this is living,
when it is really the process of dying.
They are unsuspecting victims of bondage, enslaved
by their own self-centered concepts and
convictions.

Jesus has come to set men and women and children
free from this bondage.
He does not rid people of their instincts
or eradicate their natural inclinations,
so impregnated with self-concern.
He can, infilled by the Spirit who enabled Him
to successfully confront temptation,
grant to those who seek it the power
to subdue their selfish desires and passions,
and He can bless them with the kind of joy

that will make their lives whole and abundant.

Those who continue to seek for purpose and meaning
    along other corridors of this temporal existence
    may ultimately find the door to eternal joy
    and abundance closed shut.
They remain blind to the truth,
    deaf to the word of God's love,
        numb to the movings of His Spirit in and about them.
Their good works and fine intentions avail them nothing.
They have not sought for God.
They have never found Him.

(From *Jesus/Now*, by Leslie Brandt. Copyright 1978 Concordia Publishing House. Used by permission.)

How has God made and kept you His?

In what ways has He made your life whole and abundant?

From what kinds of "bondage" are you free? Why?

Are you in the process of living or dying? In what ways?

So if the Son sets you free, you will be free indeed.
John 8:36

But now that you have been set free from sin and have become slaves to God, the benefit you reap leads to holiness, and the result is eternal life.
Romans 6:22

Session 43

The Last Laugh

Many different religions exist in the world today. Most were founded by extraordinary individuals with great capacities for influencing people. Mohammed founded the religion of Islam, which even today claims millions of followers and wields a strong influence in the Middle East and other parts of the world. Karl Marx, Nikolai Lenin, and Mao Tse Tung have spearheaded incredible advances in the last century for the communist religion, which worships the state as a god. Millions of others claim to be followers of Buddha or Confucius. In recent years, hundreds of religious cults have sprung up, each led by a charismatic leader who convinces his followers of his direct link with God. But there is at least one problem with each of these great leaders. They are all dead (or soon to be dead). Their tombs are labeled No Vacancy.

Jesus Christ is different. The millions who have visited His gravesite have found an *empty* tomb. He alone has conquered death and is alive forever. Christianity is the only religion that has a living Leader who guarantees eternal life for all His followers. Jesus and His church have the last laugh—an eternal one.

THE MESSAGE THAT SHOOK THE WORLD

Pentecost is the birthday of the Christian church. On this day long ago, Jesus' disciples were filled with the Holy Spirit, and Peter's preaching led to the conversion of 3,000 souls.

1. What was the message that climaxed Peter's sermon **(Acts 2:32-36)**?

2. In the following weeks, all the apostles went about preaching in Jerusalem a message that greatly disturbed the leaders of the Jews. What was this message **(Acts 4:1-4)**?

3. In following years, the apostle Paul went through the Roman world proclaiming a new, strange, and controversial message. What was this message **(Acts 17:18-21; 31-32)**?

4. Paul started many churches in many cities, and repeatedly encouraged and instructed them through letters which we call the New Testament epistles. What did Paul stress as of first importance **(1 Corinthians 15:1-7)**?

5. What difference would it make if Christ had not been raised from the dead **(1 Corinthians 15:14, 17)**?

ATTEMPTS TO STOP THE MESSAGE

1. In some respects, Jesus' enemies apparently paid closer attention to His words than His friends did. What did Jesus' enemies remember that His friends forgot **(Matthew 27:62-63)**?

2. What were they afraid might happen **(verse 64)**?

3. What did they do to make sure it wouldn't happen **(verses 64-66)**?

4. Read **Matthew 28:1-10** and summarize the results of Jesus' enemies' efforts.

5. What was their next plan to stop His message **(Matthew 28:11-15)**?

6. What other things did Jesus' enemies do to try to stop the message **(Acts 4:18; 5:17-20; 7:54-58; 8:1-3)**?

7. What was the result of Jesus' enemies' efforts to stop the message **(Acts 8:4)**?

WITNESSES OF THE MESSAGE

Read **Matthew 28; Mark 16; Luke 24;** and **John 20—21.** Then list all the resurrection appearances of Jesus Christ.

JESUS APPEARED

To Whom	Where	When	What Happened

To Whom	Where	When	What Happened

ONGOING WITNESSES TO THE MESSAGE

The apostle Paul tells us in **1 Corinthians 15:6** that more than 500 people saw the risen Lord Jesus Christ before He ascended into heaven.

That's not all! In the following centuries, millions of others have become witnesses to Jesus' resurrection. They may not have actually seen or touched Jesus, but they have experienced His ongoing ability to change lives through faith in Him. The world today contains millions of people who know and believe that Jesus died, was raised, and is alive today. Like the original apostles, these people would rather die than give up this faith.

In what ways can you witness to our resurrected Lord?

He is not here; He has risen!

Luke 24:6

Session 44

Famous Last Words

Imagine this. You have only a few minutes to live. Your closest family members and friends gather around you. What would you say to them? Would you talk about the weather? The latest sports scores? What color to paint your room? Or would you choose your words very carefully and tell them something of *lasting significance*?

The situation was different for Jesus. He spoke His last words to His closest friends not shortly before His death, but shortly after! Jesus remained on the earth after His resurrection for 40 days. During this time He appeared, disappeared, and reappeared to His disciples, proving to them in many ways that He really was alive, and also preparing them for the time when they would see Him no more. Toward the end of those 40 days He gathered them together to share with them what was most on His heart. The words He spoke to them were well chosen and of utmost importance. They are just as important and relevant for us today.

THE GREAT COMMISSION

Read **Matthew 28:18-20; Mark 16:15-16;** and **Luke 24:45-49.** Then answer the questions below.

1. About what great events did Jesus speak to His disciples?

2. What great commands did Jesus give His followers?

3. According to Jesus, what must one do to be saved?

4. What comfort and assurance does Jesus give to those who are called to be His witnesses?

5. Explain what happened next **(Luke 24:50-51; Acts 1:9).**

6. Final good-byes are usually tearful times. How did Jesus' disciples react to His departure **(Luke 24:52-53)?**

a. Explain why they might have reacted in this way.

b. Why can Christians today be full of joy and continually praise God when they "lose someone through death"?

THE GREAT GOOD NEWS

We've come to the end of this study of the life of Jesus Christ. Jesus was by far the greatest person to have ever walked on the earth. In the 20 centuries that have come and gone since Jesus' ascension, His influence has continually grown. History is His story. We label each year *Anno Domini* (A.D.), Latin words meaning "the year of our Lord." Today Jesus continues to be the only absolutely essential Man—the one person the world cannot do without.

Jesus' significance is explained by the eight important Scriptural truths below. Read the following passages. Then summarize each of these Scriptural truths in your own words:

1. **Ecclesiastes 7:20; Jeremiah 17:9; Romans 3:23; Ephesians 2:1, 3**

2. **Isaiah 59:2; Ezekiel 18:4; Romans 5:12; Romans 6:23a**

3. **Isaiah 53:5-6; Mark 10:45; Romans 5:8; 1 Peter 1:8-10**

4. **John 3:16; Acts 16:31; Romans 1:16-17; Ephesians 2:8-9**

5. **Proverbs 28:13; Ezekiel 18:23; Luke 13:3, 5; 1 John 1:8-9**

6. **John 10:10; Romans 6:4; Galatians 2:20; 2 Corinthians 5:15**

7. **Psalm 23:6; Daniel 12:2; John 14:1-3; Romans 8:38-39**

8. **John 5:23; John 14:6; Acts 4:12; 1 Timothy 2:5**

GO TELL, GO SING, GO SHOUT ABOUT JESUS!

What will be your message?
To whom will you tell it?
Why?

Go and make disciples of all nations.
Matthew 28:19a

Jesus said, "Feed My sheep. . . . Follow Me.
John 21:17, 19

Session 45
Review of Unit 4

Answer these questions to help you review unit 4.

1. In what ways did Jesus show He is King of kings?

2. Name at least two Old Testament prophecies (and their references) that Jesus fulfilled.

3. Describe traps Jesus' enemies set for Him and tell Jesus' answers and reactions to them **(Luke 20)**.

4. Tell how and when God's kingdom comes. Base your answer on Scripture.

5. Tell the thoughts, feelings, and attitudes you have as you look to the future, and why. How would Jesus have Christians look ahead to each day?

6. How are the problems the Jewish leaders had similar to the problems of unbelievers today? What was—and is—a solution?

7. Explain the word *covenant*. What was God's old covenant? What is God's new covenant? Describe God's covenant for you.

8. Define the word *servant*. How is Jesus a servant? How are you God's servant?

9. Why was it important that Jesus submitted to His heavenly Father's will **(Luke 22)**?

10. List five "darknesses" in your life. Then list one or more "lights" that dispel those darknesses. These may be people, thoughts, times, or things.

11. Tell why Jesus is a winner. Tell why you are a winner, too!

12. Write a short personalized paraphrase of **Romans 8:37**.

13. In what ways have Jesus' death and resurrection made you "free"?

14. What does the message in **Luke 24:6** mean to you?

15. If your friend lay dying and you had two minutes to be with him or her, what last words would you say to your friend?

SHARING THE SUNLIGHT

We each need praise and affirmation.

If we are successful by its standards, the world might give us recognition. But if we fail, it gives us the raspberries.

It stands in cold contrast to our heavenly Father who accepts us even when we fail. He loves us—not because we succeed or not because we bungle—but because He is our Father and we are His children.

God calls on us to share the sunlight as His servants. He gives us an example in Jesus, **"Who, being in very nature God, did not consider equality with God something to be grasped, but made Himself nothing, taking the very nature of a servant ... He humbled Himself and became obedient to death—even death on a cross!" (Philippians 2:6-8)**

Jesus became the Suffering Servant for you and for me. Because of Him, we live in the warm sunshine of His forgiving grace and mercy. Our sense of worth rests not in ourselves, but in God who has called us. His Holy Spirit moves in and through us. We do acts of love and mercy in Jesus' name. We serve for Jesus' sake.

We serve, not in isolation, but as members of the body of Christ. With our brothers and sisters in Christ, we share the soft, indirect sunlight of His love and mercy. You and I are never alone. Jesus and His friends are with us.

Together we sing our alleluias. Together we share His sunlight. Let us give thanks to the Lord, our God!

(From *Resources for Youth Ministry*, 82:4. Copyright 1982 Board for Youth Services, The Lutheran Church—Missouri Synod. Used by permission.)

Unit 5
The Church Begins

This unit begins the second half of this course. During this half you will learn how God has worked and still works through His people, the church, to share His Good News of salvation with the entire world. You will study Acts, quickly survey the remaining books of the New Testament, and study how the Bible was formed. Finally, you will learn about some of the events of the first 400 years of the church.

In unit 5 you will study events of the first 15 years of the church as recorded in the first half of Acts. Note how the church was able to grow, and consider how you can be an instrument to continue that growth today.

Session 46

The Roman World and God's Plan of Salvation

KEY WORDS

Pax Romana	Diaspora	Synagogue	Sanhedrin
Temple	Senate	Latin	Greek
Gentile	Caesar	Rabbi	Sadducees
Pharisees			

THE PAX ROMANA

God is Lord and Master over all creation, including human history and secular government. He uses all of history, both our glories and our tragedies, for His gracious purpose. God uses human history to help His church carry the Good News of salvation in Christ to all people.

During the time of the early church God used both the glorious Roman Empire and the tragic *diaspora* (dispersion, or scattering) of the Jewish people to further the spread of the Good News.

At this time the Roman Empire had just embarked on one of the greatest periods in human history: the *Pax Romana* (Roman peace). For more than 200 years, from 27 B.C. until A.D. 180, the Roman Empire enjoyed peace, prosperity, and stability. Several factors contributed to the Romans' ability to establish peace, order, and unity among a variety of people.

First, Rome rid the Mediterranean of pirates and built many roads. This tied the empire together by making travel possible and trade profitable, including trade with surrounding regions such as India.

Second, the diverse people could communicate with one another through one of the two common languages of the empire, Greek and Latin. The ruling class and legal system used Latin, the dominant language of the western half of the empire. The scholars and philosophers spoke Greek, the dominant language of the eastern half of the empire. With these two languages a person could communicate with anyone throughout the empire.

Third, as Rome expanded its territory, it granted citizenship to people throughout the empire, thus strengthening the bonds of loyalty between these people and Rome. People could acquire citizenship through birth, purchase, military service, or a proclamation by Caesar. A Roman citizen could request a trial before a Roman judge and appeal to a higher court or to Caesar himself. Roman citizens could not be whipped, tortured, or crucified.

Fourth, Rome's highly advanced system of laws and courts brought order and stability to the empire. A given law applied wherever one traveled in the empire. Many nations in the empire adopted Roman law, thus enabling the common people there to enjoy the benefits of Roman law, too.

Fifth, Rome used several ways to rule a local area, all designed to keep an area loyal to Rome. When Rome conquered an area, they often let a local person rule. Thus the people would be less likely to feel that an outside power, Rome, was dominating them. The least important of these rulers was a tetrarch, literally "a ruler of one-fourth." Herod Antipas, who ruled Galilee while Jesus lived, was a tetrarch. The next highest position was an ethnarch, literally "a ruler of the people." Herod the Great's son, Archelaus, was the ethnarch of Judea from 4 B.C. until A.D. 6. The most important position was that of a king. This position was rarely used, and was awarded for great service to the empire. Herod the Great was such a king. Tetrarchs and ethnarchs were often called kings, even though they actually held lesser positions. As a local ruler proved himself to be a competent and loyal Roman ruler, he could be promoted from tetrarch to ethnarch to king.

Rome ruled some areas directly. A civilian governor ruled a senatorial province—a peaceful, well-established area that remained loyal to Rome. A military governor ruled an imperial province—a newer territory, a troublesome territory, or a territory along the border of the empire. Judea was a small, troublesome imperial province; Syria was a large, border imperial province.

The greatest privilege for an area was to be a colony. The people in a colony were directly under Caesar and had the right to rule themselves and to appoint their leaders. The Decapolis, a group of ten cities located east of Galilee, and Philippi, a city Paul visited and to whom he wrote a letter, were both colonies.

THE DIASPORA

During this time a small group of Jewish people was scattered throughout the empire and beyond. The *diaspora* of the Jewish people began with their exile in Babylon almost 600 years before the birth of Christ. As the result of conquest and oppression by others, the desire to find a better or safer place to live, and as a result of commerce, Jewish communities became scattered across southern Europe, northern Africa, and western Asia—as far west as Spain and as far east as India.

The diaspora changed many aspects of Jewish life. Since people lived so far from the temple in Jerusalem, the sacrifices and position of the priests lost significance. The dispersed Jewish people gathered at synagogues and learned from rabbis. Learning and living the Torah replaced temple sacrifices as the foundation of Jewish life. Synagogues became gathering places where news was shared and traveling Jews could meet and find a welcome among local Jews.

The Pharisees developed to preserve the tradition of the Jewish people despite their scattered existence. Pharisees taught among the Jewish people and organized synagogues wherever five or more Jewish males lived. They were strongly anti-foreign, seeking to preserve their Jewish identity among the diverse people of the world. They accepted the entire Old Testament plus the oral tradition of the rabbis; they believed in the resurrection of the body; and they looked for a Davidic Messiah to save God's chosen people, the Jews, and to restore an independent Israel.

The Sadducees developed to preserve the temple and everything associated with it. Consequently, most priests were Sadducees. Sadducees were willing to work with foreigners to keep peace in Judea and thereby preserve the temple. They accepted only the first five books of the Old Testament, and they rejected the ideas of resurrection, angels, spirits, and souls. They did not go out to the Jewish people in the diaspora; instead, they expected the scattered Jewish people to come to Jerusalem to worship at the temple, the only place where true worship could occur.

The Sanhedrin in Jerusalem developed as the ruling body for the Jews. This council of 70 men consisted of both Pharisees and Sadducees. In theory, it ruled the spiritual and traditional lives of the Jewish people. Under the Romans, however, it had little power, especially outside of Palestine. Yet it provided a model for local government that many Jewish communities followed.

Though the Pharisees and Sadducees were very influential groups, they were extremely small when compared to the entire Jewish population. The common Jewish people simply struggled to live and survive as best as possible. Some supported the Romans because this meant peace and prosperity. Others supported the Zealots (see session 3) and other terrorist groups that sought to overthrow the Roman rule over the Jews. Most were, as Jesus said, **"sheep without a shepherd" (Matthew 9:36),** fumbling blindly for a better way to live.

In fact, most Gentiles (non-Jews) were **"sheep without a shepherd,"** too. Greeks, Romans, and others did much spiritual searching at the time of Christ. Romans believed that religion in general was important for preserving the empire, but most Gentiles did not believe that the traditional Greek and Roman gods had any power. Many Gentiles, therefore, sought new or different religions and philosophies. Mystery religions from Egypt and Mesopotamia became popular because of their secretive nature. Zoroastrianism (from Persia) and Judaism were other popular religions. Popular Greek philosophies included Platonism, Cynicism, Stoicism, and Epicureanism. Still many Gentiles believed that something more was needed to explain life and the purpose of human existence.

It was this setting that Paul called **"the fullness of the time" (Galatians 4:4 KJV).** Everything was ready for God to reveal His plan of salvation to the world.

LET'S TALK ABOUT IT

1. Considering what you have read, explain how each of the following helped fulfill God's plan to spread the Gospel rapidly and broadly:
    a. The size of the Roman Empire
    b. The diversity of people in the Roman Empire
    c. Roman roads
    d. Safe waterways
    e. Trade
    f. The common use of Greek and Latin
    g. General peace and order in the empire
    h. Roman citizenship
    i. The Diaspora of the Jewish people
    j. Synagogues
    k. The Roman occupation of Judea
    l. The common Jewish people being "like sheep without a shepherd"
    m. The Gentiles being "like sheep without a shepherd"

2. List other items from this time period and explain how they fit into God's plan to reveal His Gospel to the world.

3. What does all of this say about God's role in history? How does He control history? For what purpose does God control it?

4. God continues this same role in history today.

How has God used history recently to spread the Gospel?

5. Tell how God can use the circumstances around you to enable you to share the Gospel.

When the time had fully come, God sent His Son, born of a woman, born under law, to redeem those under law, that we might receive the full rights as sons.

Galatians 4:4-5

Session 47

An Overview of Acts
Read Acts 1

AUTHOR

1. Compare **Luke 1:1-4** with **Acts 1:1-2**. Why do you think most Bible students assume that Luke wrote Acts?

Actually, the above evidence tells us only that the same person wrote both Luke and Acts. The early church identified that person as Luke. The use of "we" in Acts **16:10** indicates that the author began traveling with Paul at Troas in western Asia Minor. Luke was a Gentile physician who became a co-worker of Paul **(Colossians 4:10-14; 2 Timothy 4:11; Philemon 24)**. He is the only known Gentile author in the Bible.

Because Acts does not describe how Paul's case in Rome was resolved, we assume Luke wrote Acts before the case was resolved. It appears that chapter 28 ends about A.D. 60 to 62.

2. To whom did Luke write the book **(Acts 1:1)**?

PURPOSE FOR WRITING

1. Look again at **Luke 1:1-4** and **Acts 1:1-2**. What purpose for writing do you find there?

2. We can consider the Book of Acts to be a direct continuation of the Gospel of Luke. Again Christ is the dominant figure. Luke showed the impact of the risen Christ on the whole world. Christ comes to all people in the inspired Word of the messengers He Himself had chosen. He comes to ALL people. Christ brings salvation by grace to each man, woman, and child on earth.

The Book of Acts is not a comprehensive history of the first church or of early missions. It's more. It's the continuation of the story of Jesus Christ and the impact of the triumphant Word among people. Tell how you know that Jesus' crucifixion, resurrection, and gift of salvation to you was not a fairy tale but was indeed part of God's definite plan.

3. As Luke wrote, he also defended the church and Paul's life and ministry from various accusations. First, he defended Christianity against charges that it was atheistic and seditious. Atheism and sedition were both criminal offenses in the Roman Empire.

Second, Luke defended the practice of bringing the Gospel to Gentiles. This practice offended many Jewish people and led to Paul's arrest in Jerusalem **(Acts 21)**.

Third, Luke defended Paul against several charges:

a. Paul was a traitor to Judaism because he stressed salvation by grace through faith in Jesus, rather than by works of obedience to the mosaic law, and because he claimed salvation was won for all Gentiles as well as Jews.

b. Paul was a second-rate apostle because he was not a disciple during Jesus' earthly ministry.

Speculate a bit. On the basis of what you have learned so far, expand on Luke's reason for writing. You might use a study Bible or commentary to help you find his purposes.

4. Find out how powerful the Word of God was then and how powerful it is in your life today. Divide your class into six groups. Each group should quickly skim one of the following parts of the Book of Acts:

1:1—6:7
6:8—9:31
9:32—12:25
13:1—16:5
16:6—19:20
19:21—28:31

As you skim, look for answers to these questions:
a. What important events do you find?
b. In what ways can you identify the progress of the Word?
c. In what ways (if any) did Luke defend Paul?
d. Provide a one- to three-sentence statement to summarize your section of Scripture.

Ask a spokesperson to share your group's findings with the class.

OVERVIEW OF ACTS

1. Note the gradual expansion of the church—like a ripple after a pebble is dropped in a pond—that Jesus describes in **Acts 1:8**. Use a Bible with a good outline to help you list the chapters in Acts that describe the sharing of the Good News in:

a. Jerusalem
b. the rest of Judea
c. Samaria
d. the rest of the world

2. Divide the class into two groups. Have group 1 skim **Acts 1—12** and identify the main characters. Have group 2 do the same with **Acts 13—28.**

ACTS OF THE SPIRIT TODAY

1. Many Bibles title the book we are studying, "The Acts of the Apostles." Luke does tell how God used the apostles to cause His church to spread. But the book could also be titled, "The Acts of the Holy Spirit." Why?

2. Is the church growing today? Give examples that show it is or is not growing.

3. What are some places in the world whose people still need to be reached by the Gospel?

4. What can you do now to continue the sharing of the Gospel?

But you will receive power when the Holy Spirit comes on you; and you will be my witnesses in Jerusalem, and all Judea and Samaria, and to the ends of the earth.

Acts 1:8

Session 48

The Acts of the Holy Spirit

STUDY QUESTIONS

1. Skim the entire Book of Acts. List the chapter and verse(s) where you find the Holy Spirit doing something. Write one sentence to tell what the Holy Spirit is doing in each reference.

2. On the basis of your response to the item above, describe briefly the role of the Holy Spirit in spreading the Gospel and in empowering us to do God's will.

3. What role, then, do people have in spreading the Gospel and doing God's will?

THE HOLY SPIRIT ACTS TODAY

The Book of Acts describes the acts of the Holy Spirit working through the apostles to spread the Gospel during the first decades of the church. However, the Holy Spirit did not stop working after those first few decades. He continued to work through Christians throughout the history of the church, and He continues to work through Christians today.

Think of all the activities that Christians around the world are involved in today. Look at some of the activities described in church bulletins, newsletters, newspapers, magazines, etc. Remember that the church is made up of human beings who still sin and who don't always do things God desires.

1. List activities of Christians that are activities of the Holy Spirit.

_____

_____

_____

_____

2. How can you tell whether or not the Holy Spirit is at work in these activities?

_____

_____

_____

_____

As you consider those questions, remember the many ways you saw the Holy Spirit act in Acts. Also remember that through Christ's saving death and resurrection you can act to give honor to God, but without Christ those same actions become worthless, self-serving deeds.

THE HOLY SPIRIT ACTS THROUGH ME

The Holy Spirit doesn't just act through the church in general. He acts through individual Christians, like you.

1. Think of all your activities. In which has the Holy Spirit been involved?

_____

_____

_____

_____

2. Now consider both the activities where the Holy Spirit **has been** involved and those where He **could have been** involved. In which activities has the Holy Spirit not been involved?

_____

_____

_____

_____

3. What makes the difference? Why is the Holy Spirit sometimes involved in things you do, and why do you fail to involve Him at other times? As you think about these questions, look at Bible passages like **Romans 7:18-19** and **8:9-10**.

_____

_____

_____

_____

4. Do you feel depressed because Satan, rather than the Holy Spirit, seems to influence too many of your actions? When this happens, remember that Jesus earned forgiveness for all of your sins. What assurance do you find in **1 John 1:8-9?**

_____

_____

_____

_____

Think again of the many individuals you saw the Holy Spirit working through in Acts. Remember, also, that He can be involved in every activity of a Christian, no matter how mundane or "secular," so that each action can be for the glory and honor of God.

The Counselor, the Holy Spirit, whom the Father will send in My name, will teach you all things and will remind you of everything I have said to you.
John 14:26

Session 49

Pentecost
Read Acts 2:1-41

STUDY QUESTIONS

1. During which Jewish feast did the "birth" of the Christian church occur?

2. With what event did the the church begin? Compare the actions of the disciples before and after this event. Why was this even necessary for the church to begin?

3. Many foreigners were in Jerusalem at the time of this event. What were their religious beliefs? Where did they come from? How did the Holy Spirit use them to cause the Gospel to spread?

4. Who preached the sermon to these people? What are the key items he proclaimed in this sermon?

PENTECOST

When God gave the Law to the people of Israel at Mount Sinai, He told them to observe three festivals each year **(Exodus 23:14-17):** the Feast of Unleavened Bread (the week after the Passover), the Feast of Harvest (also known as the Feast of Weeks and as Pentecost; the feast being observed in **Acts 2**), and the Feast of Ingathering (also known as the Feast of Booths).

Pentecost, the second festival, began 7 weeks (or 50 days) after the end of the Passover. Read **Leviticus 23:15-23; Deuteronomy 16:9-12, 16;** and **Exodus 34:22-23** for a description of this festival. Notice that this was a joyous festival in which the people thanked God for the first harvest of the year (thus the term, Feast of Harvest). The common Hebrew name used is **Shabuoth** (weeks), because it occurs 7 weeks after Passover. The Greek-speaking Jewish people of the Diaspora had a similar name for the festival. They called it Pentecost, which literally means "50 days."

At the time of Christ, Jewish people from Persia, Arabia, Europe, and Africa still came to Jerusalem to celebrate Pentecost. It was on the morning of this joyous setting that Christ sent His Holy Spirit upon His followers. Even though the disciples had seen and spoken with Jesus since His resurrection, they remained confused, frightened, and silent during this time. The Jewish authorities hoped that the talk of Jesus' resurrection had ended and that Jesus Himself had been forgotten. Then the Holy Spirit came, with Jewish people present from around the known world.

Notice how well God planned the proclamation of His salvation. Not only were the disciples empowered by the Holy Spirit to have courage and to speak of Christ's life, death, and resurrection, but the Spirit empowered them while people were present who could spread the news throughout the known world. These people had gathered for a harvest festival. On this Pentecost God showed the disciples the most important harvest—the harvest of souls.

"PENTECOST" FOR ME

1. Sin and its consequences (such as selfish desires and doubt) had prevented the disciples from doing God's will. On their own they could not live the new life that God desired for them. But with God's Spirit in them, they could do what God willed.

So it is for us today. Without the Holy Spirit we can only be guided by our sinful, selfish spirit. Because we know we are not perfect, and because we have seen how our spirit has misguided us at times, we will have doubts and will not be able to trust our decisions and abilities. But what happens when the Holy Spirit lives in us? What does each of the following tell you?

a. **Acts 2:17-21**

_____

_____

_____

_____

b. **John 3:5-8**

_____

_____

_____

_____

c. Luther's explanation of the Third Article of the Apostles' Creed

_____
_____
_____
_____

2. We know we have the wisdom and power of the almighty and everlasting God to guide us. This is the true meaning of Pentecost. God's own Spirit is now given to each believer so that we can have the power to believe and to boldly live and proclaim salvation through Christ. The world is full of sin, doubt, and selfishness. But the Holy Spirit makes us Christians alive, bold, and filled with care for others.

Tell how the Holy Spirit has made a difference in your life.

_____
_____
_____
_____

PETER'S PENTECOST SERMON

Review Peter's sermon in **Acts 2:14-39**.

1. What does the power of the Holy Spirit working through Peter mean to you?

_____
_____
_____
_____

2. Find Peter's words that condemned people for things they did. Before people repent, they must recognize their sin. Suppose a modern-day Peter would come to your town. What would he condemn?

_____
_____
_____
_____

3. Find Peter's words of Gospel—of Good News that through Jesus, the people may receive forgiveness. What Gospel message would you expect to hear from a modern-day Peter?

_____
_____
_____
_____

4. In the previous section we looked at Peter's quotation from the prophet Joel **(Acts 2:17-21)**. To whom do you intend to be God's witness?

_____
_____
_____
_____

And afterward, I will pour out my Spirit on all people.
Your sons and daughters will prophesy,
your old men will dream dreams,
your young men will see visions. . . .
And everyone who calls
on the name of the Lord will be saved.
Joel 2:28, 32a

Session 50

The Church in Jerusalem After Pentecost
Read Acts 2:42—6:7

STUDY QUESTIONS

1. Describe the activities of the early church. Describe the activities of Peter and John. What activities are similar to things Jesus did while He was on earth?

2. Which group was the first to oppose the church **(Acts 4:1)**? Why did they oppose the church **(4:4)**? What were some things they did to try to stop the church?

3. Even people from which group of Jews became believers according to **6:7**? Why was this significant?

4. Which Pharisee from the Sanhedrin defended the Christians **(Acts 5:33-40)**? Why did he say the Christians should be left alone? Who was a student of this Pharisee **(21:39—22:3)**?

5. Summarize the story of Ananias and Sapphira **(Acts 5:1-11)**. What sin did they commit?

6. **Acts 6:1-7** describes the appointment of seven deacons. Why were these men needed? What job was assigned to them?

7. In which city did all the above events occur?

THE EARLY CHRISTIAN CHURCH

The disciples apparently did not consider themselves to be a completely new religious group when the Holy Spirit came upon them in Jerusalem. They simply believed that they were proclaiming the Messiah that Judaism had long awaited. Consequently, the disciples did not immediately make any drastic breaks from, nor any radical changes in, the basic religious and social life of Judaism.

From **Acts 1—6** it appears that the first Christians were either Jews or *proselytes* (Gentiles who had converted to Judaism). Peter, John, and the other believers still continued Jewish customs, still gathered at the temple, still believed the Jewish sacred writings, and were still subject to the high priest and the Sanhedrin. From the problem described in **Acts 6:1-6** it appears that many early Christians even retained Palestinian-Jewish prejudice against Greek-speaking Jews and proselytes.

The Jewish people of that time apparently were not completely shocked by a group like the followers of Christ, because several small Jewish sects also existed then. These included the Essenes, the Qumran community (from whom we have the Dead Sea scrolls), and the followers of John the Baptizer. These sects all had fundamental differences from the mainline Judaism of the Pharisees and Sadducees, yet they were considered Jewish. Two major differences, however, distinguished these sects from the Christians. First, these groups generally isolated themselves from society to prevent being corrupted. Second, they were waiting, searching, and preparing for a savior yet to come. Christians, on the other hand, stayed in Jerusalem, the center of Jewish life, and proclaimed that the Savior had come.

The early Christians were, in effect, a distinct Jewish synagogue. Like other synagogues, the Christians were a community. They gathered to pray, worship, study, and socialize. Like other synagogues, the first Christians seem to have been inclined to let others come to them rather than to reach out to others. Because they were in Jerusalem, this worked out well. Jewish people from around the world came to Jerusalem, even between the three major festivals. These people were anxious to hear the words the apostles proclaimed—that the Messiah had come. Rich men like Barnabas, poor Greek-speaking widows, and even priests believed that Jesus was the risen Messiah who had come to save them. We see evidence of the power of the Holy Spirit working through these early Christians as we read that the number of disciples grew to about 5,000 men **(Acts 4:4)**, to even larger numbers of men and women **(5:14; 6:7)**.

Talk about the actions of the Holy Spirit in these chapters. Find at least one significant thing He caused to happen in each of the following sections:

2:42-47	4:1-22	5:12-16
3:1-10	4:23-37	5:17-42
3:11-26	5:1-11	6:1-7

THE CHRISTIAN CHURCH TODAY

1. Read **Acts 4:10-12** and **5:29-32**. What message spoken by Peter should the church today continue to share?

_____

_____

_____

2. Paraphrase this message into words you think would be meaningful to other teenagers today.

_____

_____

_____

3. Why can we be sure God will bless our efforts to share this message?

_____

_____

_____

_____

Peter and the other apostles replied: "... The God of our fathers raised Jesus from the dead.... God exalted Him to His own right hand as the Prince and Savior that He might give repentance and forgiveness of sins to Israel...."

Then [Gamaliel] addressed them: "... If their purpose or activity is of human origin, it will fail. But if it is from God, you will not be able to stop these men; you will only find yourselves fighting against God."

Acts 5:29-31, 35, 38-39

Session 51

Persecution
Read Acts 6:8—8:4 and 12:1-24

STUDY QUESTIONS

1. Who opposed Stephen **(Acts 6:8-10)**? What charges did they bring against him **(6:11-14)**?

2. Summarize Stephen's sermon **(7:2-53)**.

3. Why was Stephen stoned **(7:48-60)**?

4. What happened to the church after Stephen's murder **(8:1b)**?

5. Who was a leader of these persecutions **(8:3)**?

6. Who led the persecutions in **Acts 12**? Whom did he kill? Whom did he have arrested? What happened to the man they arrested? What happened to the man who did the persecuting?

7. Why did the persecuters attack the church?

8. How did the persecutions actually help the church to grow **(8:1-4)**?

ARE YOU PERSECUTED?

We in the United States do not have to fear the persecutions faced by the early Christians and by many Christians in other parts of the world today. Laws in the United States prevent Christians from being fired, arrested, tortured, or executed because of their faith.

However, persecutions do exist in the United States. For example, has someone ever teased you for going to church? Has a friend ever tempted you to do something else instead of going to Bible class? Has a classmate ever accused you of being a hypocrite for sinning one day and going to church the next? Has someone ever called you a "goody two-shoes" or asked you to use your offering money for a date, new clothes, a stereo, or partying? These and other attempts to get you to deny your faith in Christ are forms of persecution.

1. Think very carefully about the last two years. On a sheet of paper list the persecutions you have faced.

2. Now look over your list. How have you fared? Have you withstood the persecutions or have you caved in to the pressure? (Just think about your answers. You don't have to share them.)

3. If you're honest, you undoubtedly have to admit that at times you failed God when you were persecuted. As you recall your sin, think for a few minutes about Peter and Judas on Maundy Thursday. Peter denied his Lord vehemently with cursing and swearing. Cer-

tainly his behavior was every bit as bad as that of Judas! The difference took place after the sin. Peter turned to Jesus for forgiveness and renewal. Judas despaired instead.

You have already seen how the Holy Spirit made a difference in Peter's life. You might review his life after the Pentecost activities in **Acts 2:14-41; 3:1—4:31; 5:29-32;** and **12:1-17.**

You, too, can experience the same difference Peter did. Do not resist Him when He tries to guide you or work through you. Pray regularly, and listen and watch for God's response. Read and familiarize yourself with God's Word so you know what He desires and so you can use His Word to stop the challenges to your faith. Participate frequently in Holy Communion and daily renew your baptismal vows with the Lord. Seek the Lord regularly for forgiveness and renewal.

Christians need to be in the world in order to do God's will. But God does not want us to drift away from Him and become part of the world. Persecution is real, even in the United States. With God's power, however, you can withstand those persecutions. God can bring blessings through them, just as He did for the early church.

We know that in all things God works for the good of those who love Him, who have been called according to His purpose.

Romans 8:28

Session 52

The Church Grows Beyond Jerusalem and Judaism
Read Acts 8:3—11:30

STUDY QUESTIONS

1. Name the person sharing the Gospel in **Acts 8:4-13, 26-40**.

2. What did this person do before the persecution began **(6:5-8)**? How was this person similar to Stephen?

3. To which two countries did this man help bring the Gospel? What was significant about sharing the Gospel with these two countries?

4. Who converted Saul to Christianity **(9:1-19)**? Describe his conversion experience. Tell what Saul did after his conversion *before* he became a missionary **(9:19-30; 11:25-30; 12:25—13:4; 21:39—22:31; Gal. 1:15—2:2)**.

5. Why did Saul have to leave Damascus and Jerusalem **(Acts 9:19-30)**?

6. Describe Peter's experience with Cornelius **(10:1—11:18)**. What was Cornelius' ethnic background? What was significant about sharing the Gospel with Cornelius? Describe the controversy Peter's actions caused **(11:1-18)**.

7. Find Antioch on a map. With whom was the Gospel shared there **(11:19-30)**? What was significant about sharing the Gospel with these people? What name was first given to the followers of Jesus in Antioch? Name the two people who worked with the church in Antioch.

8. List the miraculous occurrences you find in **Acts 8—11**. Who was directly involved in the activities of the church? What comfort can that give to us today?

9. How was the church able to grow **(9:31; 11:23-24)**?

10. Notice the variety of people with whom the Gospel was shared in **Acts 8—11**. What does this tell us about the salvation God offers through Jesus Christ?

GOD SENDS HIS WORD OUT TO ALL PEOPLE

The persecution that began after Stephen's murder did not destroy the church. It did, however, lead to some radical changes in the church. First, the church was no longer firmly rooted in Jerusalem. Christians left the city for the Judean and Samarian countryside and for Damascus. As the Gospel was shared with more people, it spread further from Jerusalem, like a ripple moving out from the point where a pebble falls into the water. By the end of **Acts 11** the Gospel had reached as far north as Antioch and as far south as Ethiopia. Find these places on a map to get an idea of how far Christianity spread during the period of about 10 years.

At the same time something more important happened. Christianity grew beyond Judaism. Gradually Christians realized that Christ came to save all people, not just the Jewish people or people who accepted Judaism. The change did not happen easily. For several decades Christians would argue whether or not they should be Jewish. But when the persecution drove the Christians out of Jerusalem and into the world, the change had begun.

The cleanliness laws of Judaism became a major obstacle for Jewish Christians. The original cleanliness laws, given by God at Sinai, were designed to protect the Israelites and to show that they were a distinctive people, set apart by God from other people in the world. The Pharisees had greatly expanded these laws to insure that the outward, ritualistic conditions of purity were kept. They believed this purity would lead to the coming of the Messiah and the beginning of the new Israel. The emphasis changed from a community showing they were God's people to an individual trying to prove he or she was pure enough for God. As a result, anyone following the pharisaic tradition did not dare to be associated even remotely with anything or anyone considered unclean.

The early Christian church, therefore, had to deal with the question of which cleanliness laws were no longer needed (because Jesus died to free people from slavery to the Law) and which cleanliness laws they should still follow (to show that Christians were God's special people, set apart to serve Him in the world).

Many early Christians from the pharisaic tradition believed they should keep all the laws strictly because Christ came so people could keep the Law. But, through the events described in **Acts 8—11,** the Holy Spirit showed the church that God had other ideas.

Most of the people mentioned in **Acts 8—11** would have been considered unclean by the pharisaic Jews. Anyone associating with them would also have been considered unclean. The Samaritans **(8:5-25)** were archenemies of the Jews. Jewish people and Samaritans had quarreled for more than 500 years over the proper way to worship God. Jewish people felt that the Samaritan way was an evil corruption and that Samaritans should be avoided at all costs.

The Ethiopian **(8:26-40)** would have been considered unclean because he was a foreigner. Even worse, he was a eunuch, which would have prevented him from joining the Lord's assembly **(Deuteronomy 23:1)**. Simon the tanner **(Acts 9:43)** would have been avoided by most Jewish people because his work with dead animals would continually keep him unclean **(Leviticus 11:39-40)**. Cornelius **(Acts 10:1—11:18)** was not only a foreigner, but also a Roman soldier, the captain of the hated troops that occupied and dominated Judea. The Gentiles in Antioch **(11:19-24)** followed the Greek culture. The pharisaic Jews abhorred the Greek culture because most things the Greeks enjoyed and did went against the cleanliness laws of the Jews.

Yet despite their uncleanness, God dramatically showed the church that He accepted these people. He accepted them because they were made clean through Christ's suffering and death. God promised in **Isaiah 56:4-8** that foreigners and eunuchs would have a place with Him and would worship Him. **Acts 8—11** shows how this promise was fulfilled.

Today we still have ideas about what is clean or unclean, acceptable or unacceptable. *Look at the people in your school. Who is allowed into your church or circle of friends and who is not? Why? How are the nerds or outcasts of the school determined? How are minorities treated? What do people think about cafeteria workers and custodians?*

The early church struggled for some time trying to understand who should be acccepted into the church. We will see later that this problem came up again and again in the New Testament. And it still comes up today. Therefore we may need to remind one another that Christ died for *all* people; *all* are acceptable in His sight—tanners and Samaritans, nerds and custodians, eunuchs and Romans, freshmen and seniors, black and white. Also, no sin can prevent God from loving us. God does not want us to stop loving people because of rumors we have heard about them or because they have offended us. God, through His grace and the power of the Holy Spirit, has cleansed us from our sin and helps us share this cleansing with others.

The Holy Spirit made it possible for Philip, Peter, Saul, Ananias, and the apostles in Jerusalem to accept people who they previously thought were unacceptable.

1. How can a change like that take place in you?

_____
_____
_____
_____

2. What change do you wish the Holy Spirit would work in you?

_____
_____
_____
_____

Do not conform any longer to the pattern of this world, but be transformed by the renewing of your mind. Then you will be able to test and approve what God's will is—His good, pleasing and perfect will.

Romans 12:2

Session 53

Review of Unit 5

Complete the matching activities that follow.

PEOPLE

Cornelius
Peter
Stephen
Matthias
Caesar
Paul
Luke
Barnabas
Saul
Theophilus
Gamaliel
Ananias
James, the brother of John
Philip, the evangelist

1. The man who replaced Judas Iscariot as one of the 12 apostles.

2. The first of the 12 apostles to be executed for his faith.

3. The Pharisee who, in **Acts 5,** persuaded the Sanhedrin to tolerate Christians.

4. The Pharisee who, in **Acts 8—9,** led the persecution against Christians.

5. The Greek name for this Pharisee **(4).**

6. The deacon who became the first Christian martyr.

7. The deacon who shared the Gospel with Samaritans and an Ethiopian.

8. The title for the Roman emperor.

9. A Roman officer who became a Christian.

10. The man who, with his wife, Sapphira, tried to deceive the Holy Spirit.

11. The author of Acts.

12. The person Acts was addressed to.

13. The disciple who was the spokesperson for the early church and is the leading human character in **Acts 1—2.**

14. A Christian Levite from Cyprus who brought Saul to the apostles in Jerusalem and who helped establish the church in Antioch.

PLACES AND THINGS

Jerusalem
Diaspora
Pax Romana
Antioch
Proselytes
Sanhedrin
Damascus
Pentecost
Caesarea
Gentiles
Synagogue
Sadducees
Pharisees
Temple

1. People who are not Jewish.

2. Non-Jewish people who have converted to Judaism.

3. 200 years of peace, prosperity, and greatness in the Roman Empire.

4. When the church was brought to life by the Holy Spirit.

5. The city where the followers of Christ were first called Christians and where many non-Jews became Christians.

6. The city where the church began and where it was concentrated until Christians were persecuted there.

7. The city Saul was going to when Jesus appeared to him.

8. The scattering of the Jewish people around the world.

9. The city where Cornelius lived.

10. Located in Jerusalem, this was the principal place of worship for Jewish people and the only place for sacrifices.

11. The local place for learning and worship for Jewish people.

12. The ruling council of Jews located in Jerusalem.

13. A Jewish group that was antiforeign and strove to preserve Jewish traditions among the scattered Jewish people of the world.

14. A Jewish group that developed to preserve the temple and that did not believe in the resurrection.

Unit 6
God's Servant Paul

In unit 5 you studied **Acts 1—12,** which covered approximately the first 15 years of the church. In this unit you will finish reading and discussing Acts. **Acts 13—28** also covers approximately 15 years, A. D. 45—60. However, instead of describing how the Holy Spirit worked through the entire church, these chapters concentrate on how He worked through one servant, Paul.

Through Paul God caused the church to spread throughout Asia Minor and Greece. Through the people Paul trained it spread even further around the Mediterranean world. Paul's letters, which make up about one-third of the New Testament, have guided the church for almost 2,000 years. Yet it wasn't Paul who accomplished these things. It was the Holy Spirit working through Paul.

As you read about Paul, may the Holy Spirit guide you, so you, too, can see what service you can give God.

READING SCHEDULE

Session 55: **Acts 12:25—14:28**
Session 56: **Acts 15:1-35**
Session 57: **Acts 15:36—18:22**
Session 59: **Acts 18:23—21:6**
Session 60: **Acts 21:7—26:32**
Session 61: **Acts 27:1—28:31**

Note that not every session has a reading assignment. Some of the assignments (like session 60) are long, however. Therefore, remember to read ahead.

MAJOR HOMEWORK ASSIGNMENT

For this unit you will need to make a map and charts of Paul's four journeys. You can find most of the information in Acts. For the dates, however, you will have to use a Bible handbook or commentary.

The map in this book will help you locate the places Paul visited.

The map should include the following:
1. The area from Italy on the west to Palestine on the east.
2. The places Paul visited.
3. The route of each journey. Use a different color or symbol for each journey.

Make one large chart with all four journeys on it or make four small charts with one journey on each. The charts should include these items:
1. A title (which journey?)
2. Approximate date for that journey
3. Names of the people who traveled with Paul
4. Places Paul visited
5. Summary of significant events of that journey

Session 54

Paul's Threefold Background

STUDY QUESTIONS

Fill in the missing parts of Paul's resume. Use the Bible passages provided.

Resume
1. Name: Paul
2. Other Names: **(Acts 13:9)**
3. Date of Birth: Probably between A.D. 1 and 10
4. City of Birth: **(Acts 21:39)**
5. Skills: **(Acts 18:2-3)**
6. Ethnic Background: **(Acts 21:39; 22:3)**
7. Educated by: **(Acts 22:3)**
8. Teacher's qualifications: **(Acts 5:34)**
9. Descendant of: **(Romans 11:1; Philippians 3:5)**
10. Member of: **(Acts 23:6; 26:4-5)**
11. Roman citizen? **(Acts 16:37-38; 22:25-29)**
12. If yes, how was citizenship acquired? **(Acts 22:28)**
13. Christian? Yes
14. If yes, how did he hear of Christ? **(1 Corinthians 15:4-10; Acts 22:4-16; 26:9-18; 9:1-19)**
15. What service did God call him for? **(Galatians 1:15-16; Acts 13:46-47; Romans 1:13-15; 15:15-16)**
16. When did God begin preparing him? **(Galatians 1:15)**
17. Previous attempt to serve God: **(Acts 8:1-3; 9:1-2; 22:4-5; 26:9-11; 1 Corinthians 15:9; Galatians 1:13-14)**

PAUL'S THREEFOLD BACKGROUND

Jewish

Paul was born a Jew with Roman citizenship in the midst of the Greek culture. He was a descendant of Benjamin. He was a Pharisee and the son of a Pharisee, and was educated by one of the greatest pharisaical rabbis, Gamaliel. Paul was educated in Jerusalem, the center of Jewish life. He was proud of his Jewish heritage and zealous to defend it. He knew intimately and could use the Jewish Scriptures, our Old Testament. After becoming a Christian he was all the more proud of his Jewish background, because he saw and followed the true heritage of Judaism, Jesus Christ.

Roman

Paul was also a Roman citizen by birth. This was a rare honor for non-Latin people, and Roman citizenship by birth carried the highest status. Generally, non-Latins acquired Roman citizenship for some outstanding service to the Roman cause. Possibly Paul's father, grandfather, or great-grandfather was rewarded for supplying tents to the Roman army. People occasionally obtained Roman citizenship through bribery **(Acts 22:28)**. You read about the benefits of Roman citizenship on page 96.

Greek

Tarsus, the city where Paul was born, was a center of Greek culture in Asia Minor. It included a university of Greek philosophy. The people of Tarsus were noted for being well educated in the liberal arts. Paul was fluent in Greek and knowledgeable about Greek culture. He generally quoted from the Greek translation of the Old Testament, the *Septuagint*. He also readily quoted Greek philosophers and writers **(Acts 17:18-19, 28; 1 Corinthians 15:32-33; Titus 1:12)**.

How God Used Paul's Background

Paul's threefold background helped him in the service to which God called him: apostle to the Gentiles. Before Paul was born, God appointed him and blessed his background to fit the service he would be doing for God **(Galatians 1:15)**. As an educated Jew who was knowledgeable in the Greek culture, Paul was a bridge between two distinctly different worlds. He could explain to Gentiles God's Old Testament promises of the Messiah and could show them why they, too, needed the Messiah. He could also explain to Jews how the promises of God applied to all people. As a Roman citizen Paul had more freedom to travel, the protection of the Roman army, and special rights in courts of law. Through Paul and Paul's background the Holy Spirit spread God's Word far beyond Jerusalem and Judaism.

GOD USED A SPECIAL PAUL; GOD USES A SPECIAL YOU

People come in a variety of shapes, sizes, colors, economic classes, cultural backgrounds, educational training, and general upbringing. Consequently, each person's background is unique. God can use that unique background for His special purpose, just as He used Paul's background for the special service we will learn about in this unit.

YOUR UNIQUE BACKGROUND

Your Resume

Take a look at your life and your unique background. On a sheet of paper describe yourself and your life in outline form, similar to that used for Paul above. Include the following:

1. Name, age, date and place of birth
2. Where you live now, where you have lived, and whether the places were big towns, small towns, inner cities, suburbs, or rural
3. Other places you have been
4. Schools you have attended, and whether they were public, private, or parochial
5. Classes you have had and what subjects you enjoy most
6. Churches you have attended
7. Religious training you have had
8. Your ethnic background
9. Ethnic backgrounds you are familiar with and comfortable with
10. Languages you know
11. Traditions your family has
12. Groups you belong to (sports, Scouts, LYF, etc.)
13. Jobs you have had and skills you know
14. Experiences you have had
15. Music you like
16. People who have influenced your life
17. How you have served God in your life

Your Interests

Your resume describes your past experiences. Now, on another sheet of paper, list your interests. List the places, skills, and experiences you enjoy or would like to try. What would you like to do? Where would you like to go?

God Can Use Your Unique Background and Interests

Look at your resume and your interests. How can God use your life to share His love with others? List specific ways your experiences, interests, and abilities can be of service to God.

_____
_____
_____
_____

I have been crucified with Christ and I no longer live, but Christ lives in me. The life I live in the body, I live by faith in the Son of God, who loved me and gave Himself for me.

Galatians 2:20

Session 55

Paul's First Missionary Journey
Read Acts 12:25—14:28

STUDY QUESTIONS

1. The Christians from which city supported the missionary journey **(Acts 13:1-2)**? Why was this journey undertaken?

2. Name the three people who went on this missionary journey **(12:25)**.

3. How had Barnabas helped and worked with Saul before this journey **(9:26-27; 11:25-30)**?

4. About how many years passed between Paul's conversion and this journey **(Galatians 1:15—2:1)**?

5. Where was Barnabas from **(Acts 4:36)**? Where was the first stop on this missionary journey **(13:4)**?

6. To what building did the missionaries usually go first when they came to a new town **(13:5, 14-15, 43; 14:1)**? Why would they go there?

7. What problems did the missionaries encounter during this journey **(13:6-12, 13b, 45, 50; 14:1-2, 5, 8-18, 19)**?

8. List verses from **Acts 13—14** which show that many people, including both Jews and Gentiles, were converted to Christianity during this missionary journey.

9. What did Paul and Barnabas do to ensure that new Christian congregations would continue **(14:21-23)**?

BECOMING A MISSIONARY: HOW GOD GUIDED PAUL

When you think of Paul, you may think of a bold speaker for Christ who proclaimed Christ's love in many lands. However, Paul did not suddenly decide that this was how he was going to serve God. God gradually led him into this service. After Paul was converted on the road to Damascus, and even after his becoming a missionary many years later, God used many people and events to guide Paul into the service He desired for Paul.

After his conversion Paul zealously proclaimed Christ. However, in both Damascus and Jerusalem, he was frustrated by people who refused to believe **(Acts 9:19-30)**. In Jerusalem he even had the problem of disciples refusing to see him because they were still afraid of him. Paul then returned to Tarsus. God (through Luke) does not provide details of things that happened there **(Acts 9:30; 11:25-26)**.

We know, though, that God did not forget Paul. God worked through Barnabas to guide Paul's service. Barnabas spoke for Paul and relieved the fears of the Christians in Jerusalem **(9:27)**. Later Barnabas went to Tarsus to find Paul and bring him to Antioch. There Barnabas and Paul worked together for a year teaching and preaching **(11:25-26)**. Barnabas even led Paul and John Mark during the early part of the first missionary journey, when they went through Barnabas' homeland of Cyprus **(11:4-12)**.

God used various events to show Paul the tremendous work that needed to be done among the Gentiles. The congregation that Paul worked with in Antioch was primarily a Gentile congregation. Its founders had done on a small scale the same thing God was calling Paul to do on a large scale. At Antioch Paul realized that God's salvation applied equally to both Jews and Gentiles **(Galatians 2:11-21)**.

Paul's message, from his conversion until his death, was that people do not make themselves right with God by following laws, whether those are the laws of a person's conscience or the law of Judaism. Christ alone makes people right with God. Some Jewish leaders felt this was blasphemy because they believed that obeying the Law made them God's special people. Therefore they chased Paul from Damascus and Jerusalem shortly after his conversion, and they persecuted him during his missionary journeys. Many Jewish people accepted the message Paul brought. However, the stubborn belligerence of others forced Paul to concentrate on Gentiles.

The Gentiles, as **Acts 13:48** indicates, rejoiced to hear that God would accept them. Paul repeatedly spoke first to the Jewish people in any new town he visited. However, if they rejected what he said, he would tell the Good News to anyone who was willing to listen. By this action God did not close the door on the Jews; rather, He opened the door for the Gentiles.

BECOMING A MISSIONARY: HOW GOD GUIDES YOU

It would perhaps be unusual if more than one student from your class would go to another country as a Christian missionary to tell people about God, as Paul did. Few people become *that* kind of missionary. Nevertheless, God does call you to be a missionary for Him, to tell the Good News of Jesus' love to others in your family, your school, your job, and other places in your community. He is at work right now preparing you to do this mission work for Him.

1. God works through the means of grace (His Word and the Sacraments) to prepare you for your mission tasks. List some specific times when this happens.

_____

_____

_____

_____

2. God also provides people to guide you in the way of the Lord. Name some of those people and tell how God is using them to guide you.

_____

_____

_____

_____

In his heart a man plans his course, but the Lord determines his steps.
Proverbs 16:9

Session 56

The Council of Jerusalem
Read Acts 15:1-35

STUDY QUESTIONS

1. What complaint did some Jewish Christians have about Paul and Barnabas **(Acts 15:1, 2, 5)**? How was this complaint related to Paul's first missionary journey?

2. In which city did the Christians gather to discuss and settle this dispute **(15:4-6)**? In which year, approximately, was this council held?

3. What was Peter's opinion about the problem **(15:7-11)**? What earlier event did Peter refer to in **verse 7**?

4. James (the brother of Jesus) apparently became the earthly head of the church after Peter began traveling around Palestine to preach the Good News **(12:17; 21:18)**. Summarize what James said about the problem and summarize his solution for it **(15:13-21)**.

5. What did the council decide **(15:22-31)**? How did they send word about their decision to the rest of the church?

6. How did the Gentile Christians react to his decision **(15:30-33)**?

THE JEWISH-GENTILE CONTROVERSY

Session 52 mentioned the problem that was developing between Jewish and Gentile Christians as the church grew beyond Jerusalem. In **Acts 15** problems arose again. Paul and Barnabas' missionary journey had been highly successful among Gentiles. But many Jewish Christians and Christians who had been proselytes had some serious questions. Can Gentiles be Christians without following Jewish rituals? What is necessary for salvation? How could one determine if a Gentile's faith was sincere?

We use the name *Judaizers* for those who insisted that Gentile Christians had to follow all of the Jewish laws. Because a major sign of the Jewish covenant relationship with God was circumcision, the Judaizers insisted that all Gentile Christians had to be circumcised **(Acts 11:2-3; 15:1, 5)**. Consequently, Judaizers are also referred to as the circumcision party.

Many Gentiles in the eastern half of the Roman Empire were *Hellenists*—Greeks or other peoples who had adopted Greek culture. *Hellas* is Greek for Greece. Greeks believed that man was the greatest of all creatures. Therefore, they did much to cultivate their minds and bodies. They tried to learn all they could about earth, people, and life. They developed philosophies. They sculpted very beautiful and accurate statues of people. They exercised, and they enjoyed and participated in athletic events. They saw nothing wrong with nudity. And they abhorred anything that would mar the body, such as circumcision.

The Jewish-Gentile controversy in the Christian church was not something new. It was just a continuation of the centuries-old clash between Judaism and Hellenism. Jews thought Hellenists were idolatrous people because they emphasized the human body, and had statues everywhere. Jewish people abhorred the Hellenistic custom of eating pork and other unclean foods, and believed that nudity was sinful.

Hellenists thought that Jews were haughty, ignorant, and uncultured. Various Hellenistic rulers, beginning with Alexander the Great around 330 B.C., tried to educate, persuade, or force Jews to become Hellenists. Jews in general, and Pharisees in particular, fought hard and long to preserve Judaism. The Maccabean Revolt in 168—161 B.C., described in 1 and 2 Maccabees and celebrated with Hanukkah, was the high point of the Jewish struggle against Hellenism. Since then, many Jewish people looked for a messiah to come either to rid the world of Hellenists or to convert Hellenists to Judaism.

The Jewish-Gentile controversy was a serious problem for the early church. It forced Christians to consider clearly what the true reason was for Christ's life, death, and resurrection. Christians struggled to understand which people Christ had come to save, and what was involved in faith and salvation.

THE CHURCH GATHERS TO SOLVE A PROBLEM

Around A.D. 48 the leaders of the church gathered in Jerusalem to discuss and settle the Jewish-Gentile controversy. The Council of Jerusalem is considered the first ecumenical council of the entire church. This first gathering of the church is the only one recorded in the Bible. As we look at this council, we can find ideas that could help the church solve problems today.

One important item stands out in the words of Peter, Barnabas and Paul, and James. Each showed what God had done and what God's Word said about the problem. Peter related how the Holy Spirit directly showed that Gentiles can be saved through Christ **(Acts 15:7-11; 11:1-18).** Barnabas and Paul explained how God worked through them to reach the Gentiles during their recently completed missionary journey. James showed how this agreed with God's Word, spoken by His prophets, Amos and Isaiah **(Acts 15:16-18; Amos 9:11-12; Isaiah 45:20-22).**

God still guides the church. He speaks to us—the church—directly through His Word, the Bible. As humans, we have many thoughts and ideas. Some are from God. Others are temptations from the devil, the world, and our sinful flesh. In **1 John 4:1** God warns, **"Dear friends, do not believe every spirit, but test the spirits to see whether they are from God, because many false prophets have gone into the world."** It is God's Word that these spirits and our thoughts and ideas need to be tested against.

Whether the church is meeting on a local, district, or synodical level, it must understand God's Word to know which actions to take. The same holds true for individuals. If individuals want to speak, act, and think as God desires, we need to know those desires. Without understanding the forgiveness and reconciliation that God proclaims to all people, the church is no more than any other gathering of humans, and a Christian is no different than any other person. Even quoting from the Bible will prove nothing if God's love is not present.

THE RESULTS OF THE COUNCIL OF JERUSALEM

The Council of Jerusalem agreed with Paul, Barnabas, and the Antioch Christians. God's message of salvation was for all people, with no strings attached. It was not solely for the Jews or solely for the Gentiles.

Likewise, the Messiah did not come to keep Jews under the burden of the Law. Neither did He come to condemn Hellenists for their life-style, or to force Hellenists to follow Jewish laws. Instead, He came to free Jews, Hellenists, and all people, from every culture, from their sin. He came so that the sin which separates people from God, and, as a result, from each other, would be destroyed. Consequently, Christians can share God's love freely with all people.

The Council's decision confirmed that Christianity cannot be tied to one culture, whether that culture is Judaism, Hellenism, or today's western civilization. James stated that Christianity has a basic morality or right way to live **(Acts 15:19-20, 28-29);** however, this life-style honors the one true God and His love rather than our self-righteousness. Therefore, Christianity proclaims the one thing that can unite all cultures: salvation through Christ alone.

Though the Jerusalem Council gave the church's official decision regarding the controversy, it did not end the controversy. Judaizers continued to plague the church through the apostolic age. Many of the New Testament epistles, including **Galatians, Colossians, Romans,** and **1 Corinthians,** refer either in whole or in part to the controversy.

Today there are still "Judaizers" who try to add rules for people to follow in order to be saved. As long as sin exists, "Judaizers" will exist. But, in the words of Jesus to Martha, **"Only one thing is needed"** (Luke **10:38-42),** and that is Christ Himself.

1. How do "Judaizers" of today tempt you to turn away from the Gospel of Christ?

_____
_____
_____
_____

2. How can you help one another resist those temptations?

_____
_____
_____
_____

Here there is no Greek or Jew, circumcised or uncircumcised, barbarian, Scythian, slave or free, but Christ is all, and is in all.

Colossians 3:11

Session 57

Paul's Second Missionary Journey: Europe
Read Acts 15:36—18:22

STUDY QUESTIONS

1. Why did Paul want to go on another missionary journey **(Acts 15:36; 16:4)**? From which city did this journey begin **(15:35-40)**?

2. What caused a problem between Paul and Barnabas, and what was the result of that problem **(15:37-39; 13:13)**? Read **Colossians 4:10** and **2 Timothy 4:11**. How do these verses show that Paul and John Mark resolved their differences?

3. During this missionary journey Paul was led into a totally new region: Europe. How did God lead Paul to bring the Good News to Europe **(Acts 16:6-10)**? Read **Acts 14:27; 1 Corinthians 16:9; 2 Corinthians 2:12;** and **Colossians 4:3**. What phrase does Paul use to show that God's Word can spread to a new region or group of people?

4. What building did the missionaries usually visit when they arrived in a new town **(Acts 17:1, 10, 17; 18:4)**? Where would the missionaries go if this building was not in a town **(16:13, 16)**?

5. What cities did Paul visit in Greece **(16:12—18:18)**? Which city did Paul stay in the longest, at least 1-1/2 years **(18:11)**? What city in Asia Minor did Paul visit near the end of this journey **(18:19-21)**? Locate these cities on a map.

6. List the problems Paul faced in the Greek cities **(16:12—18:18)**. Why did these problems occur **(16:19; 17:4-5, 13, 32; 18:5-6)**? Describe how God's Word spread as a result of the problems Paul faced.

A NEW DOOR IS OPENED

After the Council of Jerusalem, Paul, Barnabas, Judas Barnabas, and Silas brought the letter describing the council's decision to Antioch. A short time later Paul and Barnabas decided to make a second missionary journey, returning to the places they had visited during the first journey, to share the council's decision with those Christians also **(Acts 15:36; 16:4)**.

However, the Lord works in mysterious ways. Sometimes the weaknesses and sins of people seem to close doors, but God uses them to open new doors that allow His Word to spread to more people and places than we would have imagined.

Notice the poor beginning of this missionary journey. Paul and Barnabas quarreled before the journey even began. Fortunately, this did not end their missionary work. Instead, they divided the territory. Barnabas and his cousin, John Mark, went to Cyprus, Barnabas' homeland. Paul went through his homeland, Cilicia, to the mainland cities they had visited during the first missionary journey.

But Paul needed an assistant for the journey. As the next session will show, God provided plenty of assistants. The first was Silas, one of the men who had come to Antioch with Paul and Barnabas to deliver the decision of the Council of Jerusalem. Silas, like Paul, was a Roman citizen. Together, Paul and Silas revisited and encouraged the congregations Paul had established in south-central Asia Minor. They even added another companion, Timothy.

Then another problem occurred. As the three missionaries tried to share the Gospel in western and northern Asia Minor, they discovered that God would not let them. As each region was closed to them, they kept going until they reached Troas, the last town, located in the far northwestern corner of Asia Minor. Here God invited Paul to go through a new door He opened for the missionaries so they could bring Christianity to a new continent: Europe.

The Closed Door/Open Door

Probably a few Christians already lived in Europe when Paul arrived. People from Rome were included among the Pentecost crowd **(Acts 2:10)**. Likely other Jewish people living in Europe had traveled to Jerusalem in the 20 years since Pentecost, had heard about Christ, and had even become followers of Christ. However, Christians did not discover the tremendous field for God's work in Europe until other doors had temporarily closed.

Doors continued to close at times while Paul traveled through Europe. After he gathered a group in Philippi, the door was slammed shut on Paul, so he moved on to Thessalonica. Again, Paul gathered a group, and then had the door slammed shut on his work again. Once more he moved on.

Notice, though, that this did not limit God's Word. In fact, just the opposite occurred. Each time a door was shut, God opened new doors. The groups Paul gathered continued to grow in faith, and Paul continued to gather more groups. In less than one year Christianity had spread throughout Macedonia and Achaia, the very heart of Hellenism.

Christ Opens the Doors

Christians live in a sinful world. We are freed from sin, but while we live on earth, we are not immune to it. The Jewish-Gentile controversy, the argument between Paul and Barnabas, and the closed doors Paul encountered on this missionary journey resulted from sin.

Yet the renewal Jesus won on the cross overcame these sins. The Gospel of Christ worked through the Council of Jerusalem to show that Christ was for all people. Later it healed the rift between Paul and Barnabas and created two missionary teams that could more effectively reach more areas. It also flowed through the doors that were closed on Paul, spreading the Good News of salvation to more and more people. Therefore, both Paul and Luke declared that God opens the door for His Word to be spread **(Acts 14:27; Colossians 4:3).**

TAKE ADVANTAGE OF THE OPEN DOOR

God is still opening doors so His people can share His saving love with others. Look over the past day, month, and half-year carefully. Think of the many opportunities you had to share God's Gospel love with someone. These are the doors God has opened through which you can take part in accomplishing His will.

1. On a sheet of paper for your own use (and not to share with anyone except God) list the opportunities to share God's Gospel love under two categories: *did* and *could have.*

_____

_____

_____

You probably feel disappointed in the way you responded to the opportunities above. As you think about this, remember that Paul, Peter, and the other apostles did not always have the ability to share God's love. Like you, they were humans, too. After Paul's conversion and initial enthusiasm, many years passed before his missionary journeys. Also, both Peter and Paul continued to be sinful humans **(Acts 15:37-39; Galatians 2:11-13).**

Our sins need not keep us from sharing God's love. Instead, God gives us the power, as He gave it to the apostles, to turn to the Lord, seek His forgiveness, and let His forgiveness flow through us to others.

2. According to **Romans 3:22-24,** what happens when we trust in ourselves to accomplish the tasks God gives us? What happens when we trust in God instead?

_____

_____

_____

Remember that God may not call you into a mission like the one He gave to Peter or Paul. Rather, He called you to be you. Ask God for His guidance so you can honor Him with the service He desires from you. Read God's Word regularly so you can recognize His guidance and can speak His message when He opens doors around you. Look at the resume and interest list you developed in session 54. Recognize your talents and gifts so that you can serve the Lord through them.

Also remember that it is the Spirit of God who speaks and reaches out through you. You do not have to worry about what to do or say. Trust God to provide the right words and actions so His will can be done. As Luther states in his explanation to the Third Petition of the Lord's Prayer, "The good and gracious will of God is done even without our prayer, but we pray in this petition that it may be done among us also."

3. Look at your life right now, and at what tomorrow, this month, and this next half-year have in store. What types of doors might God open for you, so you can serve Him? What opportunities will He make available? How can you determine how and where God is guiding you? What can you say or do when the door is open?

_____

_____

_____

God is opening doors for you. Go through them and serve the Lord, in Jesus' name.

Thanks be to God, who always leads us in triumphal procession in Christ and through us spreads everywhere the fragrance of the knowledge of Him.
2 Corinthians 2:14

Session 58

Paul's Helpers

STUDY QUESTIONS

1. Who was Paul's partner on his second missionary journey (**Acts 15:40**)? What was this man's citizenship **(16:38)?** What were his positions in the church **(15:22, 32)?** With whom did he later work **(1 Peter 5:12)?**

2. Who joined Paul at Lystra **(Acts 16:1-3)?** What was his family background? Paul mentioned this person in the first verses of six of his epistles. Read **2 Timothy 1:5-14.** What is this person told to do with the faith he has in Jesus? How will God enable him to do this? Read **Hebrews 13:23.** Where did this person apparently spend some time?

3. In **Acts 16:10-16** the pronoun "we" indicates that the author went with Paul from Troas to Philippi. Who is believed to be the author of Acts?

Read **Colossians 4:14; Philemon 24;** and **2 Timothy 4:10.** What was this man's profession? How does Paul describe this man?

Acts 20:6—21:26 and **27:1—28:16** are two other "we" sections. Read just the headings in your Bible for these sections. Then write a one to three sentence summary of the events in Paul's life that the author witnessed.

4. Which couple assisted Paul in Corinth and Ephesus **(Acts 18:1-3, 18-19; Romans 16:3-5)?** What were their backgrounds? How did they help Paul **(Acts 18:3, 18; Romans 16:3-4)?** How did they serve fellow Christians **(Romans 16:5; 1 Corinthians 16:19)?**

5. Apollos was a Christian Paul became acquainted with during his third missionary journey. Paul refers to Apollos frequently in **1 Corinthians (1:12; 3:4-9, 21-23; 4:6; 16:12).** Read **Acts 18:24—19:1.** What was Apollos' background **(Acts 18:24)?** Who helped him understand God's salvation better **(Acts 18:26)?**

6. Titus was another person associated with Paul. What was his ethnic background **(Galatians 2:3)?** In which city did Titus serve God for a time **(2 Corinthians 8:6, 16-17)?** Where did Titus later serve God **(Titus 1:5)?** Still later, where did Titus serve God **(2 Timothy 4:10)?** Locate these places on a map.

THE FAMOUS AND THE NOT-SO-FAMOUS

How many people from school or church can you name? Do you know even the "prominent" students and church members? If you know the names, can you also associate a face with the name?

Don't be surprised if you cannot name even all of the prominent students and church members. Don't be surprised if you cannot identify whom some of the names belong to. Likewise, don't be surprised if a few other individuals can be named by almost everyone in your school or church.

Throughout history certain people have become famous, while most people remain relatively unknown. Even among the most prominent people in history, there are only a few that almost everyone can identify. Most prominent people from history are simply a reference in a textbook or encyclopedia today.

It's the same way in the church. Almost all of us can identify some Christians, like Paul and Peter. Others are prominent, but not known by everybody. Most Christians, however, are known only among their closest friends and relatives. Yet whether a Christian is famous or not-so-famous, God has a job for that person to do in His kingdom.

PAUL'S HELPERS, AND MORE

God chose Paul to do a tremendous task: to share the Gospel of Christ with Gentiles. But God did not choose Paul to do this task on his own. God chose many people to help Paul reach the Gentiles. You may have heard about a few of Paul's helpers before. Others may be completely new to you. But each had a task as important as Paul's, and each was called to that task by God.

In sessions 55 and 57 you learned about the roles of Barnabas and John Mark in the first missionary journey. The study questions above refer to seven other people who assisted Paul during his other missionary journeys. Acts and Paul's epistles mention other helpers, such as Aristarchus, Epaphroditus, Erastus, Stephanas, and Tychicus.

1. Look through the references given in the study

121

questions and skim the last chapter of each of Paul's epistles. How did Paul's helpers help him share the Gospel?

_____
_____
_____

2. Read **1 Corinthians 3:5-11.** Who are these people really serving? In fact, who is really doing the work through these people?

_____
_____
_____
_____

WHO'S WHO IN THE LOCAL CONGREGATIONS

In a typical congregation almost everyone knows one person: the pastor. He has been called by God to do a prominent job in a congregation. Like Paul, the pastor was not called to do the job on his own. God called each member of the congregation to assist the pastor in reaching out with God's Word of salvation.

1. Make a list of the workers in your congregation and the jobs that they do. Who are the ushers, the janitors, the people who set up dinners, and the people who clean up after them? Who are the secretaries, the envelope stuffers, the choir members, and the handymen? Who are the elders, the Sunday school and Bible class teachers, the youth leaders, and the altar guild members? Who witnesses door to door, who greets people at the church services, who takes care of the finances, and who takes care of the nursery? What are the numerous other jobs at your church and who does them? Most important, how can the Gospel be shared and God's kingdom be strengthened and encouraged through the people doing each of these jobs?

_____
_____
_____
_____

2. Read **1 Corinthians 12** and **13.** God does not call every person to do the same job. But He does call everyone to serve in His kingdom **(12:7).** By allowing the Spirit to flow through each job, God's will is accomplished. Look again at the jobs listed above. What would each of those jobs be like, and what would the growth of God's kingdom be like, if people prayed earnestly that the Lord would work through them in each job?

_____
_____
_____
_____

THE KINGDOM OF GOD AND YOU

1. God did not call only the other person. God also called you to have an important role in His kingdom on earth. You are not too young to do God's will. Note that God called Isaiah, Jeremiah, John the Baptizer, and Paul before they were born **(Jeremiah 1:4-8; Isaiah 49:1; Luke 1:15; Galatians 1:15).** What are some possible things God may have called you to do for Him?

_____
_____
_____
_____
_____

2. Look again at your resume and interest list from session 54. Right now you are a student and a son or a daughter. You may play sports, enjoy your schoolwork, have a job, spend time with friends, or pursue other interests. What are some specific things you can do to share God's love in the roles you have now? Look at your future plans and interests. What are some ways God can work through those plans to accomplish His will?

_____

_____

_____

_____

Whether you are famous or not-so-famous, there are many jobs to be done in God's kingdom. Let the Spirit guide you to your task and flow through you in your task so God's will may be done.

You are the body of Christ, and each one of you is a part of it.

1 Corinthians 12:27

The goal of this command is love, which comes from a pure heart and a good conscience and a sincere faith.

1 Timothy 1:5

Session 59

Paul's Third Missionary Journey and Letter Writing
Read Acts 18:23—21:6

STUDY QUESTIONS

1. From which city did Paul begin this missionary journey (**Acts 18:22-23**)? Why did he undertake this journey?

2. In which city did Paul spend much of his time during this journey (**19:1—20:1**)? Where was this city located? At least how long did Paul stay there (**19:10**)?

3. Where did Paul go first in this city (**19:8-9**)? Why did Paul go elsewhere after three months?

4. What problems or events occurred during this missionary journey (**19:1—20:12**)? Describe how God's Word spread through these problems or events.

5. **Acts 20** describes the final visit Paul made to the churches he had established around the Aegean Sea before going to Jerusalem. Which city is mentioned in **verses 1-3**? Which city did Paul hope to visit after going to Jerusalem (**19:21**)? Where did he hope to go after visiting that city (**Romans 15:23-24, 28**)?

6. Why was Paul in a hurry to reach Jerusalem (**Acts 20:16**)?

7. Summarize Paul's farewell sermon to the leaders from Ephesus (**20:17-38**). What words of warning and advice did he give to them? What words of hope?

8. What did Paul do while waiting for his ship to be unloaded and made ready to sail again (**21:3-6**)?

9. Name the seven cities or regions to whom Paul wrote an epistle (letter). Locate them on a map.

THE GOSPEL IS SHARED THROUGH THE WRITTEN WORD

Several factors led Paul to begin writing his epistles. For example, his missionary travels carried him over a wide area, and the pressing needs of various congregations prevented him from traveling to each place whenever he wanted to. Paul could not be at each congregation he had started at all times. The several congregations begun during the first two missionary journeys were spread over an area about 600 miles long and 300 miles wide—tremendous distances in those days. The number of congregations was increasing as the early congregations began ministering in neighboring towns, thus establishing new congregations. In addition, the problems that called for Paul's guidance often occurred when Paul was far away and could not easily go to visit them.

Epistles, then, became an efficient way for Paul to shepherd the growing flock the Lord placed under his care. God now used both Paul's spoken and written words to proclaim His Gospel message. In fact, God essentially opened a whole new mission field for Paul, because through the epistles God made Paul a missionary to the entire world for the remainder of time. Once more God turned one of Paul's problems into a tremendous blessing. Through writing, Paul declared God's Word not only over a broader geographic area, but also over a broader span of time.

ANCIENT LETTER WRITING

Epistle is simply Greek for "letter" or "message." Epistles were a common method of communication at the time of Paul. They were used for official and private correspondence and for literary essays. They resembled what we today traditionally think of as a letter.

Epistles averaged about 90 words, which would easily fit on one papyrus sheet. They had a specific addressee and were begun with a greeting, which included the name of the sender, the name of the addressee, and wishes for good health. This was followed by the main body of the letter and a farewell (which could include greetings from others and a signature). We find two examples of epistles in **Acts 15:23-29** and **23:26-30**.

Literary epistles were essays written for general publication, but they included an artificial addressee to make them appear like personal letters. Orators and philosophers in the first century A.D. used them to make their views known. They averaged about 200 words in length, which would fit on one or two papyrus sheets.

Letters were usually dictated to an *amanuensis*, or

professional writer. Because of the coarse grain of the papyrus (which made writing tedious) and the illiteracy of much of the population, there was a great demand for amanuenses. He would usually take the dictation in shorthand, using a stylus to write on a wax tablet. He then would rewrite the text in longhand, using ink on a papyrus sheet. These sheets averaged about 9½" x 11". If more than one papyrus sheet was required, they were joined at the side and the finished copy was rolled into a scroll.

There was no postal service for private correspondence at that time. Consequently, letters were sent by travelers. Often someone would write a letter because he or she knew a traveler was bound for a certain destination.

PAUL'S EPISTLES

Paul's epistles follow the format of the private correspondence, yet they fall into a class by themselves. They range from 335 words **(Philemon)** to 7,101 words **(Romans)**. In one sense Paul's epistles are essays, but they were much longer than the common literary *epistle* and they are addressed to real people. Paul's epistles are rich in theology, which makes the ancient Greek word *epistle* seem an appropriate term for them. Yet in these writings Paul shows a deep concern for each individual and clearly speaks to each person today. Therefore, the more personal and modern term *letter* is also very appropriate.

Paul probably used an amanuensis when writing his letters. From **Romans 16:22** we know Tertius was the amanuensis for this letter. Paul's comment that he is writing a greeting with his own hand **(1 Corinthians 16:21; Galatians 6:11; Colossians 4:18; 2 Thessalonians 3:17; Philemon 19)** implies that an amanuensis wrote the rest of those letters. Paul's signature with those letters helps guarantee their authenticity.

The Roman world was one of the earliest mobile societies, and Christians were a part of the mobility. Paul used these mobile Christians to carry his letters to their various destinations. Phoebe, a Christian from Cenchreae (port city for Corinth) carried the letter to the **Romans (16:1-2)**. Tychicus carried Paul's letter to the **Ephesians (6:21-22)** and **Colossians (4:7-8)**. The run-away slave, Onesimus, brought Paul's letter of **Philemon (verses 10-16)**. Epaphroditus, who was returning to his hometown of Philippi after being with Paul for a while, brought Paul's letter to the **Philippians (2:25-30)**. Some Christians traveled from Corinth to Ephesus to inform Paul about the events occurring there **(1 Corinthians 1:11; 16:17)**. Undoubtedly they or other Christians returned with the letter Paul wrote to Corinth.

PAUL'S EPISTLES AND GOD'S WORD

1. Note similarities between God's work through Paul's missionary journeys, His work among the original readers of Paul's letters, and His work among people today through Paul's letters.

_____
_____
_____
_____

2. How do you know these epistles are God's Word and not just human words from Paul?

_____
_____
_____
_____

3. List three blessings you have received from God through Paul's epistles.

_____
_____
_____
_____

Bear in mind that our Lord's patience means salvation, just as our dear brother Paul also wrote you with the wisdom that God gave him.
2 Peter 3:15

Session 60

Paul's Arrest and Imprisonment
Read Acts 21:7—26:32

STUDY QUESTIONS

1. What were three reasons Paul wanted to go to Jerusalem (**Acts 20:16; 21:17-19; Romans 15:25-27; 1 Corinthians 16:1-4**)?

2. Read **Acts 20:22-23; 21:4, 10-14**. What did God warn Paul about concerning going to Jerusalem? What wrong idea did some Jews have about what Paul was teaching **(21:21)**?

3. Why did Paul go to the temple **(21:18-26)**? Why do you think Paul would observe a Jewish ceremonial law?

4. Who stirred up the crowd against Paul and what charge did they make against him **(21:27-29)**? How was Paul saved from being killed **(21:30-36)**? Why was Paul arrested?

5. Whom was Paul speaking to in **Acts 22:1-21**? In what language did Paul speak to them **(21:40; 22:2)**? Summarize Paul's speech in one or two sentences. What caused the Jews to start the noisy tumult again **(22:21-22)**?

6. What caused Paul to be saved from a whipping and to receive better treatment **(22:23-30)**?

7. Whom was Paul brought before for trial in **Acts 22:30—23:10**? How was Paul able to divide this group so that they could not judge him?

8. What good was God going to bring from Paul's problem **(23:11)**?

9. Read **Acts 23:12-35**. Why was Paul taken from Jerusalem to Caesarea? How did the Romans ensure Paul's safety?

10. Whom was Paul brought before for trial in **Acts 24:1-27**? What charges were brought against Paul? What was Paul's defense? What was the verdict and why was this verdict given?

11. How long was Paul in prison **(24:27)**? What could Paul do in prison **(24:23-26)**?

12. Why was a new trial held **(24:27—25:5)**? Who held his trial? List the similarities between **Acts 25:1-9** and **23:12—24:23**.

13. Why did Paul appeal to Caesar **(25:8-12)**?

14. Read **Acts 25:13—26:32**. Why was this hearing held? Whom was this hearing held before? Summarize Paul's defense. What was the verdict **(26:30-31)**? Why was Paul not set free?

PAUL'S PROBLEMS IN JUDEA

Paul's third missionary journey was very successful. Though he spent most of his time in Ephesus, it appears that he also trained others to lead the numerous congregations that had been established. By the end of the journey the congregations in Asia Minor and Greece were well established. Paul now began plans to use Rome as a support base to reach a new mission field: Spain.

Before going to Rome, Paul wanted to go to Jerusalem to celebrate Pentecost, to present the offering of the Gentile congregations, and to explain all the Lord had done among the Gentiles. The support of the leaders in Jerusalem would be important for getting the support of the rest of the church for mission work in Spain. The Jewish-Gentile controversy was still plaguing the church in general and Paul in particular, so Paul also had some false rumors with which to contend **(Acts 21:20-22)**.

Paul's stay in Jerusalem went smoothly until near the end of Pentecost, when events happened that began a new phase in Paul's life. Paul was falsely accused of defiling the temple and was nearly killed in the ensuing riot. Subsequently, he was accused of being a troublemaker and the cause of riots. For at least the next four years Paul endured imprisonment and a repetition of trials that found him not guilty, but did not release him.

Paul's plans went awry. His trip to Rome was delayed, and when he went, it was not in the manner he intended. But, through all the problems Paul suffered, he knew that God was with him. Paul had followed God's guidance during the three missionary journeys. Now, during his most trying journey, he continued to follow God's guidance, and proclaimed the Good News of God's love wherever he was taken.

We also rejoice in our sufferings, because we know that suffering produces perseverance; perseverance, character; and character, hope. And hope does not disappoint us, because God has poured out his love into our hearts by the Holy Spirit, whom He has given us.

Romans 5:3-5

Session 61

Paul's Fourth Journey: To Rome
Read Acts 27:1—28:31

STUDY QUESTIONS

1. Why did Paul have to go to Rome (**Acts 25:9-12; 26:32**)? What was Paul's classification during this journey **(27:1, 42-43)**?

2. Note the use of the pronoun "we" in these two chapters. Who went with Paul to Rome?

3. Describe the difficulties Paul faced on this journey and explain how God used them to spread His Gospel (**Acts 27:1—28:15**).

4. How did God use fellow Christians and other people to comfort and aid Paul on this journey **(27:3, 42-43; 28:2, 7, 10, 14-15)**?

5. Describe Paul's imprisonment in Rome **(28:16, 30)**. How did Paul use his time **(28:31)**?

6. How long had Paul been imprisoned in Rome by the end of **Acts (28:30)**? Approximately what year does Acts end? Had Paul been on trial before Caesar by that time?

7. Why was Paul able to speak and act with confidence in spite of the hazards and circumstances of his journey?

PAUL AFTER ACTS

Paul finally made it to Rome. He did not come the way he planned, but he did make it. Most important, he was able to serve God both on his journey to Rome and while waiting for his trial in Rome.

We know very little about Paul after this. Acts ends in A.D. 61 with Paul under house arrest, still waiting to see the emperor, Nero. The pastoral epistles, **1** and **2 Timothy** and **Titus,** appear to be the only epistles Paul wrote after Acts ends. Early church history and tradition generally state that around A.D. 62 Nero heard Paul and released him, only to arrest him again about two years later. **Titus** and **1 Timothy** both seem to be written by a freed Paul; in **Titus 3:12** Paul even discusses his travel plans. Paul may have realized his dream of reaching Spain **(Romans 15:23-24, 28)**.

Other things may have happened between the end of Acts and Paul's death besides release and a second imprisonment. Paul may have been exiled (some think to Spain) or simply left in prison waiting to be tried.

Regardless, **2 Timothy,** which appears to be Paul's last letter, indicates that Paul's later imprisonment was worse than the house arrest described in **Acts 28.** Paul describes himself in chains, apparently locked deep in a prison, suffering, facing death, and alone **(2 Timothy 1:8, 12, 15-18; 2:9; 4:6-18).** Yet **2 Timothy** is filled with hope. Paul had faith in God, who sent His own Son into the world to save all people. Paul knew that Christ took away the power of death, and through the Holy Spirit, the Spirit of power, he would finish the race and reach his heavenly goal **(1:7-14; 2:8-13; 4:6-8, 17-18).**

Secular history tells how Nero persecuted Christians after the great fire in Rome (A.D. 64). It appears that Paul was beheaded (the way Roman citizens were executed) during this persecution, probably in 65 or 66.

I have fought the good fight, I have finished the race, I have kept the faith. Now there is in store for me the crown of righteousness, which the Lord, the righteous Judge, will award to me on that day—and not only to me, but also to all who have longed for His appearing.

2 Timothy 4:7-8

We know that in all things God works for the good of those who love Him, who have been called according to His purpose.

Romans 8:28

Session 62

Review of Unit 6

Short Answer

Write answers to these questions on a separate sheet of paper.

1. Describe Paul's threefold background and explain how God used it to bring the Gospel to Gentiles.

2. Describe Paul's life from the murder of Stephen until the first missionary journey. Name and describe the people and events God worked through to lead Paul to become the apostle to the Gentiles, and explain how God worked through these people and events. What are the approximate dates for these early events in Paul's life?

3. What was the significance of each of Paul's four journeys, especially with regard to the spreading of the Gospel? How was Paul's fourth journey different from the three previous journeys and how was it similar to them?

4. What was the Jewish-Gentile controversy? Why did it occur? How did it affect the early church and Paul's work?

5. What was the Council of Jerusalem? Why was it held? What decision did it make? How can a Christian tell whether or not God is working through a church council meeting, regardless if it is on a local, district, or synodical level?

6. How did God guide Paul throughout his life? How does God guide you throughout your life?

7. Why, in general, did Paul write the letters he wrote? Name the people and places to whom Paul wrote letters. Why can letters Paul wrote 1,900 years ago still be used authoritatively by the church today?

8. Why was Paul able to speak and act with confidence in spite of the hazards, persecutions, and problems he faced? Why can you have this same confidence? How can you receive this confidence?

9. What were Paul's talents? How did Paul use them to serve God? What were the talents of any one of the people who helped Paul? How did this person use those talents to serve God? What are your talents? How can you use them to serve God?

10. How can you apply **Acts 13—28** to your everyday life today?

MATCHING PEOPLE

Festus Silas Felix
Timothy Titus Nero
Barnabas Apollos Agrippa II
Luke Aquila James, the
John Mark Saul brother of
Gamaliel Jesus

1. Paul's Hebrew name.

2. The man who was Caesar when Paul appealed his case and when Paul was executed.

3. The renowned pharisaical rabbi who was Paul's teacher.

4. The Roman governor, whose wife was Jewish and sister of Agrippa II, and who left Paul in prison for two years so the Jewish leaders would remember him for a kindness.

5. A Jewish Christian from Alexandria who served in the congregation in Corinth for a while, and to whom Paul refers frequently in 1 Corinthians.

6. A Greek helper of Paul who served in congregations in Corinth, Crete, and Dalmatia, and to whom Paul wrote an epistle.

7. A Greek doctor who helped Paul; he apparently traveled with Paul when Paul first went to Europe and when Paul was arrested and taken to Rome.

8. The Roman governor who was going to take Paul back to Jerusalem to be tried by the Sanhedrin. This incident caused Paul to appeal to Caesar.

9. A man of Jewish and Greek ancestry who joined Paul on his second missionary journey and to whom Paul wrote two epistles.

10. A man who, with his wife Priscilla, was from Rome and assisted the congregations in Corinth and Ephesus. This couple, like Paul, made tents and was Jewish.

11. A Roman citizen who helped bring the decision of the Council of Jerusalem to Antioch and who joined Paul for his second missionary journey.

12. The descendant of Herod the Great who declared Paul innocent after hearing Paul's case. Paul still had to sail to Rome, though, because he had previously appealed to Caesar.

13. The cousin of Barnabas who went on the first

129

missionary journey, but who quit halfway through. He and Paul later worked together again.

14. The man who apparently was the earthly head of the church during the time Paul was making his missionary journeys. This man proposed the solution at the Council of Jerusalem.

15. The man who brought Paul from Tarsus to Antioch, guided Paul's early ministry, and went with Paul on the first missionary journey.

TERMS

Council of Jerusalem	Roman	Hellenism
Synagogues	Jewish	Judaizers
Amanuensis	Pharisee	Greek
	Epistles	

1. The religion into which Paul was born.
2. The sect of the above religion to which Paul's family belonged and in which Paul himself was educated.
3. The group of which Paul was a citizen.
4. The culture with which Paul was very familiar because he grew up in an area where this culture dominated.
5. Another name for this culture.
6. People who insisted that Gentile Christians had to follow all of the Jewish laws.
7. A gathering of Christians which decided that Gentile Christians were saved by faith in Christ alone and so did not have to follow all of the Jewish laws.
8. The place of worship where Paul usually went first when he came into a new town during his missionary journeys.
9. Greek for letter.
10. A professional letter writer.

Unit 7

The Development of Holy Scripture

During the last two units you studied how the Holy Spirit worked through the early Christian church so they could share Christ's love with the world. In session 59 you saw how He used Paul's letter writing to proclaim His Word, even to today's world.

In this unit you will study in more detail how God has made His written Word known to Christians. As you work through these sessions, notice two things in particular:

1. The Bible is the Word of God.
2. God inspired, proclaimed, gathered, and preserved His Word, and He continues to give it power.

STUDY QUESTIONS

In this unit you will find the study questions at the end of each session. The first few questions will help you review the material you have read, and the last few questions will preview the next session.

Session 63

The Old Testament Canon

WHAT IS A CANON?

We use the word *canon* to describe the collection of books that makes up the Old and New Testaments. It comes from the Greek word *kanon,* which means a measurement, rule, or standard.

Canon means, primarily, the rules or standards that were used to determine which books should be included in the Old and New Testaments. Secondarily, it means the list of books that has been accepted in the Bible. In these next three sessions we will see how the canons, or standards, for accepting books into the Old and New Testaments were developed.

Four items should be noted as we begin this study:

First, canonicity is important because it determines which books are the authoritative, infallible Word of God. Without this, people would have no clear, concrete guide for their faith and life.

Second, the Old and New Testaments have separate canons, or standards.

Third, these canons were developed by people at different times in response to problems they were facing. The Old Testament canon had been generally established by the time of Christ. The New Testament canon was formed by application of a separate set of standards established by Christian leaders and a process through which the church agreed on canonical writings by about A.D. 375.

Fourth, and most important, **God is the true Source of both canons.** Just as God inspired people to write His Word, so He also guided people to preserve His written Word for people of all time. Even though God uses weak, sinful mortals to accomplish His will, His actions are not weak or sinful. Rather, they show all the more the power and grace of God. He overcomes the weaknesses and sinfulness of humans so His Word can be known and accomplished.

THE JEWISH SCRIPTURES

In order to understand the Old Testament canon, we need to know how the Jewish Scriptures are arranged.

The Jewish Scriptures developed over many centuries, beginning with Moses around 1450 B.C. Gradually, three divisions or classes of writings appeared: the Torah, the Prophets, and the Writings. Jesus refers to this threefold division in **Luke 24:44.**

The **Torah,** which means teaching, or Law, consists of the five books of Moses: **Genesis, Exodus, Leviticus, Numbers,** and **Deuteronomy.** This division is also called the *Pentateuch* **(Greek for "five books").** These books formed the nucleus of the Jewish Scriptures because they contain God's law for His people.

The **Prophets** is a large group of books that explains and applies God's law, the Torah, to His people. They are subdivided into two groups, the Former (Early) Prophets and the Latter Prophets. The Former Prophets consist of books Christians generally call "historical books": **Joshua, Judges, 1** and **2 Samuel,** and **1** and **2 Kings.** The Latter Prophets consist of books generally called prophets today: **Isaiah, Jeremiah, Ezekiel,** and "the Twelve" (those we call minor prophets: **Hosea, Joel, Amos, Obadiah, Jonah, Micah, Nahum, Habakkuk, Zephaniah, Haggai, Zechariah,** and **Malachi**). The minor prophets were often called the Twelve because the Jews placed all 12 books on one scroll (because they were so short). **Samuel, Kings,** and **Chronicles,** on the other hand, were placed on two scrolls because of their length.

The **Writings** contain a variety of other ancient Jewish religious books. Most of the debate among Jews regarding the canon for their Scripture concerned books in this division. Ultimately, the Jews limited this division to **Ruth, 1** and **2 Chronicles, Ezra, Nehemiah, Esther, Job, Psalms, Proverbs, Ecclesiastes, Song of Solomon, Lamentations,** and **Daniel.**

A CANON FOR THE JEWISH SCRIPTURES

The books included in the Torah and the Prophets seem to have been accepted as the Word of God since the times they were first written. Thus, the Torah was used at the time of David, and the Prophets (which were written over a longer period of time) had been gathered together and generally recognized as canonical by approximately 400 B.C.

The process of gathering the Writings into a canon

moved more slowly. This was probably caused in part by the Diaspora, since that phenomenon led the members of the Jewish community to grow farther and farther apart. Religious writing continued, but the entire community was no longer available to accept these works as the Word of God. Nevertheless, the canon had been pretty well accepted by about 100 B.C.

This acceptance, however, was not universal, especially among Jewish people who lived in communities away from Palestine. One important Jewish community lived in Alexandria, Egypt, at this time. They translated the Jewish Scriptures into Greek (the common language being spoken among them) in a translation still known as the Septuagint. Most Septaugint manuscripts contain certain books that are not part of our Old Testament.

THE OLD TESTAMENT

As stated previously, by the time of Christ the Old Testament canon seems to have been established. The fact that Jesus, Paul, and others quoted most Old Testament books affirms their place in the canon. We find additional support for the Old Testament canon as we know it in the writings of Josephus, the Jewish historian of that day, and in the record of various other first-century writers.

One group of Jewish writings, however, was contested at that time, and is not generally regarded as being a part of the Old Testament canon. We usually refer to these writings as the **Apocrypha.**

The apocryphal books were rejected when the canon was finally established. Roman Catholics accept these books as part of the Old Testament, but call them *Deuterocanonical* ("second canon") to show they are disputed. Protestants and most orthodox Christians do not include them in the Old Testament. (The term *apocrypha* means "obscure" or "hidden.")

THE OLD TESTAMENT CANON AND ME

1. Jesus talked with His enemies about the Old Testament Scriptures in **John 5:31-40.** These people thought (and rightly so) that by studying these Scriptures they would find the way to eternal life **(verse 39).** But they attempted to obey all the rules they found instead of looking for the Messiah promised there. According to the last words of this verse, what is the key to understanding the Old Testament?

2. The apostle Paul talked about these Old Testament Scriptures in **2 Timothy 3:14-17.** What key message of the Old Testament did he mention in **verse 15**? How can these Scriptures be useful for us **(verses 16-17)?**

3. Finish this sentence, "I appreciate the Old Testament Scriptures because . . . ."

STUDY QUESTIONS
Review

1. What are the three divisions the Jewish people have of the Old Testament? Why did these three divisions develop? Why were the Writings the most disputed division when the Old Testament canon was being established?

2. What is the Septuagint?

3. What is the Apocrypha? Why is it not accepted by all Christians as part of the Old Testament canon?

4. Why is the Old Testament considered to be the Word of God?

Preview

1. Read **1 Corinthians 2:13** and **Galatians 1:11-12.** How did the apostles know what to say to other people?

2. Why do people write things down?

3. How do you think the apostles knew what to write to other people?

Concerning this salvation, the prophets, who spoke of the grace that was to come to you, searched intently and with the greatest care, trying to find out the time and circumstances to which the Spirit of Christ in them was pointing when He predicted the sufferings of Christ and the glories that would follow. It was revealed to them that they were not serving themselves but you, when they spoke of the things that have now been told you by those who have preached the Gospel to you by the Holy Spirit sent from heaven. Even angels long to look into these things.

1 Peter 1:10-12

We have the word of the prophets made more certain . . . . No prophecy of Scripture came about by the prophet's own interpretation. For prophecy never had its origin in the will of man, but men spoke from God as they were carried along by the Holy Spirit.

2 Peter 1:19-21

Session 64

The Books of the New Testament Are Written Down and Used

THE SPOKEN GOSPEL

When Jesus lived on earth, God's people used the Old Testament Scripture. Jesus quoted from the Jewish Torah, Prophets, and Writings. At the synagogue in Nazareth He showed how He fulfilled Isaiah **(Luke 4:18-21)**. Along the road to Emmaus He explained all that Moses and the prophets had said concerning Himself **(Luke 24:27)**. Before He ascended into heaven He again explained how the Scriptures show that He had to suffer, die, and rise again on the third day to bring forgiveness of sins **(Luke 24:44-48)**.

The early church, likewise, used the Old Testament as their written Scripture. They were not planning to change the Jewish Scripture or to write a Scripture of their own. They simply used the Jewish Scripture to show what God promised concerning the Messiah. Then they spoke words which Jesus spoke and described events from His life to show how He was the fulfillment of God's promises.

At first the apostles did not write down these words and events from Jesus' life, possibly because they expected Jesus to return very soon (within a few years, or a generation at most). The apostles simply spoke about what they had witnessed and heard. They told the Good News to other people, who told it to still others. Acts contains several examples of the spoken Gospel.

APOSTLES WRITE NEW TESTAMENT BOOKS

As you might expect from oral reports you have heard, some of those who heard this message added other narratives from Jesus' life and ministry. Since these were only more or less complete and more or less accurate, a need arose for an authoritative written interpretation of the facts in the life of Christ, together with their application to life. The epistles of Paul and other apostles were written to meet this need.

About the same time and a little later the need for authentic accounts of the life of Christ itself became apparent. The four gospels were written to supply this need. **Acts filled** the need for an authentic history of the apostolic period, and Revelation set forth God's revelation of the consummation of all things.

WHY THE NEW TESTAMENT BOOKS WERE WRITTEN

While only God can tell with certainty why He caused the various books of the New Testament to be written, we can get some ideas about their purpose from the books themselves and from the history of New Testament times.

The following is a brief summary of the purpose for writing each New Testament book. The dates listed have been taken from *The Word of the Lord Grows*, by Martin H. Franzmann (St. Louis: Concordia Publishing House, 1961).

James (about A.D. 45). James called to repentance to a church beset with temptations to relapse to worldliness, less enthusiasm for Christianity, etc.

Galatians (A.D. 48). Judaizers were insisting that Christians follow certain Old Testament ceremonial practices. Paul showed how Christ had made them free.

1 and 2 Thessalonians (A.D. 50—early and summer). Paul wrote to encourage the new converts in their trials, to give instructions for godly living, and to give assurance concerning the future of believers who die before Christ returns.

1 Corinthians (A.D. 55—spring). Paul wrote to instruct and restore the church in its areas of weakness, to correct false teaching concerning the resurrection, and to give instruction concerning the offering for poverty-stricken believers in Jerusalem.

2 Corinthians (A.D. 55—summer or fall). Paul urged the church to prepare for his visit by completing the collection they had started and by dealing with troublemakers in their midst.

Romans (A.D. 56). Paul wrote to prepare the people for his anticipated journey to Rome. He explained salvation through the Gospel.

134

Paul wrote four letters from prison (A.D. 59—61): **Colossians, Philemon, Ephesians,** and **Philippians.**

Colossians. Paul wrote to combat various Colossian heresies.

Philemon. Paul appealed to Philemon to accept his runaway slave, Onesimus, as a Christian brother.

Ephesians. Paul explained what the church is and what membership in the church involves.

Philippians. Paul thanked the Philippians for the gift he had received from them and wrote about several other topics.

Matthew (A.D. 50—60). Matthew wrote to show his Jewish readers that Jesus is the Messiah.

Mark (about A.D. 60). Mark probably wrote in Rome to provide a summary of the life of Jesus for the Gentile Christians, possibly to prepare them for anticipated persecution.

1 Timothy (A.D. 62—63). Paul gave Timothy written instructions in connection with supervising the church at Ephesus.

Titus (A.D. 63). Paul gave instructions to Titus to help him establish order in young churches.

2 Timothy (A.D. 65—67). At a time when Paul realized that he would probably be put to death soon, Paul wrote sort of a "last will and testament" to Timothy.

1 and **2 Peter** (A.D. 61—62?). In his first letter Peter told how to deal with persecutions from outside the church. In his second letter he told how to deal with false teachers and evildoers who have come into the church. In both letters he spoke about Christian faith and practice.

Luke and **Acts** (A.D. 65—69). Luke provided Theophilus (and his Gentile readers) a full account of what Jesus did (in Luke) and of the continued activity of the exalted Lord through His messengers by the power of the Spirit (in Acts).

Jude (A.D. 60—70). Jude warned his readers about false teachers who were trying to convince them that being saved by grace gave them license to sin.

Hebrews (A.D. 65—70). The writer (identity unknown) wrote to Jewish converts. He pointed out the absolute supremacy and sufficiency of Christ as mediator of God's grace.

John (A.D. 90—100). John sought to deepen and strengthen the faith of Christians by recounting and interpreting the words and deeds of Jesus.

1, 2, and **3 John** (A.D. 90—100). John warned Christians about false teachers who denied the full humanity of Jesus. He also gave instructions concerning problems among various evangelists.

Revelation (A.D. 95). John wrote to strengthen Christians in their trials, to hold before them the greatness and certainty of their hope in Christ, and to assure them of their victory, with Christ, over all the powers of evil.

WHAT THE NEW TESTAMENT SAYS TO ME

The references that follow contain important words from the New Testament. Choose three of these references. For each write a paragraph telling what these words say to you.

Matthew 1:22-23	**1 Timothy** 2:1-4
Mark 8:27-29	**2 Timothy** 3:14-17
Luke 1:1-4	**Titus** 3:4-7
John 20:30-31	**Philemon** 4-6
Acts 1:8	**Hebrews** 1:1-4
Romans 1:16-17	**James** 2:5-13
1 Corinthians 11:23-26	**1 Peter** 1:9-10
2 Corinthians 8:9	**2 Peter** 3:17-18
Galatians 2:16	**1 John** 1:7-9
Ephesians 2:8-10	**2 John** 4-9
Philippians 2:5-11	**3 John** 2-4
Colossians 2:9-10	**Jude** 17-21
1 Thessalonians 4:13-18	**Revelation** 21:1-4
2 Thessalonians 2:13-14	

STUDY QUESTIONS

Review

1. How was the Word of God originally proclaimed by Christians? What written Scriptures did they originally use?

2. Why did the apostles write the documents that eventually became our New Testament?

3. Which is your favorite New Testament book? Why?

4. Write out a favorite New Testament passage. What message from God do you receive in that passage? Why is that message so special to you?

Preview

1. Use a dictionary to define *antilegomena*.

2. Make up your own criteria to accept a book into the New Testament canon. Compare them with the criteria you find in session 65.

Jesus did many other miraculous signs in the presence of His disciples, which are not recorded in this book. But these are written that you may believe that Jesus is the Christ, the Son of God, and that by believing you may have life in His name.
John 20:30-31

Session 65

The New Testament Canon Is Formed

CHURCHES BEGIN TO USE THE NEW TESTAMENT BOOKS

What happened after a gospel or epistle had been written? Following is a likely sequence of events:

The Gospel or Epistle would remain for some time the treasured possession of the individual or the church that had received it. In some cases the originals would be passed from church to church (for example, maybe Colossians and Ephesians), but they would find their way back to the original recipient.

As time passed, originals were more freely circulated and copied. Gradually, churches all over the world would obtain a more or less complete set of the inspired writings.

Because the limits of the canon had not been established, a number of other writings were also being circulated. These included *1 Clement, 2 Clement, The Teaching of the Twelve Apostles,* the *Epistle of Barnabas,* and *The Shepherd of Hermas.*

CRITERIA FOR A CANON

At times it was hard for faithful Christians to determine which writings were God's Word and which were mere human books, especially since not all churches agreed. Some read from certain noncanonical writings mentioned above, and others did not include in their readings certain writings now in the New Testament. At the same time some heretics developed their own lists of New Testament books.

Following are criteria that were applied to determine whether a writing should become part of the canon:

1. Apostolic Origin (the most important criterion). The material had to be written by or authorized by an apostle. (**Mark, Luke,** and **Acts** are books not written by an apostle. They were apparently authorized by Peter and Paul, respectively.) In addition to establishing the canon in the first place, this criterion causes the canon to be closed. Because the apostles died centuries ago, no recent book, no matter how faithful to their teaching or how widely used, can become part of the canon.

2. Faithfulness to Apostolic Teaching. The contents had to reflect as nearly as possible the content and intentions of the apostles. This criterion eliminated heretical books.

3. Extent of Use. The particular writing had to have extended acceptance and use.

HOMOLOGOUMENA AND ANTILEGOMENA

The early church fathers easily agreed upon the inclusion of certain books in the canon. These books are termed *homologoumena* ("agreed upon"). Seven of the 27 books, however, were for a time disputed or doubtful. These books are *antilegomena* ("spoken against"). They are **Hebrews, James, 2 Peter, 2 John, 3 John, Jude,** and **Revelation.**

A CANON DEVELOPS

We find only a sketchy history of the development of the New Testament canon before 325. The church fathers of those early days (such as Clement of Rome, Barnabas, Ignatius, Polycarp, and Hermas) quoted or alluded to the books that were destined to become the New Testament canon, so we know the books were *there.* Also, the thought and life of the church were being shaped by the content of the New Testament writings.

Actually, a heretic forced the church to take steps to form an authoritative canon. In about 170 Marcion constructed a canon of his own: Luke (radically revised by himself) and 10 letters of Paul (not including the pastoral letters).

The lists from church fathers shortly after Marcion generally contained all the *homologoumena* books, but did not agree on the *antilegomena* books.

Nevertheless, the canon as we know it was developing. In 325 the historian Eusebius of Caesarea provided a historical survey of what had happened to the various books in the church. Eusebius showed how the 27 books we still accept in the canon had come to that position, though he referred to six as *antilegomena.* (He mentioned that some considered **Revelation** as *homologoumena* and others considered it *antilegomena*.)

By 367 Athanasius referred to all 27 books as "wellsprings of salvation, from which he who thirsts may take his fill of sacred words." Athanasius made no mention of *homologoumena* and *antilegomena* books. Thus, the New Testament canon as we know it had been established. Other church fathers of that day, such as Jerome and Augustine, added their voices to this canon, and later challenges to it failed. (Jerome also translated the 27 canonical books into Latin.)

GOD PROVIDED THE CANON

If you had been God, how would you have established the canon? Maybe by causing some great miracle and saying to everyone there, "Here it is"? (That's the kind of human logic—"guaranteed by its miraculousness"—that Joseph Smith, for example, used when he claimed he received the Book of Mormon.)

But God chose not to work in that way. Quietly, without fanfare, the church received the canon.

Martin H. Franzmann describes this action as "a miracle of another sort, a miracle like the incarnation of our Lord, a miracle in servant's form. Only a God who is really Lord of all history could risk bringing His written word into history in the way in which the New Testament was actually brought in. Only the God who by His Spirit rules sovereignly over His people could lead His weak, embattled, and persecuted churches to ask the right questions concerning the books that made their claim upon God's people and to find the right answer: to fix with Spirit-guided instinct on that which was genuinely apostolic (whether written directly by an apostle or not) and therefore genuinely authoritative. Only God Himself could make men see that public reading in the churches was a sure clue to canonicity; only the Spirit of God could make men see that a work which commands the obedience of God's people thereby established itself as God's Word and must inevitably remove all other claimants from the scene." (From *The Word of the Lord Grows* [St. Louis: Concordia Publishing House. 1961, 294-95]. Used by permission.)

Thus, it is **God** who has given us the New Testament books as "the wellsprings of salvation" (as Athanasius called them). It is **God** who promises to bless your reading of these books, strengthening your faith and leading you to eternal life.

WHAT THE NEW TESTAMENT SAYS TO ME

Look again at the Bible references listed under this section in session 64. You were asked to write what the words in three of the references mean to you. Now choose three different references and tell what those words mean to you.

STUDY QUESTIONS
Review

1. What criteria did the early church fathers use to help them determine whether a writing should be part of the New Testament canon?

2. How did the 27 New Testament writings become the New Testament canon?

3. What was God's role in the development of the canon?

4. How can you be sure that the 27 books in our New Testament are the books God intended to be in the canon?

5. In question 4 of session 64 you were asked to write out a favorite New Testament passage. Now write out a different passage. What message from God do you receive in that passage? Why is that message so special to you?

Preview

1. What problems could occur when someone transcribes a book? Translates a book?

2. In spite of problems like these, how can we be sure we have an accurate copy of God's Word?

I am not ashamed of the Gospel, because it is the power of God for the salvation of everyone who believes: first for the Jew, then for the Gentile. For in the Gospel a righteousness from God is revealed, a righteousness that is by faith from first to last, just as it is written: "The righteous will live by faith."

Romans 1:16-17

Session 66

Scripture in My Language

HEBREW

When you say, "Please put that into a language I understand," you are talking about English. Maybe you even mean English expressions that you use.

For Moses, David, Elijah, and others in Old Testament times, however, this language would have been Hebrew. Therefore God caused almost all the Old Testament Scriptures to be written in Hebrew. Because of this, many seminaries today train their students to read and understand Hebrew. This ability enables them to read the Old Testament in its original language.

ARAMAIC

During later Old Testament times Aramaic became the language of official diplomacy **(2 Kings 18:26)** and was spoken by many of the residents of Palestine. Sections of the Old Testament were written in Aramaic **(Ezra 4:8—6:18, 7:12-26; Daniel 2:4—7:28; Jeremiah 10:11).**

Jesus and His disciples probably spoke Aramaic (perhaps along with Hebrew and Greek). Mark records Aramaic words that Jesus spoke in **5:41** and **15:34**.

Since more and more people spoke Aramaic after the return from the Babylonian Captivity, rabbis began using this language in the synagogues to explain the Scriptures. Gradually Aramaic paraphrases of the Scriptures, called *Targums*, appeared. Some Targums were created before the time of Christ, but manuscripts used today by Bible scholars are generally from the third to the fifth century after Christ.

GREEK

In session 63 you learned about the *Septuagint*, a translation of the Old Testament Scriptures into Greek, perhaps about 250 B.C.

During the early days of the church many people in Palestine generally spoke Aramaic among themselves, but Greek became the language by which they could communicate with people in other parts of the world. Probably for this reason the apostles used Greek when writing the New Testament books. As they wrote, they usually used the Septuagint translation when quoting Old Testament Scriptures.

For people in other parts of the world, the Old Testament (and later the New Testament) was also translated into languages such as Syriac and Egyptian.

LATIN

By A.D. 200 Latin had replaced Greek as the language of the people in much of the European Christian world. For a time the reading of the Scriptures in Greek was probably followed by a reading in Latin during worship services.

For this to happen, someone had to translate the Scriptures into Latin. We use the term *Old Latin* for a number of versions prepared from about 150 to 350. (If there was one version, it was probably not the work of one man, but rather the result of a process of accretion and revision, book being added to book, and the resulting whole subjected to constant revision in various localities to meet local standards and needs.)

Whatever the situation had been earlier, in 382 Pope Damasus called upon Jerome to produce a revision of the Old Latin Bible.

Jerome worked from the original languages (Hebrew and Greek) to prepare a Latin translation now known as the *Vulgate*. (Apparently Jerome translated the Old Testament and the gospels, and others completed the rest of the New Testament.) Because of the ways the Vulgate differed from the Old Latin, this translation encountered stubborn opposition. Not until the sixth or seventh century did it win general acceptance in the church.

The Vulgate remained the Bible translation widely used until the time of the Reformation.

ENGLISH

Since Latin no longer remained the language of the people at the time of the Reformation, new translations appeared. Perhaps most notable of these were Martin Luther's translation into German during the 1520s and the King James, or Authorized Version, into English in 1611.

The 20th century has seen masses of Bible translations into English. Individuals and groups have attempted accurately to translate Scripture into the vernacular of the people. By 1970, for example, the *Revised Standard Version* was widely used in the United States, and many Christians in Great Britain used the *New English Bible.*

Other recent English translations include *Today's English Version, An American Translation, New American Standard Version, New International Version,* and *New King James Version.*

OTHER TRANSLATION WORK TODAY

Christian churches today are working vigorously to fulfill Christ's command to be His witnesses **"to the ends of the earth" (Acts 1:8).** As we perform this task, we find that people who speak more than 3,000 languages do not have God's Word in their language.

Since the Holy Spirit works faith through the Word of God, we find a very strong relationship between making this Word available to people in their own language and the process of nurturing Christians and allowing them to grow in their faith. Therefore many groups are working to translate Scripture into some of those 3,000 languages. Here are three examples:

Wycliffe Bible Translators. This nondenominational group is the largest group doing Bible translation. They work only among people not being served by missionaries from any denomination.

Lutheran Bible Translators. This independent group is a listed service organization of The Lutheran Church—Missouri Synod. Some of their Bible translators work independently, while others carry out cooperative ministries with LCMS missionaries.

LCMS Missionaries. In 1986 10 Bible translation projects were being carried out by LCMS missionaries. These missionaries carry out this translation work alongside of their evangelistic ministries.

You Can Help

God can use everyone, including high school students, to assist with this Bible translation ministry. Consider, for example, the following:

Prepare to become a Bible translator. Bible translators need to have a good knowledge of Scripture and a good grasp of the spoken and written language (English and others). Concentrate on these subjects during your high school and college years. For more information write to Mission Education, Board for Communication Services, The Lutheran Church—Missouri Synod, 1333 South Kirkwood Road, St. Louis, MO 63122-7295. Ask for *God Opens Doors Through Bible Translations* and for other information about becoming a Bible translator.

Pray for Bible translation projects. If you want to learn more about individuals or projects for whom you wish to pray, ask for this information from the address above or from Lutheran Bible Translators Inc., 303 North Lake Street, Box 2050, Aurora, IL 60507-2050.

Write to Bible translators. God encourages these people through you when you tell them that you appreciate their work and that you are praying for them.

Support Bible translators through special offerings. Perhaps your class or your whole school can sponsor one Bible translator. In addition to the prayers and letters, take regular offerings to support this translation work.

What can you do? After you pray about this, write on a separate sheet of paper the way you intend to let God use you in His work of bringing the Gospel to those who do not know Jesus as their Savior.

STUDY QUESTIONS
Review

1. In what languages was the Bible originally written?

2. Why were (and are) translations of the Bible necessary?

3. In **Romans 10:14** Paul wrote, **"How can they believe in the One of whom they have not heard?"** How are these words related to the subject of Bible translation? To the fact that an estimated 200 million people have no part of the Bible recorded in words they can understand?

4. How did God work through the Septuagint, Vulgate, and other Bible translations?

Preview

When you study the Bible, how do you know what message God intends to give you through the passage you are reading? List some guidelines for interpreting Scripture.

Go and make disciples of all nations.
Matthew 28:19

You will be My witnesses in Jerusalem, and in all Judea and Samaria, and to the ends of the earth.
Acts 1:8

How, then, can they call on the One they have not believed in? And how can they believe in the One of whom they have not heard?
Romans 10:14

Session 67

Interpreting the Bible

REVELATION

When you read about the history of the Soviet Union, some information about the author and the time of writing will help you interpret what you read. You can expect, for example, that information written during World War II will emphasize favorable aspects of Soviet history, while information after the construction of the Berlin wall will give more emphasis to negative aspects of their history. In a similar way, you can assume that "liberal" and "conservative" writers would slant the information they provide about Soviet history to support their points of view. Thus, as we read secular literature, we need to find out something about the writer, the time of writing, and other information before we can make good judgments about how well we can trust the writer to present an accurate picture of a situation.

Fortunately, such is not the case when we interpret Scripture. As has been stated frequently in this unit, we can trust the truth that Scripture is God's Word. See, for example, **Luke 24:44-45; Galatians 1:11-12;** and **2 Timothy 3:16-17.**

Secular critics might respond to the paragraph above by saying, "But you are using words from the book itself to justify the way you interpret that book. You need external evidence to determine if the words in any book are accurate."

This is where Biblical interpretation differs from the interpretation of other books. Because we believe the Bible is God's Word, we can use it to interpret itself. Any other approach to Biblical interpretation questions the accuracy of what God has given us—and thereby really questions God Himself!

Thus, any sound method of Bible interpretation must accept the principle of *revelation:* The Bible is "God-breathed." It is the true and inerrant Word of God.

Therefore, we must reject interpretation principles (often labeled as *historical critical*) that lead Bible students to test the validity (accuracy) of portions of Scripture or to interpret the Bible as a human book describing a religion shaped by other religions and philosophies of the times.

HERMENEUTICS

Seminaries offer an entire group of courses called *hermeneutics.* In these courses future pastors learn *principles of Biblical interpretation* and learn to apply these principles. In this session we offer a brief summary of these principles. As you follow these principles, you can be sure that the Holy Spirit will open many truths of God's Word to you.

At times, however, you will still have trouble understanding what God is saying to you in some parts of Scripture. When this happens, you will need to get help from a person (such as your teacher or pastor) or from a reliable study Bible or Bible commentary. Some good books are the *Concordia Self-Study Commentary, Kretzmann's Popular Commentary of the Bible* (four volumes), and the *Concordia Self-Study Bible.*

Assumptions

As you apply the principles of interpretation that follow, you will need to make certain assumptions. Some of these were suggested in the previous section. Here are some assumptions:

1. The entire Bible is the verbally inspired, inerrant Word of God.

2. The dominant and unifying theme of Scripture is the story of salvation, of God acting to save sinful people.

3. God has three purposes for His Word:

a. He reveals His judgment upon sin and His plan for our eternal salvation **(Luke 16:27–29, 31; 2 Timothy 3:15; John 20:31).**

b. He speaks His judgment upon us and creates and preserves in us a saving faith **(Romans 10:17; James 1:21; 1 Peter 1:23-24).**

c. He instructs us in a God-pleasing way of life and gives us the power to live it **(Psalm 119:9, 105; John 20:31; 2 Timothy 3:16; Romans 1:16).**

4. God spoke so the people could understand; the Scriptures are clear.

5. The Old Testament and the New Testament belong together. Therefore, proper Bible interpretation seeks to learn how parts of Scripture support one another.

6. The obscure parts are to be understood in the light of the clear ones.

Principles

Following are five important principles of Biblical interpretation:

1. Take the words of Scripture in their normal, literal, intended sense unless preceding or following verses or sections compel a figurative understanding (which then is the "intended" sense).

This principle leads us to say, for example, that Jonah really did spend three days and three nights inside a fish **(Jonah 1:17—2:10)**. On the other hand, the words of **Matthew 13:3** indicate that we should not take literally the story Jesus told in **verses 3-9**.

2. Let the Bible interpret itself.

Do not read your opinions into it. One passage casts light on another, the clear verses on the difficult. Use the reference or parallel passages, a concordance, a dictionary, and other Bible helps.

For example, a reading of **James 2:14-26** can give the impression that God saves us by our works instead of through faith in Jesus as our Savior. Since you have learned otherwise, you immediately ought to look elsewhere for passages that clearly state what you believe. Maybe you will quickly find these clear statements in verses like **John 3:16, Romans 3:28, Galatians 2:15-16,** and **Ephesians 2:8-10**.

In this case you may still ask, "If James didn't mean what he seemed to mean, what DID he mean?" Both the *Concordia Self-Study Bible* and *Concordia Self-Study Commentary* suggest that when James used the word *faith,* he meant a mere intellectual acceptance of certain truths without trust in Christ as Savior, while we today generally use *faith* the same way Paul did in the passages above—as complete trust in God, including a life that demonstrates our trust **(Ephesians 2:10)**.

The process for this principle may take a while, but the Holy Spirit can use the result to open our hearts to a closer relationship with our Savior.

3. Never tear a passage out of its context; the parts are to be understood in the light of the whole.

Many sections of **Ecclesiastes** give "false" messages apart from their context. In **2:24**, for example, we read that **A man can do nothing better than to eat and drink and find satisfaction in his work.** The words that immediately follow in **verses 24** and **25** show that the enjoyment has to come from God, and the entire book illustrates that all life is meaningless, useless, hollow, futile, and vain if it is not rightly related to God. (See **1:2** and **12:13**.)

4. No passage should be understood in a way that contradicts another clear statement of Scripture.

The illustration given for number 2 shows a process to use when you find an apparent contradiction.

5. Interpret the Scripture historically (in the light of history) and evangelically (in the light of the Gospel and the person of Christ). Everything must be seen in the light of God's redeeming and sanctifying activity in Christ.

Interpreting the account of the Flood **(Genesis 6—9)** illustrates the second part of this principle. Apart from the rest of Scripture one might have trouble applying this account to the Gospel and the person and work of Christ. A knowledge of Christ's saving work will help us bring a sin and grace perspective to these events. In this case God provides even more help; in **1 Peter 3:20-21** He shows how the Flood account symbolizes the salvation we all receive through Baptism.

(The principles of Biblical interpretation in this section are taken from *Teaching the Word to Adults* by Harry G. Coiner [St. Louis: Concordia Publishing House, 1962]. Used by permission.)

PRACTICE IN THE APPLICATION OF HERMENEUTICS

1. In **Matthew 8:22** Jesus said, **"Let the dead bury their own dead."** What did He mean?

2. In **Matthew 16:18** Jesus said, **"You are Peter, and on this rock I will build My church."** What did He mean?

3. In **Exodus 12** God gave instructions for the Passover. How does the New Testament (for example, **Matthew 26:26-28**) help interpret this chapter?

4. In **John 6:35** Jesus said, **"I am the Bread of life."** How does your understanding of the implication of these words grow when you examine **John 8:12; 9:5; 10:7, 9; 10:11, 14; 11:25; 14:6; 15:1-2;** and, especially, **Exodus 3:14?**

STUDY QUESTIONS

1. Why do we use different principles for interpreting the Bible than we use for interpreting secular documents?

2. What part does faith play in interpreting Scripture?

3. Summarize the assumptions we use as we interpret Scripture.

4. Summarize the principles of Biblical interpretation.

He [Jesus] said to them, "This is what I told you while I was still with you: Everything must be fulfilled that is written about Me in the Law of Moses, the Prophets and the Psalms." Then He opened their minds so they could understand the Scriptures.

Luke 24:44-45

Session 68
Review of Unit 7

1. How does the process by which the Old and New Testament canons developed show the power and grace of God?

2. What were the three parts of the Jewish Scriptures? Which two parts were recognized as canonical almost immediately when they were written?

3. Why do we not accept the apocryphal books as part of the Old Testament canon?

4. What is the key to understanding the Old Testament?

5. Why was it necessary for the apostles to write the New Testament books?

6. Which is your favorite New Testament book? Why?

7. What three criteria determine whether a book should be in the New Testament canon?

8. Define *homologoumena* and *antilegomena*.

9. Which are the seven antilegomena books? Why do we have them in our canon?

10. Why can books written today *not* become part of the New Testament canon?

11. What seems most remarkable to you about the way the New Testament canon developed?

12. In what languages was Scripture originally written?

13. Describe two translations of the Bible.

14. Why is Bible translation work so important today?

15. What are six assumptions to remember when we interpret the Bible?

16. What are five important principles of Biblical interpretation?

[Jesus said,] "The Scripture cannot be broken."
John 10:35

[Jesus said,] "I tell you the truth, until heaven and earth disappear, not the smallest letter, not the least stroke of a pen, will by any means disappear from the Law until everything is acccomplished."
Matthew 5:18

Unit 8
An Overview of the Epistles and Revelation

In the last unit you studied how the books of the Bible were written and gathered together, and how they should be studied. In previous units you studied the gospels and Acts. During this unit you will be taking a quick look at the remainder of the New Testament (the epistles and the Book of Revelation, also called the *Apocalypse*). This unit is designed to give you background material that will equip you to use your hermeneutical skills from session 67 to study these books. The purpose of this unit is that you will hear and understand what God is saying to you and the church through His Word.

As you study these 22 books, enjoy the variety and distinctiveness of the six different authors who wrote them for widely varied reasons. At the same time, note and marvel at the unity God has given these books through His inspiration. God is the true Author of these books; each is His infallible all-powerful Word. Let the Holy Spirit guide you as you read God's Word so this Word can renew you and flow through you to people around you.

READING ASSIGNMENTS

Since this unit provides an overview of a large portion of Scripture, you will not be expected to read everything being covered in a session. Instead, read just the selections necessary to answer the study questions and to complete the other suggested activities.

Your teacher will give you instructions for the study questions at the beginning of each session.

MAJOR HOMEWORK ASSIGNMENT

Make a chart for the books of **Hebrews; James; 1 and 2 Peter; 1, 2, and 3 John; Jude;** and **Revelation** containing the following information for each book:

1. The author
2. To whom the book was addressed
3. Approximate date when the book was written
4. Why the book was written
5. Primary theological concern(s) of the book
6. If applicable, why the book is considered antilegomena and why it is still included in the Bible

You can find this information in the reading sections of this unit. You may also use a Bible commentary, Bible handbook, or a New Testament textbook to find the information.

Session 69

The Pauline Epistles (Part 1)

STUDY QUESTIONS

1. Make two lists. In the first, list the epistles Paul wrote to a city or a place, and be able to locate these on a map. In the second, list the epistles Paul wrote to a person.

2. Paul hoped Romans would prepare Christians there for what future event **(1:9-15; 15:22-24, 28-29; Acts 19:21)**? What theme did Paul keep emphasizing **(Romans 3:21-26)**? Also see **1:16-17; 3:21-26; 4:4-8, 13, 22-25; 5:1-2, 8-9, 18-21; 8:3-4; 9:22-24;** and **10:12-15.**

3. The Christian church at Corinth had many problems. It appears that Paul wrote at least four letters to them, 1 and 2 Corinthians and two "lost" letters. Paul also sent several workers there to help solve the problems, received several letters and reports from the Corinthians, and traveled there several times himself. Skim **1 Corinthians 1, 5, 6, 7, 8, 9, 11, 12, 13, 14,** and **15** and list some of the problems the Corinthians had.

4. Read **Galatians 1:6-9; 2:15-16;** and **3:1-5.** What problem did the Galatian Christians have? (You may recall a similar problem at the Council of Jerusalem—**Acts 15:1-19**). What truth did Paul emphasize in **Galatians 2:15-16?.** You can also find this theme in such verses as **1:1-15; 2:17-21; 3:10-14;** and **5:1, 5-6.**

5. Where was Paul when he wrote **Ephesians, Philippians, Colossians,** and **Philemon (Ephesians 6:19-20; Philippians 1:12-14; Colossians 4:10, 18; Philemon 1)**? Why does it seem likely that **Colossians** and **Philemon** were written at the same time **(Colossians 4:10-14; Philemon 23-24)**? What are at least two similarities you find between **Colossians** and **Ephesians** in **Ephesians 4:1-3; 22-32; 5:3-6, 21-33; 6:1-9, 21-22;** and **Colossians 3:1—4:1, 7-8**?

6. Why does it seem likely that Paul wrote 1 and 2 Thessalonians while he was in Corinth during the second missionary journey **(Acts 17:1-10, 13-15; 18:5; 1 Thessalonians 1:1; 2:17; 3:1-2, 6; 2 Thessalonians 1:1; 2:15)**? What is a major topic of Paul's letters to the Thessalonians **(1 Thessalonians 4:13—5:11; 2 Thessalonians 2:1-11)**?

7. Scan **1 Timothy 3:1-15; 4:6-16; 5:1-2. 17-22; Titus 1:5-11; 2:1-10, 15;** and **2 Timothy 1:6-14; 2:1-2, 15, 22-26; 4:1-5.** Why are 1 and 2 Timothy and Titus called the pastoral epistles?

A SUMMARY OF THE PAULINE EPISTLES

We do not know precisely when or why Paul wrote each epistle. He did not date them, and Acts makes no mention of Paul writing epistles. Likewise, we do not have the conversations, letters, and reports that informed Paul about problems and caused him to write the epistles. To determine approximate dates we read the epistles and compare them with each other, with Acts, and with the known events of Paul's time.

Likewise, we're not sure which questions or problems caused an epistle to be written. We can only speculate by reading Paul's answers and comments in the epistles.

Following is a brief summary of each of Paul's epistles. They are listed in possible chronological order.

Galatians

To: The churches in Galatia **(1:2; 3:1)**.

When? About A.D. 48, based on the dates of the Jewish-Gentile controversy, the Jerusalem Council, and Paul's visits to Jerusalem and Galatia **(Acts 15; Galatians 1 and 2)**. Because of the well-constructed thoughts and the similarities with Romans, some argue that Galatians was written later in Paul's career, around A.D. 55.

Purpose: To correct and encourage the Galatians who were being plagued by Judaizers. The Judaizers were undermining the Gospel message in Galatia by adding works of the Law to the free salvation Christ offers all people.

Theological concerns: Soteriology (describing salvation) and sanctification (to be made holy, that is, to be set apart for a special purpose). Paul shows that only through Christ can people be saved and live as God desires them to live. The Law can neither save people nor make them live as God desires.

1 and 2 Thessalonians

To: The Christians of Thessalonica (**1 Thessalonians 1:1; 2 Thessalonians 1:1**).

When? About A.D. 50, during Paul's second missionary journey. Both letters apparently were written while Paul was in Corinth (**Acts 17:1-10, 13-15; 18:5-11; 1 Thessalonians 2:17; 3:1-2, 6**).

Purpose: To encourage and answer some questions for the new congregation in Thessalonica, which Paul was forced to leave abruptly. 1 Thessalonians was written just after Timothy returned from Thessalonica with a report about the congregation (**3:6**). 2 Thessalonians was written a short time later to reemphasize what was said in the first letter, and to combat a forged letter or false reports about what Paul had said (**2:1-3, 15; 3:17**).

Theological concerns: Eschatology (**describing the end times**). The Thessalonians had several wrong ideas about Christ's second coming and about what they should do until He comes. Paul explains what Christ's second coming will be like, and why Christians can live and die for Christ now, before He comes again.

1 and 2 Corinthians

To: The Christians of Corinth (**1 Corinthians 1:2; 2 Corinthians 1:1, 23; 6:11**).

When? About A.D. 55. 1 Corinthians was written before Pentecost, towards the end of Paul's stay in Ephesus during the third missionary journey (**Acts 19:21; 1 Corinthians 16:5-9**). 2 Corinthians was written several months later while Paul was traveling through Macedonia from Ephesus to Corinth (**Acts 20:1-3; 2 Corinthians 1:15-16; 2:12-14; 7:5-7; 8:1; 9:1-4**).

Purpose: The congregation in Corinth had many problems—wicked living, abuses of God's gifts, problems of cliques and factions, and various theological questions. 1 Corinthians was written because some Christians from Corinth reported that a previous letter from Paul did not solve their problems, and because other Corinthian Christians sent a letter to Paul (**1:11; 5:9-10; 7:1; 16:15-18**). 2 Corinthians was written because Paul received good news from Titus about the Corinthian Christians, and because he wanted to clarify a fourth letter he had written to Corinth and explain why he was sending more workers to Corinth (**2:1-10; 7:5-7, 8, 12-13; 8:6, 16-23; 9:1-4**).

Theological concerns: Sanctification. Paul gives many examples of what Christ's death and resurrection mean to a Christian's personal, congregational, and civil life. Paul shows what true Christian love is and does.

Romans

To: The Christians of Rome (**1:7, 15**).

When? About A.D. 56, at the end of Paul's third missionary journey, just before Paul left Corinth to begin his return to Jerusalem (**15:25-27; 16:1; 1 Corinthians 16:1-6; Acts 20:1-3**).

Purpose: Paul hoped to go to Rome to obtain the support of the Christians there to begin missionary work in Spain. Because he had never met the Roman Christians, Paul was writing to explain salvation through Jesus Christ so the Romans could understand that he was speaking for God and not creating a new religion on his own (**Acts 19:21; Romans 1:9-17; 15:22-29**).

Theological concerns: Soteriology. Throughout Romans, Paul emphasizes that it is purely by God's grace (absolutely free gift), through Christ's redemption (ransom payment), that all people, both Jews and Gentiles, are justified (declared right) before God.

Ephesians

To: Some early manuscripts do not mention "**to Ephesus**" **in 1:1**. Ephesians appears to be a circulating letter which was intended to be passed around to all the surrounding congregations. This letter may have been the Laodicean letter Paul referred to in **Colossians 4:16**.

When? Called a prison epistle because Paul wrote it while he was in prison (**Ephesians 3:1, 13; 4:1; 6:19-20**). The similarities of topics, exhortations, and people in Ephesians, Colossians, and Philemon suggest that they were written at the same time. Philippians was probably, but not necessarily, written during the same imprisonment. These letters may have been written while Paul was imprisoned in Rome, about A.D. 59–61.

Purpose: We find no specific problems or circumstances. Possibly Tychicus was traveling through the region with Paul's letters for Philemon and Colossae, and Paul took the opportunity to provide encouragement for Christians who heard about his arrest (**Ephesians 3:13; 6:21-22; Colossians 4:7-8**).

Theological concerns: Christology (describing Christ). Paul encouraged the people by showing that the church is the body of Christ. Christ alone saves people and makes them a part of His body. Therefore, Christians need not fear imprisonment or assaults by the enemy, and all aspects of their life can be lived in Christ.

Colossians

To: The Christians of Colossae (**1:2**).

When? About A.D. 59-61. Another prison epistle (**4:10, 18**).

Purpose: Paul had never visited Colossae. However, in prison, Paul met Epaphras, a prominent Christian from Colossae, and Onesimus, a slave who had run away from a Colossian Christian. From Epaphras and Onesimus Paul learned that the Colossians had blended various Greek philosophical ideas, Eastern mystical elements, and Jewish laws into Christ, weakening the gift of salvation God sent through Christ alone **(1:6-8; 2:1-5, 8; 4:7-9, 12-13)**.

Theological concerns: Christology. Paul described the preeminence of Jesus in all things, throughout all creation. Jesus is fully God and fully supreme, so He is the only wisdom and the only law people need.

Philemon

To: Philemon **(verse 1)** and the people who worshipped at his home, which apparently was in Colossae **(verse 2; Colossians 4:9)**.

When? About A.D. 59–61. Another prison epistle **(verses 1, 9, 10, 13, 23)**.

Purpose: Paul sent Onesimus, Philemon's runaway slave, back to Colossae with the epistle to the Colossians. In Philemon Paul interceded for Onesimus, asked forgiveness for him, and introduced a converted Onesimus to his owner **(Colossians 4:9; Philemon 8-21)**.

Theological concerns: Reconciliation. Paul shows God's grace in action, bringing two brothers in Christ together again.

Philippians

To: The Christians of Philippi **(1:1; 4:15)**.

When? About A.D. 59–61. Another prison epistle **(1:7, 12-14, 17; 2:17-23; 4:22)**.

Purpose: A "thank you" letter written because the Philippian Christians sent Paul a gift through Epaphroditus. Epaphroditus became ill and near death while with Paul, but he had now recovered and was going home, so Paul sent this letter with him **(2:25-30; 4:10-20)**.

Theological concerns: Christology. While encouraging the Philippians, Paul described the servanthood of the divine Jesus becoming human and the joy we receive by living in Christ.

1 Timothy and Titus

To: Timothy **(1 Timothy 1:2, 18; 6:20)** and Titus **(Titus 1:4)**.

When? About A.D. 62–63. The similarities between 1 Timothy and Titus suggest that they were written at the same time. The travel Paul described indicates that he was a free man, but it does not fit any of Paul's travels described in Acts. He may have written these letters after Nero freed him **(1 Timothy 1:3; Titus 1:5; 3:12)**.

Purpose: Timothy and Titus were being sent out by Paul to be pastors (shepherds) of their own congregations. Both faced opposition and problems **(1 Timothy 1:3, 20; 4:12; Titus 1:5, 10-16)**. Paul offers words of advice and encouragement to these two new pastors and authorizes them to carry out their tasks. Consequently, these two letters are called pastoral epistles.

Theological concerns: Ecclesiology **(describing the church)**. Paul explains why the church must have strong leadership, a solid organization, sound doctrine, and a God-pleasing lifestyle.

2 Timothy

To: Timothy **(1:2, 5)**.

When? Probably shortly before Paul's death **(1:8, 12, 15-18; 2:9; 4:6-18)**, possibly A.D. 65–67.

Purpose: To strengthen and encourage Timothy now that Paul, his spiritual father, was imprisoned and facing death. Paul also had some personal needs he wanted to take care of before his death.

Theological concerns: Ecclesiology. Paul stresses the need for strong, sound leadership in the church, especially in the face of danger, persecution, and hardships. Paul also stresses the victory Christ has already won for His servants.

We proclaim Him [Christ], admonishing and teaching everyone with all wisdom, so that we may present everyone perfect in Christ.

Colossians 1:28

Session 70

The Pauline Epistles (Part 2)

STUDY QUESTIONS

1. Use a dictionary to define *doctrine*.

2. Use the information from session 69 or a dictionary to define the following words:

    Christology   redemption   sanctification
    soteriology   grace   ecclesiology
    justification   eschatology

3. What does Paul say about Jesus in regard to God, creation, the church, and His mission on earth **(Philippians 2:5-11; Colossians 1:13-20)**?

4. What has separated people from God? What is the condition of the human race as a result of this separation **(Romans 1:18-32; 3:9-20, 23; Galatians 3:10-11; Ephesians 2:1-3)**?

5. Describe how God saved people from the condition they were in **(Romans 3:21-26; 5:1-11; Galatians 3:13-14; 5:1; Ephesians 2:4-10)**. How do people become the children of God **(Romans 8:13-17; Galatians 3:24—4:7)**? How does Baptism cleanse and renew a person **(Romans 6:3-11; Galatians 3:26-27; Ephesians 5:26)**?

6. What does it mean if a court justifies a person? How are people justified before God? What does not justify people **(Romans 3:20-24; 4:1-3; Galatians 2:15-16)**?

7. Who redeemed (bought back, ransomed) all people **(Romans 3:24; 1 Corinthians 1:30; Galatians 3:13; Colossians 1:13-14)**? What did He have to pay to redeem all people **(Romans 3:24-25; Ephesians 1:7; Titus 2:14)**?

8. Use a concordance to find how many times Paul uses the word *grace* in his epistles. What is grace **(Ephesians 2:8-9)**? What do people deserve **(Romans 6:23)**? What has God graciously (freely) given to people instead? What, then, does it mean when Paul writes or a pastor says "The grace of our Lord Jesus Christ be with you?"

9. From what is the sanctified life set apart **(Romans 12:1-2)**? How do sanctified people want to live? How can people live the sanctified lives that God desires **(Romans 8:10-12; and 1 Thessalonians 5:23)**?

10. Read **Ephesians 1:22-23; 4:11-12, 15-16; 5:21-30; and Colossians 1:18, 24.** How does Paul describe the church? How is this similar to what Paul said regarding Baptism and being children of God? How close a relationship does a Christian have with Christ?

11. Read **1 Thessalonians 4:13—5:11** and **2 Thessalonians 2:1-12.** How does Paul describe the end of the world? What words of hope does he give? What warnings does he give?

12. Read **Romans 1:2-6.** What is the central purpose for the whole Bible, including the Old Testament?

CHRISTIAN DOCTRINE

What It Is and Where It Comes from

Doctrine is simply the Latin word for *teaching*. Christian doctrine, therefore, refers to what Christians teach. If you went through confirmation instruction, you were learning Christian doctrine. You were learning what Christians teach regarding God, people, sin, death, Jesus Christ, salvation, the Holy Spirit, living with God, and so on. Likewise, when you say the Apostles' or Nicene Creed, you are proclaiming the beliefs that Christians teach.

Christian doctrine is not the ideas of one person, or of a group of people. Christian doctrine comes from God Himself through His inspired Word (the Holy Bible) and His living Word (Jesus Christ). Because Christ is not visibly present on earth to teach people, the Bible is the sole source of Christian doctrine and the sole norm for judging whether a teaching is Christian or not.

Some people claim that an angel or even Christ Himself spoke a new teaching to them. However, these new teachings are false (unless they agree with the teachings God has already proclaimed through His Word, in which case they are not new). God warns that even an angel will be condemned if it comes with a new message **(Galatians 1:8)**. Jesus also warns that many false christs will appear who will try to lead God's people astray **(Matthew 24:23-27; Mark 13:21-23; Luke 21:8)**.

The Purpose of Christian Doctrine

Christian doctrine is not a new set of laws Christians must follow in order to get into heaven. Instead, it is the teachings God gave to people to help lead them to Christ and preserve them in Christ. Through Christian doctrine, Christians learn what God has done for them and for others; they learn of the ongoing spiritual war between God and Satan that still threatens to overcome them; they learn how God has saved them and will preserve them; and they learn how God can use them to share His Gospel-love with others.

One way God uses Christian doctrine to preserve a person in Christ is by helping him or her to judge what is God's will and what is not. Through God's teachings we know how to live so that God's will is done and His kingdom is strengthened and increased. Likewise, through God's teachings we learn about God's Spirit, who gives God's wisdom to His people; we learn what thoughts and actions show rebellion against God and should be avoided. Finally, through God's Spirit, we receive wisdom from God so we can judge which way is God's will and can have the strength to follow it.

Christian Doctrine and Paul

Through Paul's epistles God has given us a rich source of Christian doctrine. Paul had to explain to the Gentiles who Christ is, what He did, and how and why He did it. In the process, God used Paul to explain many important Christian doctrines for all people of all time.

Most important, God used Paul to describe vividly how Christ could save the entire world—people in the past, present, and future. To describe what God did through Christ, Paul used a marketplace word, *redeem;* a courtroom term, *justify;* a word of pure love and generosity, *grace;* an Old Testament concept, *atonement;* and many other terms. In this way all people, whether Jew, Greek, Roman, or barbarian; whether educated or illiterate; or whether an aristocrat or a commoner; could picture and understand what God's love for them was like.

Christian Doctrine and Me

1. Paul usually defined Christian doctrines to protect the early Christians from opposition and heresy. What kinds of opposition and heresy do you face today?

___

2. Which Christian doctrines are especially important to you in these situations? How does God use your knowledge of Christian doctrine to guard and guide you?

___

3. Who are some people in the world today who need to hear of the love of Christ proclaimed through the Christian doctrines you have mentioned?

___

All Scripture is God-breathed and is useful for teaching, rebuking, correcting and training in righteousness, so that the man of God may be thoroughly equipped for every good work.
2 Timothy 3:16-17

He [an overseer] must hold firmly to the trustworthy message as it has been taught, so that he can encourage others by sound doctrine and refute those who oppose it.
Titus 1:9

Session 71

Hebrews and James

STUDY QUESTIONS

1. Hebrews shows that Jesus fulfilled the entire Old Testament, and, therefore, is superior to all the Old Testament offices, laws, and traditions. What is Christ shown to be the fulfillment of or to be superior to in each of the following verses of Hebrews?

   a. **1:1-2**
   b. **1:4 (1:4-14)**
   c. **3:3 (3:1-6)**
   d. **4:15 (4:14—5:5)**
   e. **5:6 (5:5-10; 7:1-28)**
   f. **8:1-5; 9:1-8**
   g. **8:6 (8:6-13)**
   h. **9:11-13 (9:11-28)**

2. Hebrews shows the superiority of Jesus' fulfillment of the Old Testament in order to strengthen and encourage the faith of Christians who were facing persecution, pain, and death. Read **Hebrews 11**. How does Hebrews define *faith*? List the Old Testament people who are given as examples of faith. What can people do and endure because of faith? Why is Christian faith so powerful **(10:19-23; 12:1-2; 9:11-15)**?

3. Read **James 2:14-26** and **3:12**. Why does Christian faith produce good works and why is it true that faith without works is dead?

4. James is loaded with advice telling Christians how we can live our faith. Read the following sections and tell what advice James gave for each of the following topics:

   a. **1:12 (1:2-15)**: Trials and temptations
   b. **2:8-9 (2:1-9; 5:1-6)**: Rich and poor people
   c. **2:17 (2:14-26; 1:22-27)**: The relationship between faith and works
   d. **3:5-6 (3:1-12; 4:11)**: One's Tongue
   e. **3:13 (3:13-18)**: True Wisdom
   f. **4:13-17 (5:7-11)**: Patience
   g. **5:16 (5:13-18)**: Prayer

5. Read **Hebrews 13:1-19**. What advice does Hebrews give for Christian living?

6. In general, how should Christians live? Why can we live this way **(Hebrews 2:14-18)**? (See also **James 1:5, 18; 2:1; Hebrews 4:14-16; 9:11-15; 10:19-23; 12:1-2;** and **13:20-21**.)

THE GENERAL EPISTLES

After Paul's 13 letters we find eight shorter letters written by at least four different authors. Unlike Paul's letters, these eight either have no addressee or are addressed to a very broad audience. Consequently, we call them *general epistles*.

The general epistles are generally less well known than the Pauline epistles. In fact, in some cases we are not sure who wrote the epistle. Six of the seven antilegomena books of the New Testament are general epistles; thus, six of the eight general epistles are considered antilegomena.

This does not mean, however, that we should consider the general epistles to be worthless, or should avoid them. No, the early church included these letters in the New Testament because they believed the importance of the messages of these letters outweighed the disputes over who wrote them. As you study these letters, focus on their messages and discover how they apply Christ's saving love to your life today.

HEBREWS

Hebrews describes Christian faith and emphasizes Christ's fulfillment of and supremacy over the Old Testament and Jewish tradition. Christ is God's final Word in these latter days and our only source of salvation **(1:1-3)**. He is the perfect high priest, who offered Himself as the totally sufficient sacrifice for all people, and who continues to serve as humanity's link with God forever **(4:14—5:10; 7:1—10:23)**.

The original readers needed to hear about the superiority of Christ because they were becoming weak in their faith, immature in their spiritual growth, and lax in attending services **(5:11—6:12; 10:23-31)**. The author of Hebrews presented the one, true, all-supreme Christ, and gave numerous examples from the Old Testament of the value of remaining faithful to Christ. His cry for faithfulness climaxes in **Hebrews 11** with the great roll-call of God's faithful people.

Bible scholars generally consider this to be one of the later books of the New Testament because of the reference to Timothy's imprisonment **(13:23)**. The present tense references to the priests and temple worship **(8:4-5; 9:6-10)** and the lack of references to the destruction of the temple indicate that Hebrews was probably written before A.D. 70.

Although Hebrews is a true letter **(13:20-25),** it has no salutation at the beginning to tell who wrote it or to whom it was written. The author, whoever it was, had a thorough understanding of the Old Testament and of Jewish theology, yet could also write very correct and exact Greek. He also had visited the original readers and knew Timothy **(13:19, 23).**

Some have suggested Paul as the author because the theology of Hebrews is similar to his. However, Paul's Greek was much more rugged than that found in Hebrews, and all of Paul's known letters contain a salutation. The author of Hebrews also writes that he heard of the Gospel secondhand **(2:3),** while Paul was a firsthand witness of Christ. Other suggestions for the author include Barnabas, Apollos, Luke, Silas, Priscilla, Philip the Evangelist, and Clement of Rome, an early church father. But this is only speculation; we do not know who wrote this letter.

Likewise, we do not know who was the addressee. It seems that the book was written to Jewish-Christians, possibly in Rome, who were lapsing back into Judaism.

Some spoke against including Hebrews in the New Testament because its author and addressee are unknown and because its author was not an apostle **(2:3).** However, because of Hebrews' strongly apostolic teachings and widespread use in the early church, it was finally accepted into the New Testament.

JAMES

The letter James wrote is full of practical advice for living the Christian faith. James' thesis is that "faith without works is dead," so he shows Christians how to apply their faith in everyday life.

Some people contend that James contradicts Paul's doctrine of salvation by grace through faith. However, Paul and James discussed two different topics. Paul emphasizes *soteriology* (how a person is saved), while James describes *sanctification* (how a saved person lives). James, like Paul, proclaims that Christian faith is not a static, nebulous thought; rather, it is active and alive. It produces good works because God is working through that person. Therefore, if the good works are not present, then the faith must not be present either.

James was apparently written to Jewish Christians scattered around the known world to correct some misunderstandings these people had about Christian living. These Christians gossiped, lorded themselves over poorer people, fought, quarreled, and, in general, followed the ways of the world around them. James authoritatively rebukes these Christians and shows them what the Christian life is like and how it can be lived through faith in Christ and prayer. James may have been written about A.D. 45, before Paul's first missionary journey.

James 1:1 clearly indicates that James wrote this letter, but we are not sure which James this was. It seems most likely that it was James, the brother of Jesus.

This letter was not well known in the early church, probably because it was sent to Jewish Christian congregations (which became the minority) rather than to Gentile Christian congregations (which became the majority). For this reason, and because the identity of the author was not known with certainty, some Christians spoke against including James in the New Testament. It was eventually accepted, however, because it did not contradict apostolic teaching, and because James, the brother of Jesus, was the most likely author.

Faith is being sure of what we hope for and certain of what we do not see.
Hebrews 11:1

Since we are surrounded by such a great cloud of witnesses, let us throw off everything that hinders and the sin that so easily entangles, and let us run with perseverance the race marked out for us. Let us fix our eyes on Jesus, the author and perfecter of our faith, who for the joy set before Him endured the cross, scorning its shame, and sat down at the right hand of the throne of God.
Hebrews 12:1-2

Session 72

The Epistles of Peter and Jude

STUDY QUESTIONS

1. Read **Mark 9:2-13** and **2 Peter 1:16-18**. How can a person trust that the author of **2 Peter** knew what he was talking about? How can a person trust that the words of **2 Peter** and the rest of the Bible are the truth **(2 Peter 1:19-21)**?

2. Why can Christians trust in God even when they are facing suffering in this life **(1 Peter 1:3-9, 22-25; 4:19; 5:7)**? What difference does God make in a person's life **(2:9-12)**?

3. Why does God allow Christians to suffer **(1 Peter 1:7; 2:4-5; 5:10)**?

4. Read **1 Peter 2:19-25; 3:8-17;** and **4:12-19**. Summarize what Peter writes about suffering and persecution.

5. What group of people is Peter fighting against in **2 Peter 2:1-12**? What problems can these people cause for Christians and others **(2:1-2, 18-19)**? What problems do these people cause for themselves and the world **(2:3-22)**?

6. Explain what **2 Peter 2** says about the cults of today.

7. Why do some people scoff at God **(2 Peter 3:3-4)**? Why hasn't the end of the world come yet **(3:9)**? What will the end of the world be like **(3:10-12)**? Why don't Christians have to worry about the coming end of the world **(2:5-9; 3:5-7, 13-14)**?

8. List the people or ideas you find in each of the following pairs of verses.

	2 Peter	Jude			2 Peter	Jude
a.	2:1-3	4	e.		2:15	11
b.	2:4, 9	6	f.		2:17	13
c.	2:10	8	g.		3:2	17
d.	2:12	10	h.		3:3	18

9. Read **Jude 3: 20-25**. What warning does Jude give to Christians? What encouragement does he give?

1 PETER

Some people call 1 Peter the "Letter of Hope." This epistle shows how Christians can endure suffering, and it encourages us to live the life God desires despite being tormented and ridiculed by the world. It was addressed to the many small clusters of Christians living in the various provinces of Asia Minor who were suffering persecution **(1:1, 6-7; 2:19-25; 3:8-17; 4:12-19; 5:7-11)**. The persecution appears to be the insults and abuse Christians suffer when they dare to live their faith in a sinful world **(2:19; 3:9, 16; 4:1-4, 14)**. However, this persecution still produced much suffering, and these Christians needed guidance to endure it.

Peter guided these Christians by emphasizing Christ, who overcame His sufferings and death, and whose gift of new life overcomes the sufferings and death His people face **(1:2-5, 17-21; 2:21-25; 3:21; 4:13-14)**. Christ is the Righteous One, who died once to redeem all who are guilty, and the Cornerstone, which supports God's people forever, but which the world stumbles over **(3:18-22; 2:4-8)**. Suffering does not punish or destroy God's people; instead, because of Christ's sufferings, it beautifies, purifies, and strengthens them **(1:6-7; 5:10)**. Therefore, Christians can continue to live as God's people when they face suffering, rather than return to the ways of the world **(1:17—2:3; 2:9-18; 4:1-4, 12-19)**.

1 Peter is one of the two general epistles not considered antilegomena writings. It was well known to the early church, Peter's authorship of the letter **(1:1)** was never disputed by the early church, and it was consistently included in the various canons made by the early church fathers. Based on the description of the persecution, the list of places where these Christians lived, and the similarities of style and content with some of Paul's letters, 1 Peter was most probably written during the early 60s. Babylon, mentioned in **5:13**, is probably a reference to Rome (see **Revelation 17:5, 9; 18:1-24**), the city Peter was associated with at this time.

2 PETER

2 Peter is a defense of the true Christ and of His second coming at the end of the world. It was probably written between A.D. 65 and 68, shortly before Peter died **(1:13-15)**. Though it has no specific addressee, it was probably written to the same people as 1 Peter **(2 Peter 3:1)**. These people were now plagued by false teachers who told lies about Christ's salvation and lived

immoral lives, and by hecklers who laughed at the idea that Christ would come again **(2:1-3, 3:3-4)**.

The false teachers taught that because Christ freed people from the Law, people could do whatever they pleased, including immoral and ungodly activities. To combat this idea, Peter reminded his readers about the punishments that various immoral and ungodly people of the Old Testament received **(2:4-10, 15-16)**. Peter, like Paul in **Romans 6,** showed that the Gospel frees people from the sinful ways of the world so they can follow God. The Gospel does not free people so they can continue to be slaves of their own desires in rebellion against God **(2 Peter 2:17-22)**.

In response to both the false teachers and the hecklers, Peter indicated that God's punishment had not come yet because He was patient to save those who would not reject Him. But, as surely as the flood came at Noah's time, so God's final judgment of the wicked would also come, and with it the new age for the righteous **(3:3-13)**.

Though **2 Peter 1:1, 16-18** indicates that Peter wrote this letter, many early Christian leaders questioned this claim because this letter, unlike 1 Peter, was not widely known. They were cautious to accept this book because some heretical books also claimed to be written by various apostles, including Peter. But, because 2 Peter is faithful to apostolic teaching and appears to have apostolic origins, it was eventually accepted in the New Testament.

JUDE

Jude is a small letter, relatively unknown both to the early church and to many Christians today. Yet, it is a dynamic pep talk encouraging Christians to fight for their faith against false teachers. The man who wrote this letter is Jude, the brother of James, and another brother of Jesus **(Jude 1; Matthew 13:55; Mark 6:3)**.

Jude is very similar to **2 Peter 2,** warning Christians against false teachers in the church who lived immoral and ungodly lives **(Jude 3-19)**. Like Peter, Jude used Old Testament events to show that God does punish those who rebel against His will **(Jude 5-7, 11)**. Jude also quoted from two popular Jewish religious writings of his day, the *Assumption of Moses* and the *Book of Enoch,* to show that even these books support his accusations against the false teachers **(Jude 9, 14-15)**. Jude concluded his letter with an encouraging description of how, by the Holy Spirit, people can live as God desires for them to live **(Jude 10-15)**.

Jude simply addressed his letter to all true Christians **(Jude 1)**. Because Jude continually referred to Old Testament events and to other Jewish religious writings, his readers were probably predominantly Jewish Christians. The similarities between Jude and 2 Peter suggest that Jude was familiar with Peter's letter (or vice versa) and that, possibly, his readers were, too. This does not mean that Jude's readers were the same people Peter wrote to, though that is possible.

If Jude wrote after Peter wrote his second letter, the late 60s or 70s seem probable dates for this letter, though he may have written it in the 80s.

Though the authorship of Jude was never seriously disputed, Jude is still an antilegomena book. Some early Christians spoke against Jude because it is quite short, and because so many had not heard of or seen it before. But, because it is faithful to apostolic teaching, and because we know who the author was, Jude was finally accepted into the New Testament canon.

As you come to Him, the living Stone—rejected by men but chosen by God and precious to Him—you also, like living stones, are being built into a spiritual house to be a holy priesthood, offering spiritual sacrifices acceptable to God through Jesus Christ.
1 Peter 2:4-5

To Him who is able to keep you from falling and to present you before His glorious presence without fault and with great joy—to the only God our Savior be glory, majesty, power and authority, through Jesus Christ our Lord, before all ages, now and forever! Amen.
Jude 24-25

Session 73

The Epistles of John

STUDY QUESTIONS

1. How does the author describe that he is a witness of God's salvation through Jesus Christ **(1 John 1:1-3)**? List similarities between **1 John 1:1-7** and **John 1:1-14**.

2. Read **1 John 1:1—2:2; 4:9-10; 5:1, 5, 10-15, 20**. What words are used to describe the true Christ? List at least five things that Jesus has given to us or done for us.

3. Who are antichrists **(1 John 2:18-26; 4:1-6; 2 John 7-11)**? What problems do they and their followers cause?

4. List how many times *love* appears in each chapter of **1, 2,** and **3 John**.

5. How is true love described in **1 John 2:10; 3:11-18; 4:7—5:3;** and **2 John 1-6**? How has God shown true love? Why can we show true love **(1 John 3:16; 4:7, 9-13, 16-17, 19; 2 John 1-3)**?

6. How is worldly love described in **1 John 2:15-17; 3:11-18;** and **4:8, 20**?

7. What gave John great joy **(2 John 4; 3 John 1-4)**? What good thing was Gaius doing **(3 John 5-8)**? What problem was the church having with Diotrephes **(3 John 9-10)**?

THE EPISTLES OF JOHN

1 John

1 John focuses on God's love, clearly showing the true Christ and all He has done for us. Like *2 Peter* and *Jude*, 1 John was written when false teachers were leading Christians astray. 1 John, however, does not use Old Testament examples to combat the false teachers. Instead, using very simple words, it presents the extremely complex theology of Christ, the Trinity, and the love of the Trinity which flows through Christ to make people alive.

No author is listed in 1 John; however, there was never any doubt in the early church that Jesus' disciple John, the son of Zebedee, wrote this letter. Consequently, 1 John is the second of the two general epistles that were not spoken against when the New Testament canon was formed. There is no addressee, greeting, or closing either; however, the frequent use of the word *write* indicates this was a letter rather than a sermon (1:4; 2:1, 7-8, 12-14, 21, 26; 5:13).

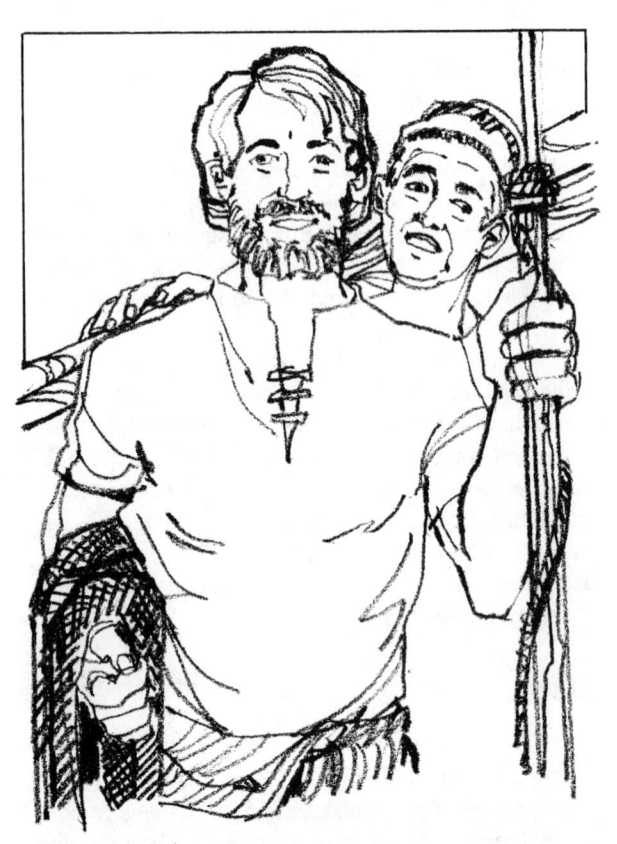

Nothing in John's epistles or his gospel provides an absolute clue to the dates they were written. Early church leaders suggest dates between A.D. 85 and 95.

2 and 3 John

2 John is an extremely condensed version of the message of 1 John. It was written to **"the chosen lady and her children"** to show the true love of God in order to oppose false teachers. Though 2 John has a more distinct letter format, its language and content are almost identical to 1 John.

3 John is almost identical in format to 2 John, though its addressee and topic are different. It encourages Christian hospitality as an example of true love in action. It was written to encourage Gaius after

some friends of the author stayed with Gaius and saw the problems he was having with Diotrephes, an inhospitable and dictatorial congregational leader. Demetrius **(3 John 12)** apparently was the carrier of this letter and one of the missionary strangers referred to in **3 John 5-8.**

The numerous similarities between 1, 2, and 3 John indicate that they were probably written by the same author at about the same time. Even so, 2 and 3 John were still spoken against when the New Testament canon was being formed. First, neither letter was widely known in the early church. Second, the author only gives his title, the elder **(2 John 1; 3 John 1),** rather than his name. This caused some Christians who were not familiar with these letters to question their apostolic origin. Third, some of these Christians thought these letters were too short to contain anything important.

2 and 3 John were accepted, however, because they are faithful to the apostolic teaching. Also, because 2 and 3 John were obviously written by the same person, and because 1 and 2 John seem to be written by the same person, the church believed that the tradition was correct that said that John wrote these two letters also.

This is how we know what love is: Jesus Christ laid down His life for us. And we ought to lay down our lives for our brothers.
1 John 3:16

Dear friends, let us love one another, for love comes from God. Everyone who loves has been born of God and knows God. Whoever does not love does not know God, because God is love.
1 John 4:7-8

Session 74

Revelation

STUDY QUESTIONS

1. Read **Revelation 1:4, 9,** and **11.** Who wrote Revelation? Where was the author when he wrote this book? To whom was it addressed? Locate these cities and the place the author was at on a map.

2. Use a dictionary to define "apocalypse."

3. Skim **Revelation 5:1-5; 5:6—6:1; 12:1-5;** and **19:11-21.** What are four symbols used to describe Jesus? Find at least three other verses that describe Christ as the Lamb of God.

4. Read **Revelation 1:12-16; 4:2-3, 5-6; 11:19; 15:8;** or **19:12.** How did John symbolize the power, majesty, splendor, and glory of God?

5. List the symbols for Satan that you find in one of the following: **9:1-2, 11; 11:7; 12:3-9, 13-18; 20:2.** What symbol do you find for hell in **19:20; 20:10, 14-15;** or **21:8?**

6. What symbol is used to describe Christians in **7:13-14?** In **12:7?**

7. List the symbols used to describe the church in **7:4-9; 12:1-6, 13-17; 14:1-5; 19:6-9;** or **21:9**

8. Read **21:1—22:5.** Which verses show heaven is being with God? A place where all things are new? A new Jerusalem? A place of tremendous splendor and beauty? A new Garden of Eden?

9. Read **19:6-9; 12:2, 9-10ff.** How are heaven and the church related to each other?

APOCALYPTIC WRITING

Revelation, "to reveal," is the Latin word for the Greek word "apocalypse." Apocalypse literally means to "uncover." At the time of Christ it was also a specific Jewish literary style. Apocalyptic writing used symbolic imagery to "uncover" or reveal the cataclysmic end of evil and the glorious beginning of the messianic kingdom. It was popular among the Jews from the Exile (in 598 B.C.) until they were banished from Jerusalem (in A.D. 135) because it proclaimed the ultimate victory of God and righteousness in spite of momentary problems and hardships. In Revelation God used the symbolism of apocalyptic literature to reveal what the end times would be like. He thereby assured His people of the complete victory Christ had won for them.

Two early examples of apocalyptic writers are Daniel and Ezekiel, both of whom wrote during the exile. Zechariah is a later prophet who also had apocalyptic visions. God frequently used these men's visions in the vision He gave in Revelation. Therefore, a study of all four books would help you better understand the message God is unveiling.

APOCALYPTIC SYMBOLISM

Apocalyptic literature used colors, numbers, and visible objects to represent many other concepts. For instance, white usually represents victory, red represents aggression, black represents famine or starvation, and pale gray represents death. The symbols also build on one another. Seven is the number of completion and perfection. Six, which is one short of seven, symbolizes incompleteness, imperfection, and sin. Three and one-half, which is half of seven, means something is very strictly limited. Likewise, the meaning of a number is intensified when it is squared or cubed, and the meanings of both numbers are present when one number is multiplied by another.

Some other numbers and common visible objects and their meanings are

lampstands—the gathered church
scroll—heavenly record
eye—knowledge
horn—power
head—ruler
12—the people of God
24—both the Old and New Testament people of God
incense—prayer
harlotry or adultery—idolatry
jewels—glory
flowing water—life or truth
sea—evil human government
land—organized, human religions
4—the created world
10—"the full amount"
10,000 x 10,000—innumerable

AN OVERVIEW OF REVELATION

More important than being rich in symbolism, Revelation is rich in Old Testament passages. It clearly shows that Christ did not replace the Old Testament; He fulfilled it. It quotes or alludes to the Old Testament far more often than any other New Testament book. As mentioned above, Revelation is closely connected with the Old Testament apocalyptic books. It also frequently refers to Joel, Isaiah, Exodus and the Psalms.

Notice especially, however, how God used Genesis in Revelation. Genesis is the beginning, where God created all things good for human beings, but where humans sinned and thus destroyed the good God had created. Revelation is the completion, showing God's re-creation.

For the first time since Genesis the tree of life appears in the garden beside the refreshing river **(Genesis 2:8-3, 24; Revelation 2:7; 22:1-5, 14, 19)**. The serpent of Genesis is defeated **(Genesis 3:1-15; Revelation 12:7-9; 20:1-10)**, death and pain no longer exist **(Genesis 3:16-19; Revelation 21:4)**, God's new creation is perfectly made once again **(Genesis 1:1—2:4; Revelation 21:1—22:5)**, the ultimate marriage has occurred **(Genesis 2:18-25; Revelation 19:6-9; 21:2,9)**, and people once more live in perfect fellowship with God **(Genesis 1:26—2:25; Revelation 21:3)**. Revelation is the perfect end to the Bible as it points back to the beginning and shows how God restored creation to the perfection He had intended for it.

Revelation shows the whole history of the spiritual struggle over people from creation through redemption to the full peace of God's new creation. However, Revelation does not do this in chronological order. Instead, Revelation is a series of seven visions which blend from one into the other. The seven visions are:

1. The seven letters **(1:1—3:22)**
2. The seven seals on a scroll **(4:1—6:17)**, followed by an interlude showing the church triumphant **(7:1-17)**
3. The opening of the seventh seal, which is a vision of seven trumpets **(8:1—11:19)**
4. A vision of the struggle between the dragon and the church **(12:1—14:20)**
5. The seven bowls of wrath poured on the earth **(15:1—16:21)**
6. The fall of Babylon, the beast, and the triumph of the church **(17:1—19:10)**
7. The final judgment and the new creation **(19:11—22:21)**

The second through seventh visions show the complete history of the struggle between God and evil from several different perspectives; yet each gradually provides more details about the last days while giving fewer details about earlier and present struggles. All of these visions have the same goal, however: to show that God is victorious and evil is defeated. Therefore, Christians do not need to fear whatever sin and Satan throw at them, because in Christ they have already won the victory.

THE HISTORICAL BACKGROUND OF REVELATION

John probably wrote Revelation about A.D. 95 during a major persecution by the Roman emperor Domitian. Revelation is a letter, complete with addressee and opening and closing salutations, specifically written to seven congregations in Asia Minor. These congregations were not only suffering various degrees of persecution by the authorities, but they were plagued by false teachers, ridiculed by neighbors, and suffered from immorality and indecisiveness. John wrote Revelation while he was exiled to the island of Patmos (in the Aegean Sea about 50 miles southwest of Ephesus).

Revelation was spoken against when the New Testament canon was being formed. Though there were a few minor questions regarding authorship, the primary concern was that Revelation was too mysterious and too hard to understand. But, because most Christians accepted its apostolic origin, because it was faithful to apostolic teaching, and because it was known throughout the church, it was finally accepted.

[Jesus said,] "I am coming soon. Hold to what you have, so that no one will take your crown."
Revelation 3:11

I saw the Holy City, the new Jerusalem, coming down out of heaven from God, prepared as a bride beautifully dressed for her husband. And I heard a loud voice from the throne saying, "Now the dwelling of God is with men, and He will live with them. They will be His people, and God Himself will be with them and be their God. He will wipe every tear from their eyes. There will be no more death or crying or pain, for the old order of things has passed away."
Revelation 21:2-4

Session 75

Concluding Activities for Unit 8

VOCABULARY

Define or describe the following words:
1. Apocalypse
2. Antichrist
3. Agape
4. Doctrine
5. Christology
6. Soteriology
7. Justification
8. Redemption
9. Grace
10. Sanctification
11. Ecclesiology
12. Eschatology
13. Pauline epistles
14. General epistles
15. Pastoral epistles
16. Prison epistles

THEOLOGICAL CONCERNS

1. Which two Pauline epistles describe the end of the world?
2. Which general epistle describes the end of the world?
3. What do Romans and Galatians describe in detail?
4. Which three Pauline epistles describe how church leaders should live and work?
5. Which two Pauline epistles emphasize what the sanctified life is like?
6. Which general epistle describes what the Christian attitude should be towards suffering and persecution?
7. Which four general epistles help Christians defend themselves against false teachers?
8. What is the primary theological concern of Ephesians, Colossians, and Philippians?
9. What is the primary theological concern of Hebrews?
10. What is the primary theological concern of James?
11. What is the primary theological concern of Revelation?

My dear children, I write this to you so that you will not sin. But if anybody does sin, we have One who speaks to the Father in our defense—Jesus Christ, the Righteous One. He is the atoning sacrifice for our sins, and not only for ours but also for the sins of the whole world.

1 John 2:1-2

Unit 9

The Church Until About 400

INTRODUCTION

During the next two units you will be studying what the Christian church was like during the first 300 years after the time of the apostles. In unit 7 you learned how the New Testament developed during this period. In this unit you will study the broader aspects of early church life, worship, history, and people.

As you study this period, notice that God continues to work through His people, the church, to accomplish His will on earth. The Holy Spirit worked through the apostles to begin spreading the love of Christ's salvation around the Mediterranean. He did not then abandon the early church when the apostles died but continued to work through Christians to share Christ's love with more people in more places. Today He still strengthens, blesses, and works through each new generation of Christians to enable God's love to reach all the more people around the entire world. Through the Holy Spirit, you, like the apostles, can be an instrument of God to share His love with the people around you.

HOMEWORK
Study Questions

The study questions are located at the end of each session for these last two units. The first few questions are a review of the material you have read, while the last few questions will help you preview the next session. Your teacher will tell you how to use these questions.

Major Homework Assignment

You will present a report about an aspect of early Christian life or life in general in Roman times, or about an early church father, a patriarchal city, or a Roman emperor. Your teacher will give you more details.

SESSION 76

The Apostolic Fathers

The Apostolic Age

The first century A.D. was the period when Christ lived on the earth and when the apostles and the first generation of Christians lived and shared the message of salvation Christ proclaimed. Consequently, it is called the *Apostolic Age. Apostle* is Greek for "one who is sent," and refers to those people who were directly commissioned by Christ to proclaim His Gospel message. The apostles were highly esteemed by Christians because they had firsthand knowledge of Christ's message of salvation. Later, the congregations that were begun by the apostles and the people who were taught by them were looked to for guidance and wisdom because of their closer connection to the message Christ had proclaimed.

During the Apostolic Age the books and letters were written that would later be gathered together as the New Testament. At this time, too, the church grew tremendously as it spread from the upper room in Jerusalem to many areas of the Roman Empire and even to some neighboring nations. Christianity became a Gentile religion at this time, instead of simply being a Jewish sect. And Christians slowly began to realize the scope of the mission God had called them to.

Before ascending into heaven, Christ promised His disciples that He would return again. Jesus did not say when He would return, but many early Christians believed that it would be very soon. Consequently, when the first Christians began to die, some Christians began to have doubts and concerns **(1 Thessalonians 4:13-18; 5:9-11; 2 Thessalonians 2:1-17)**. Yet God had a purpose for not sending Christ back immediately. He had a lost and dying world which needed to hear His message of salvation **(2 Corinthians 5:19-20)**. Today the world still continues as God holds off His final judgement until the full number of the righteous people in Christ hear the Gospel and are saved **(Matthew 24:14; Mark 13:10; Revelation 7:1-10)**.

The Apostolic Age finally ended when John died about A.D. 95, though most of the apostles were dead by A.D. 70. Though the apostles were dead, the church was not dead because the Holy Spirit still breathed God's breath of life through it to the world. God continued to work through a new generation of Christians to share Christ's life-giving salvation with more people in more places.

CHURCH FATHERS

The most prominent Christians between 90–500 are called church fathers because of the important role they played in forming and shaping the church for its great and long mission on earth. Though these men were not directly commissioned by Christ, the Holy Spirit worked through these men to provide the church with earthly leadership, just as He had worked through the apostles previously.

The church fathers are divided into several categories. Because of the importance of the Council of Nicaea, which met in 325, the church fathers are often divided into the **Ante-Nicene Fathers,** who lived before the council met, the **Nicene Fathers,** who lived during the 300s and dealt with the same issues as the council, and the **Post-Nicene Fathers,** who lived after the council met. The church fathers are also divided into the **Latin Fathers,** who primarily used Latin, and the **Greek Fathers,** who primarily used Greek. The Ante-Nicene Fathers are further divided into the **Apologists,** who defended the church against accusations by Roman officials and philosophers, and the **Apostolic Fathers,** who are the earliest of the church fathers.

APOSTOLIC FATHERS

The earliest group of church fathers are called **Apostolic Fathers** because some had personal contact with the apostles. Though the writings of the Apostolic Fathers are limited, they do give a good description of the church after the apostles. Most important, they show that the apostolic faith continued even though the apostles were gone. Through simple explanations of life, morals, Christ, salvation, and the Christian faith, the Apostolic Fathers and the second generation of the church continued the Gospel mission God had given to the church.

The three most important Apostolic Fathers are Clement of Rome, Ignatius of Antioch, and Polycarp. The **Didache** is an important anonymous writing from this time period. Other Christian literature from this period are the **Shepherd of Hermas,** the **Epistle of Barnabas,** the **Epistle to Diognetus,** and the fragments of Papias' writings.

Clement of Rome

Clement of Rome apparently was the leader of the congregation in Rome in the 90s, and may have personally known Peter and/or Paul. He is noted for writing **I Clement,** a letter addressed to the Christians in Corinth.

I Clement is similar to Paul's correspondence with Corinth. Corinth was again having problems, this time primarily regarding leadership in the congregation, especially in times of crisis such as persecution. Clement supported the office of bishop to provide strong leadership and emphasized the need for apostolic succession to provide for a strong bishop. These ideas will be discussed further in session 78. Clement also exhorted the Corinthian Christians to live the Christ-like life and provided some general information on the deaths of Peter and Paul.

Many early Christians thought I Clement should be included in the New Testament, but because Clement was not an apostle it was not included in the New Testament. There is a II Clement, but it is a sermon that was written about 50 years after Clement died and to which Clement's name was added.

Ignatius of Antioch

Ignatius, a bishop of Antioch, was martyred in Rome sometime about 107. While being sent under guard through the province of Asia he was greeted and encouraged by Christians from several local congregations. Among these Christians were Onesimus, the bishop of Ephesus, and Polycarp, the bishop of Smyrna, who influenced Ignatius to write letters of encouragement for Christians. Between Smyrna and Troas, Ignatius wrote seven letters with the help of Burrhus, an amanuensis supplied by Onesimus and Polycarp. Ignatius' letters were addressed to six congregations, Ephesus, Magnesia, Tralles, Rome, Philadelphia, and Smyrna, and to Polycarp. Almost immediately Polycarp had copies of the letters made and distributed throughout the church.

Besides providing encouragement, Ignatius proclaimed Christ to be both true God and true man in response to Docetism, which says that Christ only seemed to be man. He was the first person to use the word *catholic* to describe the universal nature of the church. (Catholic is a Greek word that means universal.) He also stessed the need for a threefold structure of ministry in the church consisting of bishops, who were to lead the church and provide unity and stability, and elders and deacons, who had various service roles.

Polycarp

Polycarp was a disciple of John and was the bishop of Smyrna from the early 100s until his martyrdom about 155 at the age of 86. Besides John, Polycarp talked with and knew many other people who had seen Jesus during His life on earth. Only one letter by Polycarp exists, which he wrote to the Philippians when he sent them copies of Ignatius' letters. But from this letter, Ignatius' letters, the writings of Polycarp's student, Irenaeus, and the written account of his martyrdom, "The Martyrdom of Polycarp," it is apparent that Polycarp was a prominent leader in the church because of his moral life-style, enthusiasm, age, and personal contact with people who knew Jesus. As such a leader, Polycarp encouraged Christian faith and Christian living, defended Christianity against Gnostic and Marcion heresies, and explained to the Romans his region's custom of celebrating Easter on Passover rather than on Sunday.

Didache

Didache is Greek for "teaching" and is the shortened title for an early Christian handbook, *The Teaching of the Lord through the Twelve Apostles.* This anonymous handbook was most likely written sometime during the first half of the second century A.D. to instruct converts to Christianity or to give practical advice to scattered Christians who may not have had access to other sources of apostolic teachings. Though a copy of the *Didache* was not discovered until 1873, the copies and fragments that have been found indicate that this and similar handbooks were popular guides for the early church.

The *Didache* is a valuable source for learning about early church practices. It describes Baptism, the Lord's Supper, fasting, prayer, worship, and general Christian conduct. It also describes a loosely structured ministry, rather than the more rigid structure Clement of Rome and Ignatius desired. This is probably because Clement and Ignatius were from major cities with several well-established congregations that needed guidance through numerous problems such as persecutions; while the *Didache* was designed for smaller congregations which had limited access to apostolic writings and fewer problems to deal with.

Summary

The Apostolic Fathers faced questions and problems regarding leadership, organization, persecutions, and heresies which the apostles did not have to deal with. But God showed this new generation of Christians how the same Gospel which the apostles proclaimed could be applied to the situations they faced. So a new generation of Christians learned to live the Gospel and share it with more people in more places. And even today God continues to show how that same Gospel message fits the modern, electronic, computerized, nuclear world, so even more people can learn of God's love and turn to Him.

I think it is right to refresh your memory as long as I live in the tent of this body, because I know that I will soon put it aside, as our Lord Jesus Christ has made clear to me. And I will make every effort to see that after my departure you will always be able to remember these things.
2 Peter 1:13-15

[Jesus said,] "And surely I am with you always, to the very end of the age."
Matthew 28:20

Session 77

Worship Life in the Early Church

FOCUS ON YOU

It's Sunday morning, just a little before 11 o'clock. You enter the church, go to your pew, and sit down. As the organ plays softly, you fold your hands, bow your head, and say a silent prayer. Soon you join the congregation in singing the opening hymn. You join in the liturgy, singing the responses. You hear the Scriptures read and listen to the sermon. You recite the Creed, place your offering in the basket, and concentrate on the prayers being spoken by the pastor. You participate in the Communion liturgy, go to the altar and receive the bread and wine, participate in the post-Communion liturgy, and receive the benediction. After saying a silent prayer, you leave the church and go home.

With some variations, that is the basic form of the Lutheran Communion liturgy. That liturgy was not a form of worship created by an individual. It evolved gradually from the worship life of the early church. The early church's liturgy, in turn, evolved from the Jewish synagogue service.

How did our liturgical worship get to where it is today? Let's take a few minutes to identify the roots of our liturgical worship.

EARLY JEWISH WORSHIP

Except on high festival days when all who were able went to the temple in Jerusalem, the ancient Jews worshiped in synagogues—meeting places in their local communities where they assembled for worship each Sabbath Day. Their worship service would progress something like this:

Invocation

Prayer

Readings from the Scriptures

Discourse on one or more of the readings

Benediction

The people did not sing hymns. However, psalms were often chanted. During prayer the people usually stood with hands uplifted to God.

To Do

1. Divide a sheet of paper into three columns. In the first column list the elements of present-day worship as described in the opening paragraph of this lesson. In the second column list the elements of ancient Jewish worship. Leave the third column blank for now.

2. Put an asterisk (*) next to those elements of present-day worship not present in Jewish worship.

3. Note at the bottom of the page any other differences you find in the worship practices in the two worship services.

EARLY CHRISTIAN WORSHIP

Christians of the early church had no building in which to gather for worship. Instead, they met for worship in private homes, in the desert, in a field, or (in Rome) in the catacombs—a series of tunnels underneath the city. They met in these places because persecution had led them to seek inconspicuous places for their corporate gathering.

They usually worshiped every day. They had a service of worship in the morning and a worship meal in the evening. The main day of celebration, however, was Sunday, for that was the day the Lord had risen from the dead.

The worship rite of the early Christians was similar to that of their Jewish ancestors. The main difference was that the Christians added Holy Communion after the sermon.

To Do

List the elements of early Christian worship in the third column on your paper. Now compare the three columns. In what ways are they the same? How do they differ? Are there parts of the worship service at your church that are different than all three of these? What are they? Why do you think they were added—or eliminated?

EARLY CHRISTIAN FESTIVALS

The most important festival in the early church was Easter. Jesus' resurrection on that day proved that He was the one He claimed to be—the Messiah and the Son of God. Other important festivals were Pentecost (the birthday of the Christian Church) and Epiphany (which declared that Christ had come not only for the Jews, but also for the Gentiles). Not until about 400 did Christians celebrate Christmas in the church. To counteract the pagan "Feast of Lights," they chose December 25 as the day to celebrate Jesus' birth.

To Think About and Discuss

At first the early church performed Baptisms only on Easter. Later they also baptized on Pentecost and, eventually, also on Epiphany. Why would these days be considered appropriate days for Baptism? Check **Romans 6:3-11; Acts 2:38-42;** and **Matthew 2:1-2.**

FOR FURTHER EXPLORATION

1. Find the meaning of the following "liturgical" words: *hallelujah, hosanna, amen.*

2. Tell when Christians began to use hymns in their worship services and why.

3. Give reasons why it is still important for us to gather for public worship today.

4. Compare Christian church festivals to Jewish festivals. How do they differ in customs and purpose? In what ways are they similar?

CONSIDER

Shout with joy to God, all the earth! Sing the glory of His name; make His praise glorious!
Psalm 66:1-2

Whatever you do, whether in word or deed, do it all in the name of the Lord Jesus, giving thanks to God the Father through Him.
Colossians 3:17

Session 78

Early Church Government

THE SOURCE OF AUTHORITY

A member of the congregation came storming into the church office. "Let me talk to someone with a little authority around here!" he demanded. "You might as well speak to me," said the pastor, who had come out of his office to see what all the commotion was about. "I have about as little authority as anyone!"

Think about it. Who has "authority" in your congregation over secular matters? Who makes decisions? How did that person or those persons get that authority?

AUTHORITY IN THE EARLY CHURCH

The apostles were the source of authority in the early church. They were respected as leaders because they had been with Jesus and were eyewitnesses to His resurrection. Jesus Himself gave the apostles authority in spiritual matters **(Matthew 28:18-20)**.

However, when it came to secular matters, there wasn't always such a clear definition of who was in authority in the church. It appears the apostles took leadership in that area of church life also for a time, but **Acts 6:1-7** seems to indicate that this was a responsibility they did not particularly care to retain.

The church in Jerusalem apparently took the lead in establishing a new leadership role in the church. They appointed seven men to handle church finances (although their exact role in the congregation is not clearly defined).

That's the way it was in the early church until about 100. It was a very loose, fluid structure. There were no job descriptions. There was no hierarchy. Down through the years, however, a formal structure of church government evolved.

To Do

Read Bible passages about Jesus giving authority to His disciples. See **Matthew 28:18-20** and **Acts 6.**
What did He give them authority to do?
Why did He give them this authority?

STRUCTURE OF THE EARLY CHURCH

Although no specific job descriptions for church officers or church leaders existed in the early church, a church government structure began to evolve. "Presbyters" or "elders" governed the church. They were usually assisted by deacons or ministers.

As time went on, one of the presbyters or deacons would assume a leadership role in the congregation. He would be considered the "primus inter pares" (first among equals). Eventually this man was called the "bishop" or the "episkopos" (overseer). He would oversee what happened in the congregation.

None of these positions in the church at this time was a full-time position. Those occupying them made their livings at other jobs. They received no pay for their positions in the church.

165

To Do

Share what you know about church government on the congregational level in various church bodies.

What is the "overseer" of the congregation called? How does a person attain that position?

What other positions are there in the church?

What are their responsibilities?

How does their form of church government compare to that of the early church?

PERSECUTION AND CHURCH STRUCTURE

Toward the end of the first century, many church leaders became concerned that the structure of church government was not rigid enough to help the church withstand the persecution that troubled it at the time. One apostolic father, Ignatius of Antioch, was greatly concerned about this. His answer was to establish a more rigid hierarchical system, which we call a "monarchial episcopate." This involved having one bishop rule over a region called a "diocese" (usually a city with surrounding countryside).

Clement of Rome was also concerned about strengthening church structure in the face of persecution. His answer was "apostolic succession." That meant that anyone chosen as a bishop needed to have a link back to the apostles. This had two very practical purposes in the view of Clement of Rome. It helped to assure that the teaching in the congregation was correct and in conformity with the teachings of the apostles, and it also gave order to the church.

To Do

1. Write a paragraph or two about how church structure changed as a result of the persecution of Christians. Indicate how you think these changes in structure would have helped the church withstand persecution. (See **Titus 1:7-9**.)

2. Talk about how the changes in church government brought about because of persecution affect the life of the church today.

FOR FURTHER EXPLORATION

1. Define and explain the church structure of The Lutheran Church—Missouri Synod.

2. Explain why some form of church government is necessary in a local congregation.

3. Present a case for what you consider to be the best form of church government for a congregation.

4. Report on patriarchal cities. How did they develop? What were their purposes?

5. Write a brief paragraph telling how you could and would serve in your church as an officer or board member.

CONSIDER

But everything should be done in a fitting and orderly way.

1 Corinthians 14:40

Since an overseer is entrusted with God's work, he must be blameless—not overbearing, not quick-tempered, not given to much wine, not violent, not pursuing dishonest gain. Rather, he must be hospitable, one who loves what is good, who is self-controlled, upright, holy and disciplined. He must hold firmly to the trustworthy message as it has been taught, so that he can encourage others by sound doctrine and refute those who oppose it.

Titus 1:7-9

Session 79

Roman Religion and Christianity

"WHEN IN ROME..."

You've heard the saying, "When in Rome, do as the Romans do." That was very good advice in the days of the Roman Empire. If you wanted to please your Roman rulers, the best way to do it was to emulate them.

In the area of religion, however, there was very little—or at least very little that was original—to emulate. The Romans did not have much of a religion of their own. In fact, they did not even have a mythology until they conquered the Greeks and made Greek mythology their own.

For this reason, when it came to religion, the Romans were fairly tolerant people. They had a state religion which included worship of the emperor as one of their gods. The countries they conquered were expected to at least pay lip service to that religion. But the Romans—who themselves were not really satisfied with their religion—allowed the people of the countries they conquered to practice their own religion as long as it did not interfere with the political situation or the state religion. The phenomenon was this: a state religion accepted in theory by all people within the Roman Empire, and legal religions in various countries which people were allowed by Rome to practice openly without persecution or restraint.

To Do

1. List as many Roman gods as you can think of. Match as many of these as you can with their Greek counterparts.

2. Explain the difference between a *state religion* and a *legal religion*.

THOSE PESKY CHRISTIANS

Rome had no problem with Christianity as long as this new religion did not interfere with affairs of state. It was not very long after Jesus' resurrection, however, that the Romans began to question whether Christianity could be considered a legal religion within the Roman Empire. Some of those problems had surfaced already in New Testament times. They led gradually to more and more persecution of Christians—not primarily because of their religious beliefs, but because those beliefs would not allow Christians to accept the state religion or acknowledge the emperor as God.

To Do

Read **Acts 13:49–14:7; 19:21-41; 22:22-29.** Why would events such as those described in these Scripture passages make Christianity a less than desirable religion? What else would have made the Christian religion less than desirable?

CHRISTIANITY VS. RELIGION

While official Rome had difficulty accepting Christianity, many individual Romans accepted it willingly. With no religion to truly call their own, these Romans found the state religion borrowed from the Greeks woefully inadequate. They sampled the religions of the East and of Egypt, but none of these seemed to satisfy completely. So in their urge to find true religion, they turned to Christianity. In Christ they found the peace that had eluded them in all other religions. They rejoiced in their newfound faith in Him.

To Do

1. Explain the difference between Christianity and all other religions. Tell why you think many Roman citizens would have accepted Christianity as their personal religion.

2. List several Bible verses you could share with someone to tell them about the peace you enjoy through Christ.

FOR FURTHER EXPLORATION

1. Write a paper as though you were a Roman investigating this new religion called "Christianity." Identify both positive and negative elements of this new religion.

2. Write a paper in which you try to convince a Roman citizen to become a Christian.

CONSIDER

Now that we have been justified by faith, we have peace with God through our Lord Jesus Christ.
Romans 5:1

Salvation is found in no one else, for there is no other name under heaven given to men by which we must be saved.
Acts 4:12

Session 80

Early Church Fathers

AFTER THE APOSTLES

The apostles were the unquestioned leaders in the early church. Their teachings were considered true and correct. So it was natural that great value would be given to the teachings and writings of those who were considered to have been associated with the apostles. They were given the title Apostolic Fathers. In this category are usually included the following:

1. Clement of Rome: a disciple of Peter and Paul; bishop of Rome 92—101; first of the Apostolic Fathers.

2. Ignatius of Antioch: third bishop of Antioch; according to tradition he was martyred under Trajan in 107.

3. Polycarp: listed about 69—155; bishop of Smyrna; disciple of John and friend of Ignatius; burned at the stake during the persecution under Antoninus Pius.

4. Papias: about 150; bishop of Hierapolis; disciple of John and friend of Polycarp.

5. Hermas: writer of *Shepherd of Hermas*, according to tradition written about 140, but probably written earlier; nothing is known about him.

6. Writer of *Epistle of Barnabas:* epistle originated in Egypt about 130; probably not by the Barnabas who was Paul's traveling companion.

7. Writer of *Epistle to Diognetus:* this epistle has been assigned to the second, third, or even fourth century; author unknown.

8. Writer of the *Didache (Teachings of the Twelve Apostles):* written about 150, this book was intended to be used in the instruction prior to Baptism; author unknown.

To Do

1. Talk about the importance the Apostolic Fathers played in the historical development of Christianity.

2. Are Christian writers today as important as they were in the early church? Why or why not?

THE NEED TO DEFEND THE FAITH

The Apostolic Fathers wrote primarily to explain or extend the teachings of the apostles. After them, between about 150 and 250, other writers wrote primarily to defend the Christian faith. They wrote in response to persecution, trying to convince their enemies of the merits of the Christian faith. They also wrote to defend the church against error within.

During this period, distinct schools of thought developed in the East and West. Two important "schools" of theology were founded in the East: one in Alexandria, represented by Pantaenus, Clement, and Origen; and one in Antioch, represented by Lucian, Diodorus, Theodore of Mopsuestia, John of Antioch, and Theodorus. These Eastern theologians were primarily philosophical. They dealt primarily with philosophical ideas about the mysteries of God. They tried to blend Christianity with Greek philosophy.

In the West, the concern was more with practical questions basic to Christianity, such as "How are we saved?" Tertullian is considered the father of Western theology, and with Irenaeus and Hippolytus, he is regarded as one of the anti-Gnostic fathers.

To Do

1. Identify people in history beyond the early church period whom you would identify as apologists. Tell why you identify them in that way.

2. Write one or two paragraphs defending your Christian faith.

THE ANTI-GNOSTIC FATHERS

One of the heresies most rampant in the early church was the heresy of Gnosticism. The roots of Gnosticism go back to the pre-Christian era, but Gnosticism flourished during the early centuries of the Christian church. Gnosticism encompassed a variety of philosophical ideas that stressed redemption—first from the material world, and then escape into a world of freedom, thus achieving the liberty implied in human spirit. The soul, escaping from matter, is united with the *pleroma* or fullness of God. This happens through secret knowledge or wisdom which is received only by a select few. This Gnosticism was applied to Christianity by early Christian heretics. The anti-Gnostic fathers countered this heresy with a simple, practical theology. An example of this is the teachings of Irenaeus, bishop of Lyon, France.

Irenaeus said that while Gnosticism claims a secret knowledge, there is only one source of knowledge about Christian faith: the public proclamation of the church. That is open and available to everyone. The tradition of the church follows the apostolic tradition, which follows the teaching of Christ. Thus, true church tradition and teaching follow from Scripture. If it doesn't, it is false. Irenaeus said that the bishop of Rome had the best link to the apostles and thus to Christ, so all Christians should look to Rome as the best source of true teachings.

To Do

1. Explain the difference between Eastern and Western thought in the early church. What do you think caused this difference?

2. At the time John wrote his epistles, a form of Gnosticism led some Christians to deny the humanity of Jesus. What message did John proclaim in **1 John 1:1; 2:22; and 4:2-3?**

FOR FURTHER EXPLORATION

1. Write a report on Gnosticism.
2. Write a biography of one of the following: Tertullian, Hippolytus, Clement of Alexandria, Origen.
3. Explain the contribution the early Christian apologists made to the life of the church.

CONSIDER

But with the help of our God we dared to tell you His Gospel in spite of strong opposition.
1 Thessalonians 2:26

I am not ashamed of the Gospel, because it is the power of God for the salvation of everyone who believes.
Romans 1:16a

Session 81

Roman Persecution—Times of Fiery Trial

YOU ARE THERE—TARGETED FOR PERSECUTION

Imagine, if you can, that the people of our country elected a president who was openly anti-Christian and wanted to stop Christians from worshiping or practicing their faith. Of what do you suppose he might accuse Christians to stir up public sentiment against them? What true things might he say about Christians that might make others turn against them? How might he twist Christian practices or doctrines to make them seem undesirable or evil?

Although this may seem preposterous to think about, it could happen. It did happen in the Roman Empire and more recently in many communist countries. We thank God for religious freedom in America, but there is no guarantee that our freedom of religion could not change.

To Do

1. Discuss why and how Christians might be persecuted by an anti-Christian government.
2. Talk about how Christians in America would react to persecution and why you think they would react that way.

REASONS FOR ROMAN PERSECUTION

At first Rome regarded Christianity as part of the Jewish religion. Since Rome considered the Jewish religion a legitimate religion, Christians were allowed to practice their religion freely. When it became clear, however, that Christianity was independent of any locality, that it cut across national boundaries, and that it was held together by distinctive beliefs and practices, it was soon outlawed by the Roman Empire. Among the reasons cited for outlawing Christianity were the following:

1. Christians would not bow down to the emperor, since they would only bow the knee to the King of kings and Lord of lords.
2. Christians were arrogant and presumptuous because they claimed to possess the only true and universal religion.
3. Christians were disloyal to Rome since they refused to give divine honors to the emperor.
4. Since they met frequently and in secret places, Christians probably had treasonable intentions against the state.
5. The absence of all visible objects (images, altars, etc.) laid Christians open to charges of atheism.
6. Their refusal to attend idolatrous ceremonies and public pagan festivals stamped Christians as antisocial and haters of society.
7. Christians were guilty of incest and cannibalism.

To Do

Participate in a roleplay between Christians and Romans in which the Romans accuse the Christians of the charges above and the Christians defend themselves.

THE PERSECUTORS

The actual persecutions of the Christians took place during a period from A.D. 64—313, when the persecutions themselves were ended by the Edict of Milan. Many of these persecutions were localized, but these local persecutions were often severe. Persecution did not take place during this entire time, but broke out sporadically in different places for various reasons. Church historians usually identify 10 specific periods of persecution:

1. Nero (64): Christians were persecuted by Nero, who, in order to point suspicion away from himself, accused them of burning Rome.
2. Flavian: Christians were persecuted as disturbers of the public peace.
3. Domitian (95): Christians were condemned as atheists because they refused to worship the emperor.
4. Trajan (98–117): Extended persecution to Asia Minor, Syria, and Palestine.
5. Hadrian (117–138): Protected the Christians against popular outbursts but punished all who were

convicted by a legal orderly procedure of being Christians.

6. Antoninus Pius (138–161): Adopted a similar course to that of Hadrian, although in the case of Polycarp, the aged bishop of Smyrna, the will of the authorities was overruled by the fury of the crowd, and he was burned at the stake.

7. Marcus Aurelius (161–180): Sought out Christians for trial and was responsible for some of the most violent and widespread persecution of Christians.

8. Decius (249–260): Determined to destroy the church as an atheistic and seditious sect, his persecution extended throughout the entire empire, was conducted with relentless vigor, and produced a larger number of martyrs than any that preceded it.

9. Valerian (260–263): Sought to undermine Christianity by banishing, and later by putting to death, the bishops and leaders of the church.

10. Diocletian (303–313): Four edicts against the Christians: all Christian churches were to be destroyed, all Bibles burned, all Christians deprived of civil rights, and all were to sacrifice to the gods on pain of death. A fifth edict was added by his co-regent Galerius in 308 in order to force heathen defilement on the Christians: all provisions in the market should be sprinkled with sacramental wine.

To Do

Read **1 Peter 4:12-19.** Tell how these words would strengthen Christians in time of persecution.

RESULTS OF PERSECUTION

Suppose the persecution you talked about in this session's first activity had actually happened. Suppose that when it happened, you refused to deny your faith and were beaten, tortured, and imprisoned because you continued to confess Jesus Christ as your Lord and Savior.

Many others like you remained firm in their faith. But some renounced their faith and were spared from persecution.

Persecution times were over. Those who had renounced the faith then said that they did believe in Jesus and had renounced their faith because they were not strong enough to withstand persecution. How do you feel about them? What would you say to them? Should they be readmitted to the church?

That was the dilemma that faced the early church concerning the treatment of the lapsed—those thousands of people who had renounced their faith during times of persecution. Conflict concerning this broke out after the Decian persecution. Bishop Cornelius of Rome (251–53) favored mild discipline for them, while Novatian, his defeated rival for the bishop's chair, advocated harsh treatment. He and his followers admitted that God might pardon the lapsed, but denied that the church should readmit them to its fellowship. They broke away from the Catholic church and called themselves *Katharoi* (Puritans), saying that the visible church should be a communion of *saints* only. They even rebaptized all who came to them from the Catholic church. They chose Novatian as their bishop against his will, and Cornelius excommunicated him. Despite opposition by churchleaders (especially Cyprian, bishop of Carthage), the Novatians spread over almost the entire Roman Empire.

To Do

Find out more about the positions of Bishop Cornelius and of Novatian concerning the lapsed. Write several paragraphs defending one side or the other. Find someone in the class who has taken the other side. Talk with each other about why you took the positions you did. Explain and defend those positions.

FOR FURTHER EXPLORATION

1. Explain the meaning of the words of Tertullian: "The blood of the martyrs is the seed of the church."

2. Refute as many of the charges as you can that the Romans made against the Christians.

3. Tell what Scripture passage(s) you would use to respond to those who said that the lapsed should not be readmitted into the church.

CONSIDER

Be self-controlled and alert. Your enemy the devil prowls around like a roaring lion looking for someone to devour. Resist him, standing firm in the faith, because you know that your brothers throughout the world are undergoing the same kind of sufferings. And the God of all grace, who called you to His eternal glory in Christ, after you have suffered a little while, will Himself restore you and make you strong, firm and steadfast. To Him be the power for ever and ever. Amen.

1 Peter 5:8-11

Session 82

In The Days of Constantine

PROBLEMS IN THE CHURCH

Someone has said that the church is a "divine-human" institution. It was instituted by Christ Himself and is sustained by the power of His Spirit, but because it is made up of humans, it is vulnerable to conflict, error, and even sin.

Already in the middle half of the third century, problems were evident in the young church. There was still persecution by the Romans, but there were also problems within. These included

1. two dominant languages—Greek in the East, Latin in the West;
2. many diverse local customs and even local doctrinal differences;
3. questions about which writings actually constituted the New Testament Scriptures;
4. divergent opinions about what form church government should take;
5. the question of whether Christianity could survive and perhaps even somehow become the state religion of the Roman Empire.

As the church struggled with these and other problems, something happened that was neither planned nor predicted by the church fathers. It was either a clever political ploy by a wise Roman emperor or a miracle engineered by God.

To Do

1. Choose one of the problems stated above that the church faced. Write a paragraph explaining how you would have solved that problem had you been a church leader at the time.
2. Identify a similar problem the church might face today. Give a possible solution for that problem.

CONSTANTINE AND THE EDICT OF MILAN

After the abdication of Diocletian in 305, the rule of the western half of the Roman Empire fell to Constantius Chlorus. At his death in 306, his son Constantine the Great was proclaimed emperor of the western half of the empire, while Licinius reigned in the east. A heathen usurper, Maxentius, however, assumed the title of Augustus and seized the government in Italy and Africa. Constantine crossed the Alps from Gaul at the head of a large army and resoundingly defeated Maxentius at the Milvian Bridge near Rome in 312.

On his way to the battle, Constantine had seen a vision in the sky of a cross bearing the Greek name of Christ and the inscription in Greek, "By this sign, conquer." Constantine attributed his victory at the Milvian Bridge to this vision. The following year, he joined with Licinius in publishing the Edict of Milan, which ended the persecution of Christians and gave freedom of worship to Christians and heathen. The triumph of Christianity was complete when, in 324, Constantine defeated Licinius, who, in the meantime, had espoused the cause of the heathen party, and issued a decree of universal toleration. The following year, Constantine convened the famous Council of Nicaea, about which we will hear more in the next unit.

To Do

1. Discuss whether you think Christians would have been more successful in gaining adherents when it became an acceptable religion compared to the years when it was unacceptable.

2. Describe the similarities between Christianity under Constantine and Christianity in the United States today.

THE TWO FACES OF CONSTANTINE

Although Constantine tolerated Christianity and considered himself a Christian, when we look at his life, we're faced with the nagging question, Did Constantine become a true convert to Christianity? Or did he simply realize that toleration of Christians was now politically expedient?

Consider these events:

1. His vision of the cross and his victory at the Milvian Bridge.

2. The Edict of Milan, which ended persecution of the Christians and granted freedom of worship to Christians and heathen alike (313).

3. His transferring of the seat of government from Rome to Byzantium, which he rebuilt with great magnificence, using primarily Christian art and architecture, and renamed Constantinople.

4. He convened the Council of Nicaea in 325 to resolve the Arian controversy.

5. He executed his son Crispus on charges brought by his wife, Fausta. He then ordered her suffocated in a hot bath when the charges were proven false.

6. He retained the title "Pontifex Maximus" until his death.

7. He erected a triumphal arch three years after his victory at the Milvian Bridge that attributed his victory to "the impulses of the deity."

8. He exempted Christian clergy from military duties.

9. He abolished rites offensive to public morality.

10. He prohibited infanticide and the exposure of children.

11. He mitigated the slave laws.

12. He issued rigorous laws against adultery and placed strong restrictions on obtaining a divorce.

13. He was baptized shortly before his death in 337, honestly admitting that in his life he had been swayed by two conflicting motives.

To Do

Identify the two conflicting motives that motivated Constantine. Decide whether or not you think Constantine was a true Christian. Defend your answer in a one-page essay or in a class discussion.

FOR FURTHER EXPLORATION

1. Write a fictional account of how you felt as a Christian in prison awaiting martyrdom when Constantine issued the Edict of Milan.

2. Explain why the city of Constantinople as built by Constantine was primarily Christian in character.

3. Describe how you think the world would be different today if Constantine were supreme ruler over all nations. Indicate why this would or would not be beneficial to Christianity.

CONSIDER

Finally, be strong in the Lord and in His mighty power. Put on the full armor of God so that you can take your stand against the devil's schemes. For our struggle is not against flesh and blood, but against the rulers, against the authorities, against the powers of this dark world and against the spiritual forces of evil in the heavenly realms. Therefore put on the full armor of God, so that when the day of evil comes, you may be able to stand your ground, and after you have done everything, to stand.

Ephesians 6:10-13

Session 83
Review of Unit 9

How well are you able to relate what you have learned in this unit to your life and to the life of the church today? Keeping this question in mind, answer the seven questions below as completely as you can.

1. Describe the basic form of worship used in the early church. Give similarities and differences between that of former worship and Lutheran liturgical worship today.

2. Tell how church government developed in the early church, beginning in apostolic times. Describe some of the ways these early developments in church government have influenced church government in various denominations today.

3. Explain the difference between Christianity and all the other legal religions in the Roman Empire. Also, explain the difference between Christianity and all other religions in the world.

4. Identify and describe one of the early apologists. Explain what it means to be an apologist for your faith. Describe a situation in which you might be one.

5. Describe the problem concerning "the lapsed" which the church faced during and after its time of persecution. Tell how you think we should treat delinquent church members who have been dropped from the church rolls and who subsequently ask to be reinstated.

6. How did God use Constantine to further the cause of Christianity? What are some ways God has used political events and world situations to further the cause of Christianity throughout history?

7. Apply this Scripture passage to the life of the early church in as many ways as you can:

"But you are a chosen people, a royal priesthood, a holy nation, a people belonging to God, that you may declare the praises of Him who called you out of darkness into His wonderful light."
1 Peter 2:9

Unit 10

The Church Responds to Heresies

This unit continues your study of early church history and how it relates to the life of the church today. It looks at how the church dealt with heresies and at how and why three major creeds of the Christian church developed.

THE NICENE CREED

I believe in one God,
    the Father Almighty,
    maker of heaven and earth
    and of all things visible and invisible.

And in one Lord Jesus Christ,
    the only-begotten Son of God,
    begotten of His Father before all worlds,
    God of God, Light of Light,
    very God of very God,
    begotten, not made,
    being of one substance with the Father,
    by whom all things were made;
    who for us men and for our salvation
        came down from heaven
    and was incarnate by the Holy Spirit of the virgin
        Mary
    and was made man;
    and was crucified also for us under Pontius Pilate.
    He suffered and was buried.
    And the third day He rose again
        according to the Scriptures
        and ascended into heaven
    and sits at the right hand of the Father.
    And He will come again with glory to judge
        both the living and the dead,
        whose kingdom will have no end.

And I believe in the Holy Spirit,
    the Lord and giver of life,
    who proceeds from the Father and the Son,
    who with the Father and the Son together
        is worshiped and glorified,
    who spoke by the prophets.
And I believe in one holy Christian and apostolic
    Church,
I acknowledge one Baptism for the remission of
    sins,
and I look for the resurrection of the dead
and the life of the world to come. Amen.

Session 84

Early Christian Heresies

STRANGE BELIEFS

If you announced that you had seen a vision from God in which He had told you that Jesus' second coming was to occur on July 4 of this year, and that you and whoever would follow you should move to Dodge City, Kansas, to await His second coming, probably a certain number of people would believe what you told them and follow you to Dodge City.

It's always been like that in the world. It's like that even in the Christian church. Some people are ready to believe and accept anything, no matter how farfetched or foolish it may seem. It was that way in the early days of the church; it's still that way today. The Jehovah's Witnesses, the Mormons, the Unification Church, and the Way members have their proponents, as do the more bizarre cults that are constantly springing up. Whatever they may call themselves, these are heretical groups, and their leaders must be described as heretics, for what they believe and teach runs counter to the true Christian teaching that Jesus Christ offers forgiveness of sins and eternal life through His death and resurrection to all who believe in Him.

To Do

1. Describe any cult you know about and tell what its basic teachings are. Tell why the cult cannot be considered Christian.

2. Give a basic statement of what a church body must believe in order to be considered Christian.

CHOOSE YOUR HERESY!

Among the many heresies that plagued the church during its early years, some were especially notable ones. These were not easily stamped out. Many of them continued to run rampant in the church even after the church declared them to be not in conformity with acceptable church doctrine. They include the following:

1. *Gnosticism:* Mentioned in unit 9. Spirit is good, matter is evil. The Father created Christ as an "intermediate being." The body is not redeemed. Only the soul is redeemed through secret knowledge revealed only to the initiated.

2. *Marcionism:* The primary purpose of Marcion was to free Christianity from the Old Testament and from Jewish influences. Yahweh was a just God; Jesus revealed the good God. The Old Testament should be rejected and the New Testament purged of all Judaistic elements.

3. *Docetism:* Christ was not really a human being; He only seemed to be one.

4. *Ebionites:* An extreme Jewish sect of the second century. They adhered to the Torah and practiced asceticism. Jesus was the promised Messiah, but neither divine nor born of a virgin.

5. *Monarchianism:*

    a. *Dynamic or Ebionite:* Christ was a pure man whom God endued with His power, thus adopting Him.

    b. *Modalistic:* The three divine persons are in some manner a manifestation of one and the same God. God revealed Himself as Father in the work of creation, as Son in the work of redemption, and as Holy Spirit in the work of sanctification.

6. *Montanism:* The Montanists were a sect founded by Montanus in the second century. Protesting against worldliness and a laxity of the church, he declared himself the instrument of the Paraclete promised by Christ. With two prophetesses, Prisca and Maximilla, he announced the speedy establishment of the millennium centered at Pepuze, in Phrygia. When this failed to happen, the movement turned to a rigorous legalism.

7. *Novatians:* Followers of Novatia who differed from the dominant church concerning the treatment of the lapsed. Although they admitted that God might pardon the lapsed, they strongly denied that the church had any right to readmit them to its communion.

8. *Donatism:* They hold essentially the same positions as the Novatians, but also held that the sacraments administered by one deserving excommunication were invalid. Since the Catholic church had failed to excommunicate such people—notably, the lapsed—it had ceased to be the true church, and its baptism was invalid. Because of their strict discipline and the absolute purity of their members and clergy, they and they alone were the true bride of Christ.

9. *Nestorianism:* There is no communion of natures in the person of Christ. Mary really could not be re-

garded as the mother of God, but only the mother of Christ. Christ was the Son of God—the Logos—in name only.

To Do

1. Choose one of the heresies described above. Tell why it would have been considered a heresy.

2. Find a Scripture passage to support the church's contention that the teaching you chose was truly heretical.

3. Create a new religion based on one of the 10 heresies. Write a few paragraphs about your new religion. Read your paragraphs to the class. Have your classmates guess on which heresy your "new religion" is based.

COMBATING HERESY

The church sought to combat heresy through convening church councils which formulated creeds—statements of what the orthodox Christians were expected to believe. The three universal creeds are the Apostles' Creed, the Nicene Creed, and the Athanasian Creed. These three creeds became the norm of faith for the church. We will study more about councils and creeds in other sessions of this unit.

To Do

Locate the three universal creeds of the church. (Use *Lutheran Worship* or *The Lutheran Hymnal.*) Look at the heresies described in "Choose Your Heresy!" Determine how that heresy conflicts with one or more of the statements of faith in one or more of the Christian creeds.

FOR FURTHER EXPLORATION

1. Write an essay about a present-day cult explaining in detail that cult's beliefs and practices. Give as many details as you can about what makes that cult's views heretical to Christianity.

2. Choose one of the heresies described above. Give as much detail as you can about that heresy. Who was its founder? When and where did it begin? How long did it flourish? How did the church try to combat it? Give any further information you can.

CONSIDER

Dear friends, do not believe every spirit, but test the spirits to see whether they are from God, because many false prophets have gone out into the world. This is how you can recognize the Spirit of God: Every spirit that acknowledges that Jesus Christ has come in the flesh is from God, but every spirit that does not acknowledge Jesus is not from God.

1 John 4:1–3a

Session 85

The Apostles' Creed

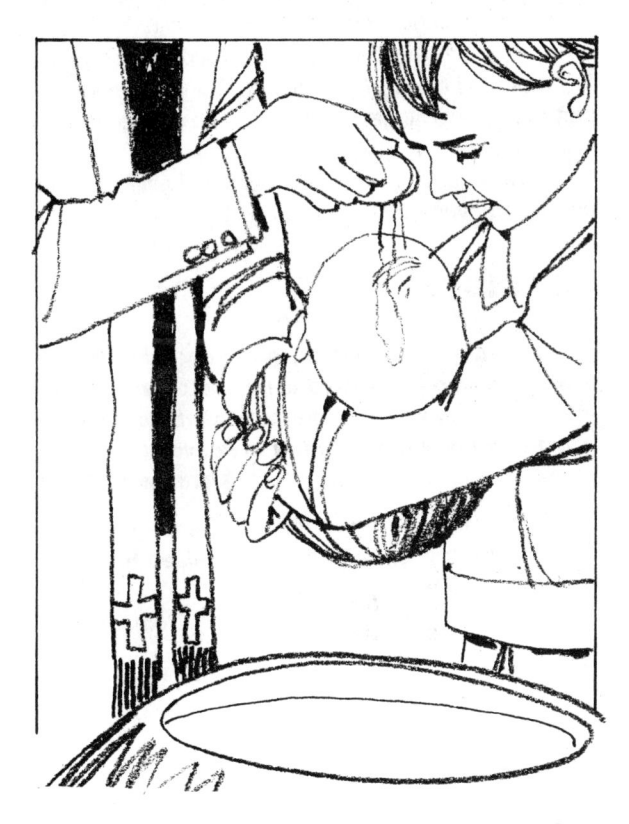

EARLY CONFESSIONS OF FAITH

Unlike the Nicene Creed and the Athanasian Creed, the Apostles' Creed was not formulated by councils of theologians, but grew spontaneously out of the needs of the early church. The tradition saying that the creed was composed by the 12 apostles on the day of Pentecost or shortly after has been discounted as fiction. However, The Apostles' Creed has its roots in the apostles' teachings and confessions of faith as recorded in the New Testament. Those confessions of faith can be found in **Matthew 16:16; John 1:49; John 6:69; John 11:27; John 20:28; Acts 8:37;** and **Acts 14:15.** Also strongly related to the Apostles' Creed is the baptismal formula in **Matthew 28:19.**

To Do

1. Look up the Bible passages listed in the preceding paragraph and tell how the apostles' confessions of faith in these passages are reflected in the Apostles' Creed.

2. Read **Matthew 28:19** and explain why you think the Apostles' Creed would have been considered a baptismal creed in the early church.

OTHER CREEDS, OTHER PLACES

The Apostles' Creed grew from its beginnings in New Testament times. Until the time of persecution ended in the West, it was usually memorized, but not written down. It was explained to the catechumens—those being instructed before being baptized and confirmed—in the last stages of their preparation. Early forms of the creed were called the "rule of faith," "rule of truth," "apostolic tradition," "apostolic preaching," and "symbol of faith."

Different creeds apparently developed in different places. An early Roman creed reads: "I believe in God the Father Almighty and in Christ Jesus, His Son, our Lord, and in the Holy Spirit, Holy Church and resurrection of the flesh."

The Apostles' Creed as we know it today developed over the centuries from all of these sources. Among the latest additions to the creed were "He descended into hell," "catholic," "communion of saints," and "life everlasting." The creed came into its present form in the West sometime between the sixth and eighth centuries.

To Do

1. Write the Apostles' Creed, omitting the words identified as late additions in the preceding paragraph. What difference does the omission of these words make? Does it make the Apostles' Creed a stronger or weaker confession of faith? Or doesn't it make any difference?

2. Write your own creed. Make it as simple and concise a statement of your Christian faith as you possibly can.

3. Explain why you think the Apostles' Creed was memorized but not written down during the time when Christians were being persecuted.

OPINIONS ABOUT THE APOSTLES' CREED

"It is a rule of faith both small and great; small in the number of words, but great in the importance of its ideas."

St. Augustine

"Christian truth could not possibly be put into a shorter and clearer statement."

Martin Luther

"We hold this to be beyond controversy that the whole history of our faith is concisely and in distinct order stated in it; on the other hand, it contains nothing which cannot be supported by sound testimonies of the Scriptures."

John Calvin

"These articles of the creed divide and separate us Christians from all other people on earth."

Martin Luther

To Do

1. Ask your pastor, principal, or a teacher (other than the teacher of this class) what he or she thinks of the Apostles' Creed as a statement of faith. Write down the answer, and bring it to the next class session.

2. Talk about why the Apostles' Creed was a good expression of faith during times of persecution. Is this creed still a good expression of our Christian faith today? Why or why not?

FOR FURTHER EXPLORATION

1. Write a paper telling how, through God's Holy Spirit working in you, the Apostles' Creed can help strengthen, defend, and proclaim your faith.

2. Explain why the Apostles' Creed is considered the baptismal creed of the church. Tell what important part this creed still has in the Lutheran baptismal service today.

3. Describe in more detail how the Apostles' Creed developed over the centuries.

CONSIDER

[*Jesus said,*] *"Whoever acknowledges Me before men, I will also acknowledge him before my Father in heaven. But whoever disowns Me before men, I will disown before my Father in heaven."*

Matthew 10:32-33

If you confess with your mouth, "Jesus is Lord," and believe in your heart that God raised Him from the dead, you will be saved.

Romans 10:9

Session 86

Arianism—a Strong Challenge to Orthodoxy

ARIANISM

Arianism, the heresy that began with Arius (256–336), was perhaps the most persistant heresy in the church. It was condemned at the Council of Nicaea in 325. Yet it continued to plague the church for many decades.

Arius and his followers believed and taught that God is one God and infinitely divine. Because God is divine, unchangeable, and infinite while creation is finite and changeable, there is an impassible chasm separating God from creation.

To bridge the chasm, the Arians said God created out of nothing "before all times and aeons" an intermediate being, exalted above all other creatures, through whom He made the world and all things. They called this being the Son of God, *LOGOS,* but believed He is not true God and is dissimilar in all respects from the essence of the Father.

The *LOGOS* is a perfect creature, yet not inherently sinless, but capable of moral progress, of choosing the good and continuing to do it. He does not fully know His Father nor His own nature. In time, this imaginary human being assumed a human body, but not a human soul. He redeemed humanity by showing how, as free moral agents, we might choose the good and become children of God.

Another name for the *LOGOS* is Christ. Arians believed that Christ and God are similar, but not alike. Because Christ is created, He is separated from God. Humanity is also separated from God, but cannot reach God through Him. We can only attain to being children of God by following His example and choosing the good.

To Do

1. Discuss where and how Arius went wrong.
2. Read **John 1:1-14.** Explain the difference between what this passage of God's Word says and what Arius taught.

THE TROUBLESOME WORDS

The basic problem Arius and his followers tried to address was the relationship between God the Father and God the Son. That relationship was described by different theological factions in the church in a variety of ways. These are best described by the Greek words and the various factions used to explain their positions. They include:

1. *homoousia*—The Father and the Son are the same substance.
2. *anomion*—The Father and the Son are unlike one another.
3. *homoiousia*—The Father and the Son have similar substance.
4. *homoios*—The Father and the Son are similar. No mention of substance is made.

These were the views expressed by various factions in the church. They caused such divisions in the church that Constantine finally called the Council of Nicaea in A.D. 325 in an attempt to resolve the differences. (We will study that council in more detail in session 88.)

To Do

1. Identify words from the list above that describe the position of Arius and his followers. Identify the word you think describes the orthodox position of the church. Tell why you believe this is the orthodox position.
2. Discuss why the Apostles' Creed alone did not solve the problem Arianism.
3. Read the Nicene Creed. List phrases that were written specifically to counteract Arianism. Save your list for use in session 89.

FOR FURTHER EXPLORATION

1. Find out as much as you can about Arius. Write a short biography of his life.
2. Write a brief essay telling about the influences of Arianism on the church today.
3. Tell exactly what is wrong with Arianism and

why it is important to have a proper understanding of who God is.

4. Explain why you think so many Christians accepted Arianism.

CONSIDER

You believe that there is one God. Good! Even the demons believe that—and shudder.

James 2:19

Session 87

Athanasius, the Father of Orthodoxy

A BRIEF BIOGRAPHY

Athanasius, one of the most important persons in the history of the early church, lived from about 296 to 373. He was responsible for combatting Arianism, making the Nicene Creed the official doctrinal position of the church, and preventing Christianity from becoming a thinly covered paganism.

Athanasius arrived at his strong, consistent understanding of God not by reason, but by faith. His special gifts attracted the attention of the Bishop of Alexandria, who appointed him a deacon in 319. In 325, he accompanied his bishop to the Council of Nicaea. Largely because he skillfully and fearlessly testified and witnessed to his faith, the Arian heresy was condemned.

In 328, Athanasius became Bishop of Alexandria, and continued his defense of the Christian faith according to the tenets of the Nicene Creed. His life was not an easy one. He was banished five times and spent 20 years in exile. He died in 373 before the conclusion of the Arian controversy, but with the final victory of orthodoxy in sight.

To Do

1. Compare the biography of Athanasius with the biography of Arius. Think about why Athanasius and Arius ended up on opposite sides of the Arian controversy.

2. Discuss various factors that influence theological positions of church leaders today.

SEMANTIC PROBLEM

One problem that made it difficult to resolve doctrinal differences in the early church really was not directly related to the church's theology. That problem had to do with the fact that the dominant language of the Eastern church was Greek, while Latin was the dominant language of the West. Thus questions always arose, "Which Latin word should represent which Greek word?"

This was important if the church was to resolve its differences. If the Greeks used a certain word to describe God, those who spoke Latin could not really know whether they agreed with that description or not, because they did not understand Greek and therefore could not really know what the Greeks were saying.

Here is where Athanasius made one of his many great contributions to the life of the church. He determined and defined which Latin words should be used for which Greek words. As a result of this, those from the Western church who spoke Latin and those from the Eastern church who spoke Greek could better understand each other, and the orthodox theologians of both branches of the church could unite in their fight against Arianism.

To Do

1. Explain why it was especially important for the church to bridge the language gap at Athanasius' time.

2. Think about and discuss why Christians must still be careful today what words they choose when they bring Christ's message of salvation to people in their own language. What are some language problems the church might have when translating its message into a different language?

ATHANASIUS FOR TODAY

As you have learned, Athanasius was a strong defender of the orthodox Christian faith. He defended Christianity from heresies concerning the nature of God based on reason, basing His defense strictly on faith. He can serve as a model and guide for us today as we defend our faith against attacks based on reason.

To Do

1. Respond to someone who rejects the doctrine of the Trinity by saying that human reason proves that one God cannot be three different beings.

2. Explain why the doctrine of the Trinity is an important article of our Christian faith.

FOR FURTHER EXPLORATION

1. Find information about one group that considers itself Christian and rejects the doctrine of the Trinity. Tell why that group cannot be considered Christian even though it claims to be.

2. Explain why The Lutheran Church—Missouri Synod does not allow members of the Masonic Lodge to be members of its congregations. Explain what this has to do with our study of Athanasius.

CONSIDER

"I tell you the truth," Jesus answered, *"before Abraham was born, I am!"*

John 8:58

Session 88

Ecumenical Councils— Doctrine by Decree

THE FIRST COUNCIL OF NICAEA

The first ecumenical church council was convened by Emperor Constantine to deal with doctrinal matters in the church. In previous sessions we have already referred to the first of these councils, the Council of Nicaea, convened in 325. From this council came the formation of the Nicene Creed. From this council also came the bad precedent of inflicting civil punishment on Arius and his followers and the beginning of many bad practices that came from the union of church and state.

To Do

1. List some of the bad practices that resulted from the union of church and state.
2. Talk about problems that affect Christianity where it is the state religion today.

THE FIRST COUNCIL OF CONSTANTINOPLE

A second church council was convened by Emperor Theodosius I in Constantinople in 381. Its main purpose was to confirm the Nicene Creed and to take up other matters relating to the Arian controversy and to the succession of bishops in Constantinople.

False teachings, such as the Macedonian opinion that the Holy Spirit held an inferior position in the Trinity, were condemned and the Nicene Creed was expanded into the form in which we know it today. Other results of the Council of Constantinople were that all heretics were anathematized, bishops were ordered to stay within their own dioceses in exercising their jurisdiction unless invited to officiate elsewhere, and the bishop of Constantinople was given the prerogative of being second in honor only to the bishop of Rome.

To Do

1. Explain why early church councils were convened by the emperor rather than by the church.
2. Discuss why it was important for the Council of Constantinople to decree that bishops should stay within their own dioceses in exercising their jurisdiction. Compare this problem to any similar situations in the church today.
3. Defend from Scripture the position that the Holy Spirit is fully God, equal with the other persons of the Trinity. Check **Romans 8:9-11; 1 Corinthians 3:16-17; 2 Corinthians 3:17;** and other Scripture references by using a concordance.

THE COUNCIL OF EPHESUS

The Council of Ephesus was convened by Theodosius II in 431 to deal with the Nestorian controversy (see session 84). Although Theodosius favored the viewpoint of Nestorius, the approximately 200 bishops present condemned his erroneous teaching, deposed and excommunicated him. The decree of the Council of Ephesus says that "Mary brought forth, according to the flesh, the Word of God made flesh."

To Do

Read **Luke 1:31; Luke 2:5-7; John 1:14.** Explain why the doctrine that Jesus was born as the son of a human mother is an important article of our Christian faith.

THE COUNCIL OF CHALCEDON

The fourth ecumenical council was convened in Chalcedon in 451 by Leo the Great to deal with the Eutychian controversy. Eutyches, a monk in Constantinople, taught that there were two natures in Christ before the incarnation and that the human nature in Christ was absorbed by the divine nature.

The statement of the Council of Chalcedon was very precise. It declared: "Following the holy fathers, we all with one voice teach men to confess that the Son and our Lord Jesus Christ are one and the same, that He is perfect in Godhead and perfect in manhood, truly God and truly man, of a reasonable soul and body, consubstantial with His father as touching His Godhead and consubstantial with us as to His manhood, in all things like unto us, without sin; begotten of His Father before all worlds according to His Godhead; but in these last days for us and for our salvation born of the virgin Mary, according to His manhood, one and the same Christ, Son, Lord, only-begotten Son, in two natures, unconfusedly, immutably, indivisibly, inseparably; the distinction of natures being preserved and concurring in one person and hypostasis, not separated or divided into two persons, but one and the same Son and Only-begotten, God the Word, the Lord Jesus Christ, as the Prophets from the beginning have spoken concerning Him."

To Do

Explain why the decree of the Council of Chalcedon got so complicated in its language and concepts. Write a short statement explaining what the decree says.

FOR FURTHER EXPLORATION

1. Write a short essay explaining the importance councils had in fighting the various heresies the church faced over the years.

2. Explain similarities and differences between these ecumenical councils and Vatican Councils I and II.

3. Explain similarities and differences between these councils and modern-day church conventions, such as conventions of The Lutheran Church—Missouri Synod.

CONSIDER

Watch your life and doctrine closely. Persevere in them, because if you do, you will save both yourself and your hearers.

1 Timothy 4:16

Session 89

The Ecumenical Creeds

WHAT'S IN A NAME?

The three ecumenical creeds of the church—the Apostles' Creed, the Nicene Creed, and the Athanasian Creed—all in a sense are misnamed.

The Apostles' Creed, written earliest of the three, was not written by the apostles. It is called the Apostles' Creed because it confesses the apostolic faith. It is considered to be the chief confessional statement of the western (Roman) church. It is the baptismal creed of the church.

The Nicene Creed is the chief confessional statement of the eastern church. It was developed in response to the Arian controversy. A first form was developed at the Council of Nicaea in 325, but this was not the Nicene Creed as we know it today. A second form, presented at the Council of Chalcedon in 451, extended the third article by asserting the true divinity of the Holy Spirit. The third form of the Nicene Creed added the "filioque" to the third article—the doctrine that the Holy Spirit proceeds "from the Father *and* the Son." The addition of this phrase to the creed in the sixth century contributed to the permanent schism between the Roman Catholic Church (western church) and the Greek Orthodox Church (eastern church) in the 11th century.

The Athanasian Creed is the third of the ecumenical creeds. It was not written by Athanasius, nor was it formulated by a church council. As nearly as can be determined, it probably originated in Gaul or North Africa as a commentary on the four ecumenical councils. Beginning in about the ninth century, the creed was ascribed to Athanasius, which caused it to be widely accepted. The creed was popular among monks of the Middle Ages who considered it well suited for meditating and memorizing. In Charlemagne's time, it came to be used as a canticle at Prime (early morning Matins). Luther called the Athanasian Creed the grandest production of the church since the times of the apostles.

To Do

Discuss briefly why the three creeds are named the *Apostles', Nicene,* and *Athanasian Creeds.*

THE CREEDS AS CONFESSIONS TODAY

The three ecumenical creeds are used by the Greek, Roman, Lutheran, and some Protestant churches. The Greek church, however, uses the Nicene Creed without the "filioque" and never officially adopted the Athanasian Creed. The Lutheran and Anglican churches have incorporated the creeds into their confessions. The Reformed churches, while agreeing to the doctrines of the Nicene and Athanasian Creeds, still formulate their confessional position primarily in the words of the Apostles' Creed.

To Do

1. Divide a sheet of paper into three sections with headings: **Father, Son,** and **Holy Spirit.** Write in each column the phrases from the three creeds which refer to that person of the Godhead. Explain which phrases

187

were added specifically to combat Arianism and which were added to combat other heresies. Use your list from session 86.

2. Explain why the Apostles' Creed is used at baptisms, the Nicene Creed is used at the Lord's Supper, and the Athanasian Creed is used on Trinity Sunday.

3. Write a paragraph about why the ecumenical creeds are important to the life of the church today.

FOR FURTHER EXPLORATION

1. Explain why some churches accept the three ecumenical creeds as their confession of faith and others do not.

2. Trace in detail the development of the Nicene or Athanasian Creed.

CONSIDER

We proclaim to you what we have seen and heard, so that you also may have fellowship with us. And our fellowship is with the Father and with His Son, Jesus Christ.

1 John 1:3

Session 90

Review of Unit 10

VOCABULARY

Define these words:
1. heresy
2. gnosticism
3. ecumenical council
4. Arianism
5. creed

IDENTIFICATION

Who are these people, places, and documents? Why are they important?
1. Arius
2. Athanasius
3. Nicaea
4. Paul of Samosata
5. The Nicene Creed

APPLICATION—SHORT ANSWER

1. Why did heresies develop in the early church? Why do heresies develop in the church today? What can you do to avoid these heresies? How can you help others avoid false doctrines?

2. Explain in detail how you can use the three ecumenical creeds to strengthen, defend, and proclaim your faith in Christ.

CONSIDER

But you, dear friends, build yourselves up in your most holy faith and pray in the Holy Spirit. Keep yourselves in God's love as you wait for the mercy of our Lord Jesus Christ to bring you to eternal life.
Jude 20–21

25 B.C.	
1 A.D.	c. 4 B.C. The birth of Christ
25 A.D.	c. A.D. 26 Christ begins His public ministry Passover c. A.D. 30 Christ's crucifixion and resurrection Pentecost c. A.D. 30 The church begins by the power of the Holy Spirit c. A.D. 32 The death of Stephen and the conversion of Paul c. A.D. 43 James, the son of Zebedee, martyred A.D. 44 Herod Agrippa I dies c. A.D. 46—48 Paul's first missionary journey A.D. 49 Council of Jerusalem c. A.D. 49—51 Paul's second missionary journey
50 A.D.	c. A.D. 52—56 Paul's third missionary journey c. A.D. 56 Paul's arrest in Jerusalem c. A.D. 58—59 Paul's journey to Rome c. A.D. 59—61? Paul imprisoned in Rome A.D. 64 Fire in Rome. Nero persecutes the church c. A.D. 64—67? Paul and Peter martyred c. A.D. 69—156 Polycarp A.D. 70 Destruction of Jerusalem
75 A.D.	
	c. A.D. 90—100 Domitian persecutes the church A.D. 92—101 Clement is bishop of Rome c. A.D. 98 John dies
100 A.D.	c. A.D. 100 Council of Jamnia c. A.D. 100—165 Justin Martyr A.D. 112—113 Trajan persecutes the Church c. A.D. 112 Ignatius of Antioch martyred
125 A.D.	c. A.D. 125 The Didache was written
150 A.D.	c. A.D. 150—215 Clement of Alexandria c. A.D. 155—230 Tertullian

175 A.D.	c. A.D. 177 Marcus Aurelius persecutes the church
	c. A.D. 185—254 Origen
200 A.D.	c. A.D. 200 Irenaeus dies c. A.D. 200—258 Cyprian
225 A.D.	
250 A.D	
275 A.D.	
	c. A.D. 292—373 Athanasius
300 A.D.	A.D. 303—313 Diocletian severely persecutes the church A.D. 313 The Edict of Milan
325 A.D.	A.D. 325 Council of Nicaea The Cappadocian Fathers — Basil (c. 330—c. 379) Gregory of Nazianzus (c. 330—c. 390) Gregory of Nyssa (c. 331—c. 396) c. A.D. 345—407 John Chrysostom
350 A.D.	c. A.D. 340—420 Jerome A.D. 340—397 Ambrose A.D. 354—430 Augustine
375 A.D.	A.D. 381 Council of Constantinople
400 A.D.	
425 A.D.	A.D. 431 Council of Ephesus
450 A.D	A.D. 451 Council of Chalcedon

The Roman Empire

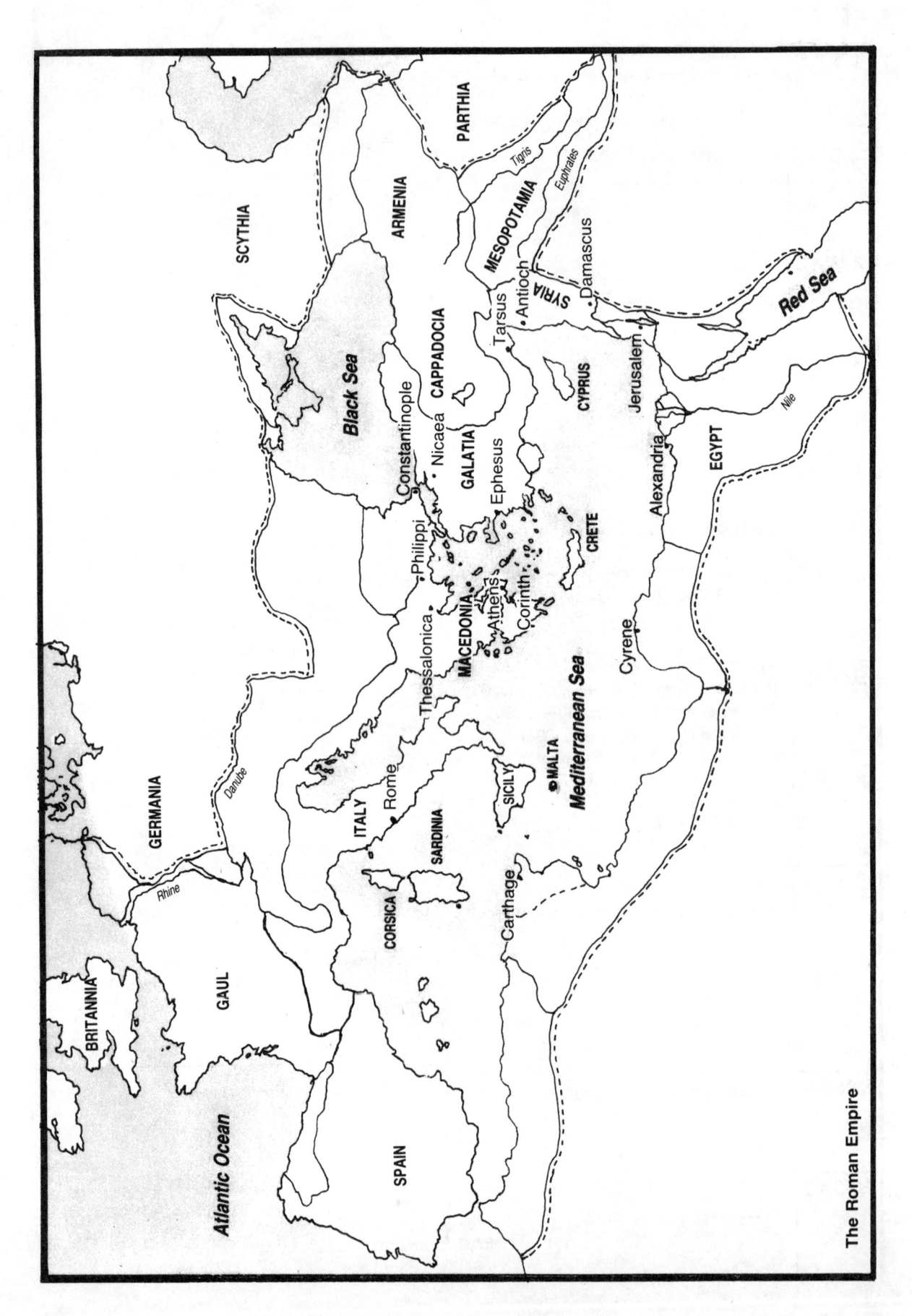